13456205

WITHDRAWN
NDSU

D1560188

THE PERFECT AGE OF
MAN'S LIFE

THE PERFECT AGE OF
MAN'S LIFE

MARY DOVE

Senior Lecturer in English, University of Melbourne

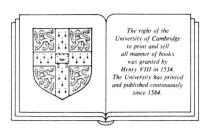

CAMBRIDGE UNIVERSITY PRESS

Cambridge

London   New York   New Rochelle

Melbourne   Sydney

Published by the Press Syndicate of the University of Cambridge
The Pitt Building, Trumpington Street, Cambridge CB2 1RP
32 East 57th Street, New York, NY 10022, USA
10 Stamford Road, Oakleigh, Melbourne 3166, Australia

© Cambridge University Press 1986

First published 1986

Printed in Great Britain at
the University Press, Cambridge

British Library cataloguing in publication data
Dove, Mary
The perfect age of man's life.
1. English literature–Middle English, 1100–1500
–History and criticism   2. Middle age in
literature
I. Title
820.9'354   PR275.M4/

Library of Congress cataloguing in publication data
Dove, Mary
The perfect age of man's life.
Bibliography.
1. English poetry–Middle English, 1100–1500–
History and criticism.   2. Middle age in literature.
3. Middle age–Philosophy.   4. Aging in literature.
5. Aging–Philosophy.   6. Perfection in literature.
7. Perfection (Philosophy)   8. Philosophy, Medieval.
9. Philosophy in literature.   I. Title.
PR317.M53D68   1986   821'.1'09354   86-9527

ISBN 0 521 32571 4

SE

Contents

List of illustrations	*page* vii
Acknowledgments	ix
List of abbreviations	xi
Note on texts and transcriptions	xiii

PART I   THE MIDDLE AGE OF MAN'S LIFE

1	In the middle of the way	3
2	Numbering ages and naming the middle age	10
3	The ages of woman's life	20
4	'Maturity, full of ripenesse'	26
5	'Secrete diminution'	37

PART II   THE PERFECT AGE OF MAN'S LIFE

6	The perfect age and the ages of the soul	45
7	The perfect age and the perfect man	53
8	The perfect age and the ages of the world	60
9	The perfect age and the image of the wheel	67
10	The perfect age and the De Lisle Psalter	80

PART III   THE PERFECT AGE IN RICARDIAN POETRY

11	*Myddel age* in *Piers Plowman*	103
12	*Hy tyme* in *Piers Plowman*	118
13	*Myhty youthe* in *Confessio Amantis*	125
14	*Hyghe eldee* in *Sir Gawain and the Green Knight*	134
15	The *ryght yong* man and Lady Perfect Age in the *Book of the Duchess*	141

Notes	148
Bibliography	167
Index	169

Illustrations

1 'Volat Irrevocabile Tempus'. Otto Van Veen, from *Quinti Horatii Flacci Emblemata . . . studio Othonis Vaenii*. Antwerp: 1607. *page* 31

2 The six ages. Rabanus Maurus, *De Universo*. Bibl. Casinensis MS 132, p. 150. 1022/3. 33

3 The 'formula of four' Wheel of Fortune from the Holkham Bible Picture Book, B.L. MS Add. 47682, fol. 1v. 1320/30. 69

4 Crowned king representing May. Bodl. MS Rawlinson liturg. f. 14, fol. 5r. French, early sixteenth century. 77

5 The Wheel of Life from the De Lisle Psalter, B.L. MS Arundel 83 (II), fol. 126v. c.1310. 81

6 The three living and the three dead from the De Lisle Psalter, fol. 127r. 82

7 The *rota altercacionis oppositorum* from Bodl. MS Laud misc. 156, fol. 66r. Early fifteenth century. 83

8 The poem *Duodecim proprietates condicionis humane, inc.* 'Parvule, cur ploras', from the De Lisle Psalter, fol. 126r. 91

9 The poem *Speculum etatis hominis, inc.* 'Parvule, quid ploras', from Camb. U.L. MS Gg. 4.32, fol. 15v. Fourteenth century. 93

10 The wheel of fortune of W. de Brailes. Fitzwilliam Museum, Cambridge, MS 330(4). Mid thirteenth century. 95

11 Three of the Ages of Man from the frescoes in the Palazzo Trinci, Foligno. c.1400. (a) The 21-year-old (b) The 40-year-old (c) The 84-year-old. 97

12 (a) The half-wheel of the Seven Ages on the north wall of the 'great chamber' of Longthorpe Tower, near Peterborough. 1330/40. (b) Detail of *juvenis*. 99

vii

Acknowledgments

The Master and Fellows of Corpus Christi College, Cambridge, and the Dean and Chapter of Lincoln have kindly given me permission to make use of unpublished material from their manuscript collections. George Russell has most generously allowed me to quote from his forthcoming edition of the C-text of *Piers Plowman*. Jacquelyn Hardwick and M.A. Martindale have given me permission to make reference to their unpublished dissertations. The editors of *The Critical Review* (Canberra) and of *Parergon* have given me permission to use material which originally appeared in a somewhat different form in their journals.

Plates 1, 3, 5, 6, 8 and 11 are reproduced by permission of the Trustees of the British Library; plates 4 and 7 are reproduced by permission of the Keeper of Western Manuscripts, the Bodleian Library, Oxford; plate 9 is reproduced by permission of the Syndics of Cambridge University Library; plate 10 is reproduced by permission of the Syndics of the Fitzwilliam Museum, Cambridge, and plate 12 is reproduced by permission of the Society of Antiquaries of London.

The University of Melbourne has given me generous financial support, for which I am very grateful.

Trevor Mills, Rare Books Librarian of the Fisher Library, the University of Sydney, has helped me with innumerable points of detail. I should like to thank him, and also the following people who have given me information, suggestions and practical help: Elizabeth Adeney, John Burrow, Philippa Crea, Florence Dove, Len Dove, Beverley Goldsworthy, Brian Hillyard, Kathryn Jenkins, Debra Knight, Gregory Kratzmann, Dora Mills, George Mills, Alexander Murray, Kevin Taylor, Stephanie Trigg and Eileen Whittaker.

In recognition of my most pervasive debt, this book is dedicated to Robin Grove.

Abbreviations

Full bibliographical details in the bibliography, where not given below

Boll, Franz. 'Die Lebensalter'.

Brown, Carleton, and Rossell Hope Robbins. *The Index of Middle English Verse*. New York: Index Society, 1943.

CCL Corpus Christianorum. Series Latina. Turnhout.

Chew, Samuel C. *The Pilgrimage of Life*.

CSEL Corpus Scriptorum Ecclesiasticorum Latinorum. Vienna: Oesterreichische Akademie der Wissenschaften.

Cuffe, Henry. *The Differences of the Ages of Mans Life*.

EETS Early English Text Society.

Eyben, Emiel. 'Die Einteilung des menschlichen Lebens'.

Eyben, Emiel. 'Roman Notes on the Course of Life'.

JWCI Journal of the Warburg and Courtauld Institutes.

MED Middle English Dictionary. Ed. Hans Kurath, Sherman M. Kuhn, *et al*. Ann Arbor: Univ. of Michigan Press. 1952—.

Milles, Thomas. *The Treasurie of Auncient and Moderne Times*.

PL Patrologia Cursus Completus. Series Latina. Ed. J.-P. Migne. Paris.

STC Pollard, Alfred W. and G.R. Redgrave. *A Short-Title Catalogue of Books Printed in England . . . 1475–1640*. London: Bibliographical Society, 1926.

Van Marle, Raimond. *Iconographie de l'Art Profane*.

Walther, Hans. *Initia Carminum ac Versuum Medii Aevi Posterioris Latinorum*. Göttingen: Vandenhoeck, 1969.

Walther, Hans. *Proverbia Sententiaeque Latinitatis Medii Aevi*. Carmina Medii Aevi Posterioris Latina II. Göttingen: Vandenhoeck, 1963—.

Wing, Donald C. *Short-Title Catalogue of Books Printed in England . . . 1641–1700*. 3 vols. New York: Index Society, 1945–51.

Note on texts and transcriptions

Unless otherwise stated, quotations from the Bible in Latin are taken from Jerome's Vulgate and quotations from the Bible in English are taken from the Authorised Version of 1611.

Quotations from Chaucer are taken from F.N. Robinson's second edition of *The Complete Works*, London: Oxford Univ. Press, 1957.

Quotations from Shakespeare's plays are taken from the First Folio; line references are to The Riverside Shakespeare, ed. G.B. Evans, Boston, Mass: Houghton Mifflin, 1974. Quotations from Shakespeare's sonnets are taken from the 1609 edition.

In quotations from early English texts, I have followed the editions cited in the notes, except that the distribution of *i/j* and *u/v* has been modernised and punctuation has sometimes been supplied, altered or lightened in order to assist ready understanding. In transcribing English texts from manuscript, I have followed the same practices.

In quotations from Latin texts and transcriptions of Latin texts from manuscript, the distribution of *u/v* has been modernised and punctuation sometimes adapted or supplied. In order to avoid annoyance to the eye, *juvenis, juventus* and related words are given their medieval *j* throughout, except in quotations from classical Latin texts and from certain secondary material.

Translations are my own, unless they are acknowledged in the notes.

PART I

The middle age of man's life

I

In the middle of the way

IN THE CHURCH at Llanelieu, Powys, a hamlet on the slopes of the Black Mountains, there is a tablet to the memory of William Davies, who died in 1808 'in the Prime of Life, aged 36'. Jane Eyre tells us that when she met Mr Rochester for the first time, in Hay-lane, he 'was past youth, but had not reached middle age: perhaps he might be thirty-five' (*Jane Eyre* was first published in 1847). In the middle of the way of our life is the best age; in the middle of the way of our life is an unnamed and indefinite period of transition: two utterly unlike attitudes are apparent in these two examples of definitions of a man's mid-life age.

Medieval and modern perceptions of the course and goal of human life often seem to co-exist uneasily in the late eighteenth and early nineteenth centuries, and it is tempting to see Jane Eyre's attitude as characteristically modern and the attitude of William Davies' commemorators as characteristically medieval. For the larger part of the middle of our lives we tend to shy away from assigning ourselves to any named age, our so-called 'middle age' having almost entirely negative associations, whereas the medieval tendency was to exalt and glory in a middle age which under a variety of age-names was represented as being possessed of exuberance, strength and maturity. One of its names was perfect age, and it is the subject of this book, but right from the start its characteristic elusiveness is worth bearing in mind. It is still possible to die in one's prime – indeed, the age-name only survives in common parlance in such a context – but it has always been easier to die in one's prime (or, in the language of earlier generations, in the perfection of one's age) than to be perceived as living in it. Even that has always been easier than it has been for a man to perceive himself, or for a woman to perceive herself, as enjoying perfect age.

From the literary point of view this has been just as well, for if Dante in the middle of his life had thought of himself as a man in his prime there would have been no story beginning in the dark wood of this world and ending in Paradise. If Mr Rochester had been perceived by the young Jane as being a perfect-aged man, the relationship between them would have been reversed: to assign her hero to a period of life without a name and without any fixed characteristics suits Charlotte Brontë's purposes very well, for it is Jane who will lead him to his age of perfected maturity, not the predictable course of life. Yet perfect age is a stage of life, one of the Ages of Man. It cannot manifest itself in complete isolation from the other ages – if it is to manifest itself at all.

Because perfect age is an age, our investigation into it will take us among encyclopedic age-schemes and the age-lore of the encyclopedias; it will also take us among visual representations of the ages and poems closely associated with the image of the procession of the ages and the image of the Wheel of Life. The idea of the perfect age of man's life, however, is most at home within man's fictions of the progress of his own life and other people's lives, and the goal of our investigation will be to recognise and interpret it there.

One of the central propositions of J.A. Burrow's important study of the characteristics Chaucer, Gower, Langland and the poet(s) of *Sir Gawain and the Green Knight* and the other poems of B.L. MS Cotton Nero A.X have in common, the study which suggested the convenient label 'Ricardian' for the literature of England in the latter part of the fourteenth century, is the proposition that the Ricardian poets share the sense that there is an 'inevitable order in the unfolding of individual experience'.[1] These poets represent the life of the individual man, Burrow argues, as a series of predetermined steps, for they accept the 'doctrine of the Ages of Man – each age with different activities and preoccupations appropriated to it' (p. 117). At the same time, the Ricardian poets seem to him, an acute and sensitive reader, to have a special kind of investment in or commitment to one particular age, the middle age of man's life.

This he interprets as being both the cause and the result of their 'mature, or one might prefer to say "middle-aged", sense of the limits of human achievement and the importance of dull, everyday duties' (p. 120).[2] He goes on to question his own choice of adjective:

'Middle-aged' is, after all, too dim and negative a term to apply to those vigorous and eminently characteristic figures no longer young but not yet old, who occupy such an important place in the poetry of this period and set its tone. These are men in the prime of active life

– and, as examples, he names Theseus, Pandarus, Harry Bailey and the Green Knight. He then proceeds to give the prime of active life guardianship, as it were, of the doctrine of age-decorum:

These figures, with their characteristic 'jovial' wisdom, embody an image of man which is not heroic, not romantic, and not at all 'monkish'. It is an image of 'high eld' which stands at the centre of Ricardian poetry, an ideal of 'mesure' which involves [a] sober acceptance of things as they are   (p. 129)

The 'dim and negative' twentieth-century associations of 'middle-aged' are specifically rejected here, but the image of the prime of active life Burrow presents, with its emphasis on wisdom and sobriety, is closely related to the *gravitas* of late classical and early medieval writers, the age which is the 'middle age' between *juventus* and *senectus* ('no longer young but not yet old', as Burrow says).[3]

Alongside Burrow's claim about the centrality of middle age in Ricardian poetry we may place a general observation on medieval divisions of the Ages of Man offered by the theologian Joseph de Ghellinck, in his article 'Iuventus, gravitas, senectus'. Whatever the particular scheme of classification adopted, he says,

one is at once struck by the protraction of the period during which a man is called *iuvenis*, the lack of significance attached to the years of maturity (l'âge mûr) and the early date assigned to the onset of old age.[4]

De Ghellinck is talking about encyclopedic schemes of the ages, not about representations of the ages in imaginative literature, but his observation that *l'âge mûr* is given relatively short shrift echoes my own response when I encountered the age-name *myddel age* for the first time in a Middle English text, in passus 12 of the B-text of *Piers Plowman*.[5] So seldom is there any explicit reference in medieval English literature to an age intervening between youth and old age that the occasional exception serves to alert us to the usual gap, inviting us to consider its implications. The invitation is particularly pressing in view of the fact that Burrow's discussion of the Ages of Man in Ricardian poetry, the fullest and most interesting discussion to date, concludes that the characteristic image of man in Ricardian poems is an image of man in his maturity.

Already it is only too evident how easily age-nomenclature and differences between (and variations within) traditional and modern divisions of the ages can stand in the way of meaningful discussion. It is probable, but not certain, that Burrow regards 'high eld' (*hyghe eldee*, an age-name occurring only once in Middle English)[6] as the equivalent of mature/middle age; it is probable that De Ghellinck's *l'âge mûr* should be understood as an exact synonym for *gravitas*, in which case the translation which immediately suggests itself, 'middle age', would be slightly misleading. Acknowledging that problems of this kind cannot be ignored without the risk of distorting every aspect of my argument, I devote the next chapter of this study to questions of terminology, and then move on to a consideration of the middle age of man's life within a broad epistemological context. The third explains why I am not using the word 'man' inclusively.

I choose to discuss a few significant (and often very well known) passages in some detail rather than to make copious reference to the large body of literature on the Ages of Man, because I hope to offer not a thickly-textured survey (far less a fully-fledged taxonomy) of the ages but a meaningful pattern composed of foregrounded moments. In this first part, I aim to establish that representations of the Ages of Man characteristically contain within themselves a response to the threat posed by the topos itself, the threat posed by the idea of an ineluctable procession of ages, ending in death. The idea that there is a *media aetas*, an age intervening between youth and old age, is one such response; the medieval idea of the perfect age is, I hope to show, another.

'Perfect age' is the age-name I have chosen for the title of this study primarily because it immediately suggests to us (though it did not necessarily do so when the age-name was in current use, as it was until the eighteenth century) the *perfecta aetas* of Christ and the Christian context within which the medieval idea of the middle age of man's life must be located. Not, however, exclusively located; in the second part of this book we see medieval Christian perfect age attempting to come to terms with Hellenistic and Arabic concepts of an age of perfection which is deferred until the bodily ages have completed their course. From Tertullian onwards, Christian writers insist, profoundly attracted and influenced by Hellenistic thought though they often are, that the perfect age of the body and the perfect age of the soul belong together, and that everlasting blessedness has been and can be achieved in the middle of man's life. The icon of perfect age as a king enthroned at the top of the Wheel of Life, reigning over the ages, mirrors this idea and reflects back the tensions within it.

Perfect age at the top of the wheel is right to call himself 'lifted up', right to proclaim his rule, as he does both in visual representations of the Wheel of Life / Wheel of Fortune and in poems associated with the image of the wheel of the Ages of Man (several of the poems belonging to this genre are discussed here for the first time).[7] His legitimate claim to kingship needs to be distinguished from the claim of the figure who pretends to his throne, the Pride of Life, whom we shall encounter in *Piers Plowman* as Pruyde-of-parfit-lyvynge, Fortune's minion in the 'lond of longyng and love'. Since the Pride of Life is already a well-known personality, far better known than kingly perfect age – and since he is only sporadically, not constitutively associated with the Ages of Man – he will only appear in this book from time to time, on those occasions when texts which are concerned with perfect age include him, too.[8] Unlike the Pride of Life, who from time to time is represented in literary texts as a king, King Perfect Age cannot exist at all unless the other ages accompany him and allow him a place in the series of the ages of man's life.

At the end of the second part of this book we shall at last find ourselves in a position to return to the Ricardian poets and to Burrow's proposition that they share the sense that there is an 'inevitable order in the unfolding of human experience'. I am fully in agreement with Burrow that the Ricardian poets are deeply interested in the Ages of Man topos. If they had not been, they would hardly have chosen to make the individual's journey through the ages play a significant part in so many of their narratives. Yet an unquestioning adherence on their part to a pre-known sequence of predictable ages and inevitable age-characteristics would have been most unlikely to result in an enthralling story. Philippa Tristram suggests that there is indeed something distinctive about the treatment of the ages in the poetry of Chaucer and Langland and in *Sir Gawain and the Green Knight*. More ordinary English poets are content, she argues, to 'maintain the distinctive virtues and vices of the ages in opposition', to abide, in effect, by Burrow's 'doctrine' of the ages, whereas the 'exceptional' Ricardians show the ages 'as consistently connected . . . to form a part of the irrepressible human continuity'.[9] Tristram is quite right, I think, to make the point that the Ricardian poets want to represent the life of the individual man as an integrated experience, an experience which can be contemplated in its entirety by the reader and, inside the text, by the person who is living it. It is a pity, however, that she takes it for granted that the ages of human life have normally been and will normally be perceived as 'consistently connected', for it seems to me that what is distinctive about the Ricardian poets' treatment of the ages is precisely that they do not anticipate consistency, or continuity, or 'inevitable order'.

The idea of the perfect age, an age to which man may hope but not expect to attain in the middle of his life, provided the Ricardian poets with just the unknown factor they needed when they were constructing narrative poems around the individual's experience of living through the stages of his life. Such subject-matter seemed to them not only possible but irresistibly enticing: it enabled them to internalise the marvels and coincidences which were the *koinē* of late medieval romance, to make man rather than narreme the structural centre of narrative. The poems discussed in the third part of this book, *Piers Plowman*, *Confessio Amantis*, *Sir Gawain and the Green Knight* and the *Book of the Duchess*, have been chosen as outstandingly bold examples of this new Ricardian internalisation of *aventure*.

If my argument about the medieval idea of the perfect age has any validity at all, it obviously has implications for a great many other literary texts; the drama and the lyric come immediately to mind. It would equally have been possible to devote Part III entirely to Chaucer, and to debate whether Theseus, Pandarus and Harry Bailey are indeed enjoying mature middle age, or perfect age, or a range of mutually incompatible ages (certainly the last of these alternatives seems to be true of Theseus, who places himself now on this side and now on that of the boundary dividing youth and old age, and who is introduced as being in his perfect age).[10] I decided, however, to select

7

texts written by four different Ricardian poets rather than to concentrate on any one poet, in order to demonstrate one more aspect of the extraordinary inventiveness of late Middle English poetry. I have every confidence that others writing on medieval ideas of the Ages of Man will remedy some of my omissions as well as calling into question some of my interpretations. (I particularly regret that I have not, at the time of writing, had the chance to benefit from J.A. Burrow's later book, *The Ages of Man: A Study in Medieval Writing and Thought*, Oxford, 1986.)

The paired portraits of the Squire and the Yeoman at the beginning of the General Prologue to the *Canterbury Tales* (1:79–117) make an appropriate miniature with which to decorate the beginning of this book about perfect age, for at this very early stage of his poem Chaucer insinuates the idea that his audience should by no means take it for granted that any part of it will represent one age of man's life succeeding another in an orderly progression.

Chaucer's portrait of the young Squire is superlatively decorous, decorous almost to the point of absurdity. He associates him with the sanguine complexion of youth ('whyte and reed', 1:90), with spring, the season corresponding to youth and with the 'yonge sonne' (1:7), making explicit the latent personification in the General Prologue's opening lines. The stages of man's life may indeed be seen to correspond to the inevitable order of the seasons or to the sun's predictable movement through the heavens, suggests Chaucer in the portrait of the Squire. The boundaries between figurative representation and shared substance, correspondence and incorporation, come close to being dissolved altogether: the May flowers, the embroidered representation of the flowers on the Squire's gown and the flower-coloured, sanguine-complexioned body on which the gown so lightly sits are as near to being substantially the same as they are to being differentiated in substance. So measured and predictable will the Squire's journey through the ages be (Chaucer leads us to the verge of thinking) that even our sense of the inevitability of the seasons' or the sun's journey would be heightened by a comparison with the journey on which this young man is setting out.

Chaucer's portrait of the Squire encourages us to expect that whatever else may or may not be made known to us about the Yeoman, who is the Knight's other attendant, we shall at least know where to place him in the series of the ages. Like the Squire, the Yeoman is virtually incorporated into the natural world he inhabits, with his 'not heed', 'broun visage' (1:109) and green clothing, but whereas the Squire is incorporated into the season to which he corresponds, the Yeoman is incorporated into the forest, a world in which correspondence, order and decorum have no place. The green he wears associates him both with vigorous life and with death.[11] He is hung round with weapons sharpened for the kill, the weight of which seems to trouble him not at all, but he wears 'a Cristopher' (1:115), a medallion representing an old man stooping beneath the weight of the Christ-child, the giver of life. Inscriptions accompanying the medieval image of St Christopher commonly guaranteed anyone who looked upon them a day's preservation from unprepared-for death.[12] In the portrait of the Yeoman, then, death and life confront us simultaneously. The pilgrim-narrator, however, contents himself with drawing conclusions about his fellow-pilgrim's *estat* – tentative ones, at that: 'A forster was he, soothly, as I gesse' (1:117).

As we pass from Squire to Yeoman, we pass from an ordered and decorous world, in which each age in turn corresponds to and is incorporated in the appropriate complexion and season, to a world in which life and death are incorporated into each other, making a nonsense of the idea of the series of the ages; yet both the Yeoman and the Squire ride with the Knight and wait upon him. The Squire–Yeoman diptych illumines the two extremes of Ricardian understanding of the way in which man experiences the course of his life, and both these extremes effectively prevent the possibility of an *aventure* based on that journey, one by removing the element of chance from the journey altogether, the other by removing all trace of a predictable pattern and, therefore, of a potential narrative structure. Appropriately enough, the Squire tells an unfinished and unfinishable story, just the kind of marvel-studded romance Ricardian poets characteristically reject; the Yeoman tells no story at all. Between these extremes of understanding of the course of man's life is another: an understanding of the course of life as an unpredictable journey among familiar landmarks, with perfect age perhaps, or perhaps not, awaiting man in the middle of the way.

2

Numbering ages and naming the
middle age

By common devision of astrologers, Arabians, Chaldeans, Greekes, and Latines, and
perticularly by Proclus, a Greek authour, Ptolemie and Halyben Razell; the life time of
man is divided into seaven ages
                                                        (Thomas Milles, 1613)[1]

I F the worthy civil servant and economist Thomas Milles were ever in a
position to compare his own account of the division of the ages with the
'Observations on the Origins of the Division of Man's Life into Stages'
of John Winter Jones (1853), he would be astonished, without a doubt, to
discover that in the intervening two-and-a-half centuries the venerable
authorities he had cited had been superseded by the 'authority' of his upstart
contemporary, Shakespeare. 'The name of Shakspere', observes Jones,
'appears to be so inseparably connected with the Seven Ages of Man in the
minds of most persons, that few have thought of inquiring how much of this
charming creation is really his own'.[2] Milles would be very startled, too, by
the adjective 'charming'.

Perhaps it is even truer now than it was in the mid nineteenth century that
for most people the ages of man means the seven ages of man, and the seven
ages of man means Shakespeare's 'All the world's a stage'. Then, many more
people would have been familiar with other traditional numerical divisions
of the ages, the most well-known, perhaps, being Ovid's four ages in
Metamorphoses 15: 199–216.[3] Many more people would also have become
acquainted at school, as Shakespeare himself did (though probably by way of
intermediaries), with such *loci classici* for the association of the ages with the
number seven as Hippocrates' unequal sevenfold division and Solon's poem
dividing life into periods of seven years, both cited by that honourable
hander-down of ancient learning Philo of Alexandria as evidence of 'the
perfecting power of the number seven'.[4] Although it is true, then, that
extreme familiarity with Shakespeare's division of the ages and relative
unfamiliarity with the tradition to which that division belongs has resulted
in some persistent oddities of emphasis in discussions of the ways in which
the ages of man have been represented, especially within the English
tradition, it is also true that the near-obsession with the number seven in
relation to the division of the ages has venerable antecedents in the
metaphysical stratum of Greek writings about the composition of the

human body and about the correspondence between microcosm and macrocosm, and in the Arabic medical writings which transmitted the ancient hebdomadal theory to western Europe in the later Middle Ages.

The number seven, as Franz Boll says in his densely-packed study of the ages of man's life, 'in its spread and influence leaves all others behind'.[5] Certainly it was alive with meaning for the writers of ancient Greece, and for those whose learning derived from them at first hand, but by the end of the Middle Ages, in England at least, seven had come to be the number so habitually associated with the Ages of Man that in that particular context its force as a numerical signifier was reduced almost to nothing. Fifteenth-century Norfolk schoolchildren learning elementary Latin from the *Promptorium Parvulorum* would have discovered under the entry *agis sevyn* an account of the six ages of man's life according to Isidore, the seventh age being 'in resurrectione finali'.[6] The poem known as 'The Myrrour of Mankind' (*c*.1400) divides man's life into eleven ages; nonetheless, it is 'clepid þe sevene ages' in the Cambridge University Library copy.[7] The 'steynyd cloth with vii agys' which John Baret of Bury bequeathed to his niece Jone in 1463, and all those other tapestries depicting the 'seven ages' which are mentioned in the inventories of the well-to-do, may have actually portrayed seven ages, or more, or less.[8]

In England, from the late Middle Ages onwards, the terms 'the seven ages' and 'the age of man' (more rarely, 'the ages of man') mean virtually the same thing; the former grows in popularity while the latter declines. It is not hard to see why 'the age of man' came to seem a less appropriate term than 'the seven ages'. Until the second half of the sixteenth century the primary meaning of 'age' was 'a stage or period in human life' (*MED*, *age*, 1a, a). As late as 1600, Henry Cuffe, writing about *The Differences of the Ages of Mans Life* (he was also busy plotting on behalf of the Earl of Essex) defines 'age' as

a period and tearme of mans life, wherein his naturall complexion and temperature naturally and of its owne accord is evidently changed   (p. 166)[9]

But the definition of age in Thomas Newton's 1576 translation of Levinus Lemnius' *De Habitu et Constitutione Corporis* (1561) reflects the changing sense of the word. Here, age is

no other thing but the race or course of life, or the time that wee have to runne from oure infancye til wee come to olde age.

Lemnius only then goes on to define age as a *gradus* 'step':

in which time, the state and constitution of mans bodye is altered, and steppeth from one temperamente to an other.[10]

The concept of age as *gradus* is completely lost in John Cowell's neat definition in *The Interpreter* (1607): '*Age*, that part of a man's life, which is from his birth unto his last day'.[11] Cowell's definition is repeated by Thomas

Blount in his *Glossographia* (1656).[12] In his *New English Dictionary* (1702), John Kersey contents himself with '*Age*, the duration of time, or the space of 100 years', a definition which has no reference to man's life at all.[13]

Once 'age' no longer unambiguously implied one of the divisions of man's life, but in common parlance meant the whole of man's life, or even just 'a long time', the term 'the age of man' was not able clearly to convey the idea that lies at the heart of the Ages of Man topos, the idea that during the course of his life man passes through several distinct states of being. The term 'the seven ages' gradually took over from 'the age of man' because it expressed this idea in a more immediate and unambiguous way; 'seven' functioning as a sign for 'several' rather than as a precise number. Indeed, the similarity in sound between these two words seems to have had something to do with the spread of the term 'the seven ages'. Cuffe differentiates 'seven severall parts of our life'.[14] Nathaniel Crouch's very popular treatise *The Vanity of the Life of Man* (1688) promises on its title-page to represent the 'seven several stages thereof, from his birth to his death. With pictures and poems exposing the follies of every age'.[15] The woodblocks used for these pictures were re-used in the pseudo-Bunyan *Meditations on the Several Ages of Man's Life* (1701), a title which later in the same work turns into 'Meditations upon the Seven Ages of Man's Life'.[16]

Given that 'the seven ages' in the late medieval period and in the Renaissance means no more than the Ages of Man, there is not much to be gained by inquiring, either in relation to 'All the world's a stage' or in relation to late medieval and Renaissance literature as a whole, whether seven is the most 'correct' number of ages or whether it is in fact the division most often encountered in art and in literature.[17] The history of number symbolism in general and the writings of the Pythagorean school in particular are of very great interest for their own sake, but discussions of the Ages of Man have often been less illuminating than they might have been, given the wealth of material which has been brought to light, because of the way in which such discussions are typically organised – according, that is to say, to the number of ages into which man's life is divided in the works being discussed. This even applies to Franz Boll's and Samuel Chew's studies of the Ages of Man, though anyone interested in the subject must of course be deeply indebted to them.

The habit of organising the argument according to numerical divisions of ages in Ages of Man studies goes back to antiquity, and it might well be argued that it is as intrinsic to the genre as is the *forest aventureuse* to Arthurian romance. A characteristically unpromising opening to a study of the ages is found in the Lowland Scot David Person's encyclopedia, *Varieties* (1635):

Severall men have severally treated of severall numbers . . .

He quickly reassures us, however, that he will confine his attention to three and seven:

> as finding maniest and most memorable things in all sciences comprehended within them; which thus pack't up together, cannot but bee infinitely delightfull, and most helpefull to the memory of every reader.[18]

The survey of the division of the ages here winningly presents itself as a micro-encyclopedia within the macro-encyclopedia, which is, in turn, a microcosm – as William Drummond points out in his dedicatory poem:

> This booke a world is; here if errours be,
> The like (nay worse) in the great world we see.

Information cunningly packaged for ready assimilation and memorising: if that is the purpose of the survey of the ages then the organisation of the material by number is apt. The wood, in that case, only exists for the trees. But if we want to work in the other direction, to ask questions about the underlying ideas associated with the Ages of Man, we need to break loose from the centuries-old bond of an overriding concern with the question 'how many?' Emiel Eyben has notably done so in his articles on the ages in the Roman world, articles which I cite again and again in the notes to this volume. Eyben concerns himself with a wide range of age-related matters and considers the beginning, middle and end of man's life. My focus here is a narrower and more purely literary one, and it is high time to ask the question 'why *perfect* age?'

> *Edmund*: I have heard him oft maintaine it to be fit that sonnes at perfect age, and fathers declin'd, the father should be as ward to the son, and the sonne manage his revennew.
> *Gloucester*: O villain, villain: his very opinion in the letter. Abhorred villaine, unnaturall, detested, brutish villaine   (*King Lear* I, ii 71–7)

Shakespeare uses the age-name 'perfect age' in this one instance only, when Edmund is pushing his father to the point where his anger can no longer be satisfied with piled-up adjectives and demands release in violent action. Gloucester's wrath is kindled not only by the 'opinion' itself, which neatly turns established social order on its head, making a child of the parent and a parent of the child, but also by the coolly objective and even pedantic terminology in which this outrageous proposition is put forward. Gloucester and (as he thinks) Edgar are generalised into 'fathers' and 'sonnes'; the more usual age-names for the age of legal majority – 'manhood', 'man('s) age', 'man's (e)state' – are rejected in favour of the English equivalent of *perfecta aetas*, 'perfect age'. In English, perfect age is an age-name associated with legal documents and with writings on the Ages of Man which rehearse Greek, Latin and Arabic divisions of the ages and translate the age-names of their authorities as exactly as possible.[19] Shakespeare's contemporary Thomas Bowes, for instance, begins his discussion of manhood, in his chapter 'Of the division of the ages of man', with a familiar age-name, 'man's estate', combined with an explanation of the age-name *perfecta aetas* (he is translating from Pierre de la Primaudaye):

Mans estate beginneth when a man is even now ripe and setled, and groweth no more in bodie.

As he goes on to specify the duties of this 'setled' stage of life, his marginal note adopts the Latin age-name: 'the dutie of a man at the perfection of his age'.[20]

If the carefully-calculated stuffiness of Edmund's age-terminology serves to madden Gloucester, it may also serve to alert us to some of the problems associated with the names of the different ages, and with the particular age-name chosen for the title of this book. The first problem is that many age-names which once carried with them more or less precise contexts (legal, medical, theological and so on), which once indicated more or less precise stages of life and which were once perceived as belonging to known divisions of the ages, now, in the second half of the twentieth century, are either unknown or seem imprecisely quaint. Editors of *King Lear* did not usually feel the need to gloss 'sonnes at perfect age' until the last twenty years or so; now, it is customarily glossed 'full maturity', but the specifically legal associations of the age-name are not noted.[21]

The glosses provided for age-names in the standard editions of late Middle English texts – the latter part of the fourteenth century in England being our principal literary focus – often reflect the classical education of their editors, reminding us that our own vocabulary of age-names is sadly impoverished. Who now would think of glossing 'al watz þis fayre folk in her first age' (*Sir Gawain and the Green Knight*, 54) as Norman Davis did in 1967, 'in the flower of their youth'?[22] Unfortunately this gloss itself now needs to be glossed before its aptness can be assessed; indeed, the vague sense of nostalgic eulogy this gloss has suggested to post-1967 readers of *Sir Gawain* has significantly influenced interpretation of the first movement of the poem, and obscured what the *Gawain*-poet is saying about the age of Arthur's court, as I shall argue when we come to discuss *first age*. Age-names in early English texts in general now need to be given detailed comment, not just in-context equivalents.

One of the problems associated with names of ages, then, is the rapidly declining awareness of classical age-names and of traditional divisions of the ages. But in a sense this can work to our advantage if it prevents us from taking it for granted that age-names refer to stages of life which are absolute and fixed, and especially if it prevents us from thinking that earlier age-names are readily translatable into modern equivalents. Although early modern English, in marked contrast to present-day English, was exceptionally rich in borrowed age-names deriving from the divisions of the ages in earlier cultures, Renaissance writers discussing the Ages of Man were acutely aware of the contradictions and ambiguities of their own age-terminology. Above all, they expressed concern about the relative vagueness of their native age-name 'youth', which could be used to refer to the whole of a man's life up to the onset of old age, or to the period after boyhood and before *adolescentia* and mature adulthood, or to the period after what we should call adolescence. John Wodroephe (1623), the scholar–soldier, is very unsure:

> [Perot says that] the age of youth ought to be put after adolescence, never the lesse it is more likely true that it ought to follow puerilitie[23]

Cuffe decides to bow to common age-name usage, and gives the name 'youth' to two different ages, the age from eighteen to twenty-five years, which is the fourth stage of 'our growing age', and the age from twenty-five to thirty-five or forty years, which is the first of the two stages of 'our flourishing and middle age', 'manhood' being the second. The second time he uses the age-name 'youth' he justifies himself by saying 'so the penurie of our English toong warranteth me to call it . . . you may call it our *prime*' (pp. 118–19).

The problem for Cuffe, Wodroephe and their contemporaries arose from the fact that the English *geogooð* > youth was not and never had been an age-name which had an exact equivalent in authoritative divisions of the ages, but yet it was obviously the nearest approximation to the Latin age-name *juventus*. In classical usage, *juventus* clearly implied mature adulthood, though in medieval usage its upward and downward age-limits were not by any means fixed, and the relationship between *juvenis/juventus* and *adolescens/adolescentia* in later Latin, in Patristic writings and throughout the Middle Ages has caused historians particularly grave difficulties in their attempts to establish exact dating by way of the age-terminology used in documents.[24] In spite of this area of uncertainty surrounding the precise signification of *juventus*, English writers in the Renaissance wanted to prove to themselves that their own 'youth' could achieve a similar authoritative resonance and at least as much definition. Walter Haddon, in his epigram 'How every age is enclined', adopts one of the commoner solutions: he distinguishes between young youth and mature, adult youth (*juventus*) by adding a descriptive adjective to the second of the two:

> From 12. to 21. *Youth*
> runnes rashly on his race:
> The *Lustie Youth* to lawles luste
> and riot runnes apace.[25]

Haddon's epigram recalls the interlude *Lusty Juventus* both in choice of age-name and in satirical content, but other English age-names for *juventus* suggest rather the physical strength and maturity of adult youth. Milton, for instance, in *Areopagitica*, sees the 'noble and puissant nation' of England 'as an eagle muing her mighty youth, and kindling her undazl'd eyes at the full midday beam' (this age-name is anticipated by Gower).[26] The 1620 recusant translation of Augustine's *Confessiones* chooses 'more confirmed youth' for the *juventus* of the original.[27] Shakespeare, in sonnet 7, speaks of 'strong youth':

> Loe in the Orient when the gracious light
> Lifts up his burning head, each under eye
> Doth homage to his new appearing sight,
> Serving with lookes his sacred majesty,
> And having climb'd the steepe up heavenly hill,
> Resembling strong youth in his middle age,
> Yet mortall lookes adore his beauty still
> Attending on his goulden pilgrimage . . .

Stephen Booth, in his edition of the sonnets, misinterprets the sixth line, taking it that 'strong youth' and 'middle age' are two distinct ages; they are in fact the same age (*juventus*) under two different names.[28]

Whereas Renaissance writers were concerned to find age-names which would unambiguously indicate mature, adult youth while still preserving the native age-name closest to *juventus*, writers in the late medieval period in England do not seem to have felt the same need to differentiate between the various stages of youth, even when youth was perceived as extending right up to the threshold of old age. When Langland defines Jesus as being 'in his juventee' (*Piers Plowman* B19:108) at the marriage-feast in Cana his choice of age-name has nothing to do with a desire to be precise about the stage of youth Jesus had reached when he turned the water into wine: he anglicises the Latin age-name because he has particular reasons for wishing to avoid using the usual English word in relation to the life of the perfect man.[29] Age-names for mature adulthood were available in late Middle English – *middel age/elde*, *manhod*, *mannes age (-stat)* and *ful age*, among others – but they were not nearly as commonly used as *youthe*.

From the outset it is as well to be clear that the rather rare Middle English age-name *middel age* is not normally the equivalent of *media aetas*, the age intervening between *juventus* and *senectus*, but rather manhood, the strongest age, the age in the middle of man's life. As John Trevisa says in his translation (1398/9) of the *De Proprietatibus Rerum* of Bartholomeus Anglicus (Bartholomew of Glanville), it is the age which is 'in þe middil amonges ages, and þerfore strengest'.[30] Between *striplynges age* (Bartholomeus' *adholescencia*) and the first part of old age (Bartholomeus' *senecta*), man 'is isette in þe ende of his ful encresinge, and þerfore he is strong to helpe at nede'. The phrase Malory uses of the pick of warrior-knights, 'within two ayges', means 'in the middle/strongest age' (not 'between youth and middle age' or 'middle-aged' as the *MED* suggests, *age*, 1a,a).[31] Unambiguous confirmation of this sense of *middel age* is provided by the fact that *adulta aetas* is translated *medil age* in a couplet accompanying an image of the Passion in a fifteenth-century Franciscan homiliary:

I am a sowl baryn and seer;
Myn medil age desyvyth me here
(Sum mens inculta, mea decipit etas adulta).[32]

In late Middle English, the age-name *parfit age/elde*, another name for mature adulthood, the stage of life lasting from the completion of bodily growth until the beginning of *elde*, came to be used in certain scholarly and professional contexts to translate *perfecta aetas* as precisely as possible. The earlier version of the Wyclifite Bible (*c.*1384) contains the earliest recorded example of this age-name in English:

[Antiochus] sente an odious prince . . . comaundynge to hym for to slea alle of parfit age.

(2 Maccabees 5:24)

As we have already noticed, it was occasionally used in legal documents to mean the age of majority.[33] From what has been said already, it is evident that a book about the use of the age-name 'perfect age' in English would be a short and dull one, but there are two reasons why this study of the middle age of man's life in medieval thought and late medieval English poetry is entitled *The Perfect Age of Man's Life*. The first reason is that this age-name does not readily bring to mind ready-made associations, as many other names for the age of completed maturity, even if they are no longer current, still do – age-names like 'acme', 'best age', 'constant age', 'firm(est) age', 'flower', 'flowering/flourishing age', 'full(est) age', 'meridian', 'prime' and 'strong-(est) age'. Literally, of course, 'perfect age' is precisely equivalent to Ælfric's Old English age-name *se fulfremeda waestm*, 'completed, perfected growth', but it does not so immediately suggest bodily strength, physical maturity or age in years.[34] It does, however – and this is the second and more important reason for choosing it – suggest a more absolute concept than names like 'flower', 'prime' (and so on) do, a concept more detached from the Ages of Man topos (with its inherent sense of a sequence of stages of life) and with more specifically Christian connotations. All these suggestions are consonant with the medieval Christian idea of the middle age of life.

The Latin *perfecta aetas* is closely (though not exclusively) associated with the perfect age of Christ's life, with his baptism, ministry and crucifixion, and with the age which resurrected and redeemed Christian bodies will enjoy for ever in Heaven.[35] These associations will be examined in chapter 7. For the moment, a glance at the one reference to man's 'perfect age' in Middle English poetry may help to direct us towards those things about this age-name which are odd, and uniquely medieval. In the early fifteenth-century poem 'The Nightingale' (beginning 'Go, lityll quayere, and swyft thy prynses dresse'), the nature of the nightingale is 'moralysyd unto Cryste', to the ages of 'every crystyn sowle, that schuld remembre the ourys of Cristys passyoun' and to the ages of the world.[36] Thus 'morrow' should make man think of the first age of the world (the creation and fall), of his birth with its woe, and his 'youth' (line 170; here, pre-adolescence) with its folly and vice, and of the betrayal of Christ: these are the correspondences of which the nightingale sings 'this oure of morow, cleped matutyne' (line 187). At prime, man should think of the wantonness of his 'adolescens' (267), at tierce of the devil's incitement to pride in his lusty youth (330), the age that 'hast reson, strenght, and hele' (317), and at sext . . . but this age, corresponding to the hour of Christ's crucifixion, is not endowed with any specific inclination to vice:

> in speciall, ye of perfyt age,
> This oure of sixt, in myddes of your lyfe,
> Aught to be war and wayte aftir þe wage
> That Crist rewardeth withoute werre or stryfe,
> Wher endles joye and blysse are ever ryfe. (358–62)

wayte aftir look for

The very name 'perfyt age' that a man is properly given in the middle of his life ought, the poet suggests, to put him in mind of Christ's perfect age, to protect him from all imperfection and prepare him for the everlasting perfect age of Heaven. Christ, and the nightingale, die at nones; no age of man's life corresponds to this hour, for perfection cannot be followed by a less perfect age, and Christ himself never knew *elde*.[37] The ages of man's life in 'The Nightingale' are accommodated to the ages of Christ's life with a boldness which, as I shall argue in the third part of this book, is characteristic of the treatment of the ages in late medieval English poetry.

The age-name 'perfect age' may, then, in certain, confined contexts mean no more than 'legal majority', as perhaps in *King Lear*, but writers using this age-name usually show that they are aware of its more absolute sense, aware that it sounds as though it ought to be an age more-than-naturally free from human vice and inadequacy. The author of *Meditations on the Several Ages of Man's Life* (1701) can scarcely believe such an age could be experienced in this fallen world:

This surely is miscalled the perfect age [the fourth age; thirty to forty years], unless by perfect, we mean only that in this age it is, that all the imperfections of this humane nature, which before this lay hid under the undisguis'd simplicity of childhood, or the more airy lightness of unbridled youth, appear in this age in their full perfection (p. 40)

18

I suspect that thoughts something like these may be assumed to be in Gloucester's mind as he listens to Edmund talking about 'sonnes at perfect age'. What is unique about the medieval idea of the perfect age is that the idea of an age of unchanging perfection is entertained not simply as fuel for satire but as a serious possibility. A man may, perhaps, reach perfection in the middle of his life. This is the idea which is reflected in the title of this book.

3

The ages of woman's life

The third age consisteth of eight yeares, being named by our auncients *adolescencie*, or youth-hood, and it lasteth from fourteene till two and twenty yeares be fully compleate . . . a man then beginneth to be prompt by Nature, powerfull and able for procreation: as enclining to love, to women, and addicted to musicke, sports, pleasures, bankets, and other worldly delights . . .

The fourth age paceth on, untill a man have accomplished two and fortie yeares, and is tearmed young man-hood, the course whereof continueth nineteene yeares . . . this age is prince of all other, and the source of life, during which time the faculties and powers of the body and of the spirit doe acquire and attaine to their strength, and man beeing then apprehensive, bold and hardy knoweth how to order and dispose of his owne affaires.

(Milles, p. 336)

THE AGE in the middle of the seven ages, which Milles chooses to call young manhood as distinct from mature manhood, the fifth age, is unmistakably represented here as the middle age of the life of *man*. His account of the first two ages, infancy and childhood, is not specifically gendered: the visible bodily changes of the first 'doe happen generally in all persons, by reason of the Moones government', while the planet Mercury, in the second, influences all young children, so that they incline towards being 'inconstant and mutable'. But, under the influence of Venus, the third age comes to be perceived as exclusively male, women no longer being part of the subject but objects of youth-hood's desire. This specificity continues into the fourth age, culminating in the image of young manhood as the age which is 'prince of all other'.

Milles is translating and adapting Pedro Mexia's version of the seven ages of man's life, and Mexia's version is an amalgam of the authorities cited in the quotation at the head of chapter 2 (and of later medieval recensions of these authorities): not Milles himself, then, but the tradition of dividing and characterising the ages assumes the centrality of man's experience. Where woman's experience of the ages is explicitly recognised, it is recognised in terms of its deviation from a masculine norm. The supposition that man's experience of the ages is normative is remarkably tenacious in writings belonging to the Ages of Man tradition: B.M. Foss, for instance, in the course of characterising infancy in a *New Society* Social Studies Reader called *The Seven Ages of Man* (1970), says 'the child's progress from the mewling, puking infant to the whining schoolboy is shaped by his environment'. If Foss was unthinkingly led into that transition from ungendered names to

20

gender-specific name through recollecting 'All the world's a stage', it is precisely the liveliness of the Ages of Man tradition that makes it necessary to point to the fact that Milles' princely age is represented as an age that only men may expect to enjoy.

During this stage of life 'the faculties and powers of the body and of the spirit doe acquire and attaine to their strength': Milles' middle age is thoroughly medieval in its yoking together of the spiritual and bodily *perfecta aetas*. Both are characterised by strength, the spiritual *perfecta aetas* by the power of the faculty of intellection and the bodily *perfecta aetas* by physical fearlessness. Neither of these is available to women. Richard Carew reminds us in his *Examination of Mens Wits* (1594), a translation of Juan Huarte's *Examen de Ingenios*, that the opening of the book of Genesis provides incontrovertible evidence that woman's wits are much inferior to man's:

> for God having fashioned [Eve] with his own hands, and that very accomplished, and perfect in her sex, it is a conclusion infallibly true, that she was possessed of much lesse knowledge than Adam . . . she was by God created cold and moist: which temperature is necessarie to make a woman fruitfull and apt for childbirth, but enemy to knowledge.[1]

That Adam was created in his perfect age was a medieval and Renaissance commonplace; Eve must therefore have been created 'perfect in her sex', in the full perfection of the female creature, woman's nearest approach to *perfecta aetas* – but, lamentably, a 'perfection' containing within it 'an impairement in the reasonable part' (p. 273).[2] The authority of Aristotle is invoked for the characterisation of the female temperament as cold and moist (p. 272), lacking the heat that is necessary if the wits are to sharpen and strengthen. The authority of Avicenna might have been invoked, too: 'for males, warmth and dryness; for females cold and moisture' he says in his *Poem on Medicine*, summarising the sexes' characteristic temperamental disposition.[3]

Thomas Aquinas seems to allow a *perfecta aetas* to all human beings when he says, in the course of his discussion of the sacrament of confirmation in *Summa Theologiae*, that it is nature's intention 'ut omnis qui corporaliter nascitur, ad perfectam aetatem perveniat' (that everyone who is born physically should reach the perfect age).[4] Interestingly, however, his concern about whether this really applies to women as well as men is displaced on to the question of whether it is appropriate for the sacrament that confers on the recipient the *perfecta aetas* of the spirit to be made available to the sex that cannot participate in activities requiring strength: 'pugnare non competit mulieribus' (p. 212). Surely it is a contradiction in terms to talk of a woman's perfect age? As much of a contradiction as it is to offer the sacrament of confirmation to a child *in aetate puerili*? Or to a man nearing death? Nevertheless, Aquinas argues, 'corporales aetates animae non praejudicant' (the ages of the body are not detrimental to the ages of the soul) and women, too, may experience spiritual maturity; indeed, many women have fought spiritually 'animo virili' (p. 214).[5] Theologically, this is a consoling and sympathetic conclusion, but the structure of Aquinas' debate serves to suggest that all the ages of woman's life and the ages at the beginning and end of man's life are aberrations from the normative age, the perfect age of man's life. It is a short step from this suggestion to the suggestion that every age but man's perfect age is dissatisfied with its condition – a step Barnabe Googe (translating Marcellus Palingenius) takes in *The Zodiake of Life* (1576):

> So women, aged men and boyes,
>   do covet most alwaies:
> Because they lack both strength and force
>   in mind, and have no stayes.[6]

In this matter-of-fact aside (Palingenius is aware that he is stating the obvious), 'well stayde age', the age-name Thomas Fortescue chooses as the equivalent of Avicenna's *aetas consistentiae*, is characterised as an age of positives, while woman is perceived as being in want in all her ages.[7] Nothing in the course of her life affords her intrinsic security. This perception informs the account of the procession of the seasons in the pseudo-Aristotelean *Secretum Secretorum* (*Kitāb Sirr al-asrār*), the 'Long Form' of which dates from the late eleventh century.[8] We shall look more fully at the image of the procession of the seasons represented as the ages of man's life in the next chapter; in the *Secretum Secretorum*, unusually, the four seasons are represented as the four ages of woman's life. James Yonge, translating the treatise as *The Governaunce of Prynces* (1422), is sufficiently surprised by this to turn the *juvencula* who represents spring into 'a fayre young man that arrayth hym well of al maner of anournement to shewe hymselfe atte the weddynge'.[9] But he reverts to the sex indicated in his original when he comes to summer. In the Latin text, summer is a woman 'corpore plena, etate perfecta', which Yonge renders 'a spouse ful woxen of body and parfite age' (p. 244).

The first two seasons–ages are purely ornamental: no age-related characteristics are associated with woman's youth or perfect age. But in the autumn and winter of her life, when woman as object is no longer pleasing to look upon, there is a lot more to be said, in the English translations of the *Secretum*, at least. Yonge's autumn presents herself

as a woman of grete age, that now wox a-colde and hade nede to be hote clothyde, for that the yowuthe is passyde, and age neghyth, wherefor hit is no mervaile yf beuté she hath lost. (p. 245)

The winter of Sir Gilbert of the Haye's Scottish version (1456) presents herself as ane ald wyf, bludelas . . . calde and dry, nakit and trembland, gray and gretand (sobbing), and all for elde drawand to the poynt of dede.[10]

For Yonge, she is 'like an old katte' (p. 246). In these descriptions we have to do with more than simply fascination with the grotesque: the elaboration of detail provides an outlet for the frustration inherent in the idea that woman exists to be decorative but cannot be so for very long. Yonge may admit that 'it is no wonder', but man's sense of woman's autumn-age throws retrospective shadows on her perfect age – something that is not true of his sense of the course of his own life, as we shall see.

One of the consequences of the ages of woman's life being perceived in this way was that it came to be regarded as a fact that the course of woman's life was shorter than man's. There was evidence to support it, too: Cuffe, discussing the length of life, points out that

those of a sanguine constitution are by nature capable of the longest life; as having the two qualities of life best tempred (pp. 97–8)[11]

Women, however, are disposed to be phlegmatic, cold and moist, and this means that

for the most part [they] are sooner perfected than men, being sooner fit for generation, sooner in the flower and prime of their age, and finally, sooner old (pp. 106–7).

Cowell tells us (1607) that as far as the law of England is concerned a woman has already lived through six ages by the time she reaches twenty-one. 'First, at 7 yeares of age the lord her father may distraine his tenents for ayde to marry her: for at these yeares she may consent to matrimonie' and lastly 'at 21 yeares she is able to alienate her lands and tenements'.[12] 'Six severall ages', Cowell calls them, linking them deliberately with Ages of Man writings.

The belief that the ages of woman's life occupy a much shorter space of time than the ages of man's life is expressed in Orsino's words to the travestied Viola in *Twelfth Night*:

Then let thy Love be yonger then thy selfe,
Or thy affection cannot hold the bent:
For women are as Roses, whose faire flowre
Being once displaid, doth fall that verie howre. (2:4:36–9)

Orsino's comparison is a well-worn one, and the 'truth' it conveys is repeated as late as 1842 in an anonymous treatise on *The Seven Ages of Man's Life* printed at the Baptist Mission Press in Calcutta. In the chapter on the sixth age, the autumn of life, the author remarks that 'one of the most painful incidents of humanity is the short duration of female beauty'.[13] The bland assumption that woman experiences the flower of her age through man's eyes is more striking in the unvarnished nineteenth-century statement than in Orsino's honeyed words, but of course Orsino is playing (or, rather, advising Viola to play) one of the best-known gambits in the game of seduction. Viola's response picks up the erotic undermeaning of Orsino's words:

> And so they are: alas that they are so:
> To die, even when they to perfection grow. (2:4:40–1)

Supposing that man's 'affection' manages to 'hold the bent', and that woman's 'flower' is indeed 'display'd', then sexual climax is the natural consequence. But Viola's lament also opens out Orsino's image and places it in a universal context, in its reference to the heart-breaking precariousness of perfection. Achieving prime and losing it occur at the same instant. The specifically sexual meaning is not cancelled out, but absorbed into a coherent sense of the course of woman's life – perceived from a man's point of view by a woman's consciousness.

Viola's 'conceit of this inconstant stay' also informs the first sequence of Shakespeare's sonnets – much more, I suggest, than does the classical sense of life's progressing ritually from one phase to the next (which we shall look at in the next chapter). The sense of ritual progression is not absent from these sonnets, but it is always undermined. In sonnet 12, for instance, there is an ordered and measured opening:

> When I doe count the clock that tels the time,
> And see the brave day sunck in hidious night,
> When I behold the violet past prime,
> And sable curls or silver'd ore with white . . .

But this calm confrontation of mutability gives way to a plangent lament for prime, helplessly and in great haste giving itself over to death:

> sweets and beauties do them-selves forsake,
> And die as fast as they see others grow (11–12)

Activity and passivity are strangely blended in this image of the death of perfection.

Shakespeare chooses to represent the course of the Fair Youth's life in terms normally appropriated to the course of woman's life. The function of his master–mistress in the perfection of his age is precisely woman's function when she is 'perfect in her sex' – to be fruitful. The first two lines of the first sonnet are as it were a gloss on the exchange between Orsino and Viola:

> From fairest creatures we desire increase,
> That thereby beauties *Rose* might never die

The natural outcome of woman's perfect age is here presented as a rational solution to the problem of the transience of perfection. The effect of co-operating with nature and with reason, however, is to ensure that woman's understanding of the course of her life will mirror man's understanding of the course of her life in an endlessly reflexive cycle:

The ages of woman's life

Thou art thy mothers glasse and she in thee
Calls backe the lovely Aprill of her prime,
So thou through windowes of thine age shalt see
Dispight of wrinkles this thy goulden time.   (3:9-12)

The only way out of this enclosed system is for Shakespeare to allow the Fair
Youth to enjoy man's princely perfect age, as he does in sonnet 37, for
instance, and in sonnet 62 – though here perfect age speaking through the
person of the lover turns into the Pride of Life:

Me thinkes no face so gratious is as mine,
No shape so true, no truth of such account,
And for my selfe mine owne worth do define,
As I all other in all worths surmount.   (5-8)

We are left asking whether it is possible for a woman to be represented as
enjoying perfect age, enjoying it not as the object of man's perception,
deprived of 'stayes', but as the 'well stayed' subject of her own experience.
Perhaps all that woman can do is interpret to man (as Viola does) his
understanding of her ages and his understanding of his own ages. That, after
all, is largely what this book is attempting to do. In the last chapter, however,
we shall encounter a woman who is in her perfect age in the fullest sense of
the age-name: she is White, in Chaucer's *Book of the Duchess*, and one of the
most astonishing of all women brought into imaginative life by men. In the
mean time, we need to remind ourselves that 'man' in the Ages of Man is not
normally an inclusive term, and that when I talk about 'man's life' I am not
being inclusive, either.

4

'Maturity, full of ripenesse'

Anything better than the anxiety dream
Of being on the stage without a part,
Especially in a long play: seven acts
Although the first and last are played in darkness.

THE English poet Patricia Beer here suggests that the tradition of codifying the ages of man's life, a tradition already old when Hippocrates divided life into seven unequal parts, is rooted in man's need to impose a knowable shape upon what would otherwise be experienced as frightening, unexpected and directionless physical and mental changes.[1] The wish to see or hear or read representations of the sequence of the ages has been so generally felt that it is tempting to fall into the supposition that the ways in which man thinks about the ages transcend the barriers of time and place, as well. The physical facts of birth and weakness, growth and vigour, decline and death, to some extent influence every representation of the ages, but where the representations of the ages in different cultures tend to have most in common with each other is at the two ends of the sequence rather than in the middle. The 'childishness' of the very young tends to be idealised, as in the avuncular couplet about what children are like in John of Grimestone's fifteenth-century preaching-book:

Children ben litel, brith and schene, and eþe for to fillen,
Suetliche pleyȝende, fre of ȝifte, and eþe for to stillen.[2]
brith bright; *eþe* easy; *fre* generous.

The 'childishness' of the extremely old, by contrast, tends to be viewed with disgust, yet it has very generally been recognised that infancy and decrepit old age, Beer's 'acts . . . played in darkness', strangely resemble each other – whether second childishness be attributed to libidinal regression or to the imbalance of the bodily humours. What happens to man's body, mind and spirit in the middle of his life, on the other hand, has been perceived and interpreted in many different ways.

The idea that there is an age of transition between youth and old age is so firmly established in twentieth-century Western culture that 'middle age' enjoys the status of a fact of life. Middle age is, nevertheless, an idea – a way of perceiving the middle of man's life which has its origins in Graeco-Roman civilisation. Although we, like the Roman physician Celsus, find it natural to divide humankind into the young, the old and 'those who are between youth and old age',[3] the age which classical writers occasionally call *media aetas*, which Renaissance writers sometimes call '(the) middle age' (but usually together with an alternative age-name) and which we habitually call middle age (the in-between age), has never had an unambiguous name of its own.[4]

The stepping-stone age between *juventus* and *senectus*, between mature adulthood and old age, has its origin, I suggest, in the desire to smooth over the transition between these two ages. This transition has been imaginatively realised in terms of unkind and inexplicable abruptness in the literatures of many times and places.[5] Within the English tradition, one of the most tantalising pieces of evidence for the relationship between 'literary' and 'real life' experience of this unkind transition is found in the autobiography of the early Tudor musician and spelling reformer, Thomas Whythorne:

I considering with my self that I was now about thirty yeers of age, and growing toward the age of forty, at the which yeers begins the first part of the old mans age, I took occasion to write therof this sonnet foloing –

> The force of yowth is welni past
> Where heat and strenth of late took place,
> And now is cumming in all hast
> The cold weak age for to deface
> The shew of yowth, wherfor I must
> Yeeld to mi chaunce and thrall mi lust.
> Now, farewell youth and all thi toies!
> I will go seek more certain joies.[6]

Not only the idea of an age of transition between mature youth and old age but also the very idea of the representation of the ages may have had its origins in man's need to be reassured that there was no unpredictable transition in store for him and that the course of his life would be a steady and measured progress. Whythorne was able to prepare himself in advance, and to write like an old man before he became one. But once the idea of a stepping-stone age had become established the inevitability associated with the movement from one *gradus* to another became a new source of disquiet – for men less complacent than Whythorne. It then became desirable to divert attention from the end of the sequence, which might or might not offer 'more certain joies', and focus attention on the steps along the way. This hypothetical chain of causes and effects is offered as one possible way of interpreting the evolution of ideas of the middle age of man's life, and of accounting for the ambiguity characterising descriptions of the age separating the passing of youth from the advent of old age.

[Middle age] at its best is the fullest and richest phase of all. And even at its average it brings a good harvest and a flowering of social and personal maturity – which is wisdom. (1970)[7]

The idea that there is a well-defined age intervening between youth and old age goes back at least as far as Aristotle's description of 'the nature of men according to their ages', directed towards rhetoricians who wish to adapt their manner of speaking to the audience and the occasion.[8] First he describes what the young are like (12); then he moves straight on to 'older men' (13) and lastly he turns to the 'character of those in the prime of life', the *akmē* (14). Aristotle gives the *akmē* extravagant praise: 'all the advantages that youth (*neotes*) and old age (*geras*) possess separately; those in the prime of life possess combined; and all cases of excess or defect in the other two are replaced by due moderation and fitness' (section 3). It is during the *akmē*, according to Aristotle, that the mind is most fully developed, 'at about forty-nine' (section 4). Here he is following Solon: 'in the seventh [period of] seven [years], he is at his prime in mind and tongue.[9]

The authority of Aristotle, confirming the statements of the Hippocratic writers, inevitably stamped on the minds of later writers discussing the Ages of Man the idea of the supremacy of the forty-ninth year. Macrobius, for instance, in his *Commentary on the Dream of Scipio*, says of it:

the number seven multiplied by itself produces the age which is properly considered and called perfect, so that a man of this age, as one who has already attained and not yet passed perfection, is considered ripe in wisdom, and not unfit for the exercise of his physical powers.[10]

The compromise implied by 'not *yet* passed . . . not *un*fit' in the context of what is apparently an absolute endorsement of the *akmē* is more obviously a source of embarrassment to Macrobius when he is describing the sixth hebdomad: from forty-two to forty-nine years 'a decline (*diminutio*) does set in, it is true, but a hidden one (*occulta*)' (section 74), Aristotle himself, following the Hippocratic writers but moving away from strictly hebdomadal numbering, concedes that 'the body is most fully developed from thirty to thirty-five years of age' (14, section 14).[11] Discussing the implications of this, in the *Politics*, Aristotle argues that the state's warriors and the state's counsellors should be the same people, 'not, however, at the same time, but in the order prescribed by nature, who has given to young men strength and to older men wisdom'.[12]

The forty-nine year *akmē* of Aristotle's *Rhetoric* is an age-concept which is deliberately dissociated from what nature prescribes, and his brief discussion of the character of men in their prime makes no attempt to disguise this. Although he professes to elevate the age which is the mean between youth and old age, having the advantages of both and the disadvantages of neither, he finds very little to say about it, and what he does say sounds aloof and perfunctory. This is the more striking because his descriptions of the characters of young men and old men are funny and wise and full of life. The young 'take pleasure in living in company and as yet judge nothing by

28

expediency, not even their friends' (12, section 13); the old 'are always suspicious owing to mistrust, and mistrustful owing to experience. And neither their love nor their hatred is strong' (13, sections 3–4). Men in their middle age, though, 'are neither over-confident, which would show rashness, nor too fearful, but preserving a right attitude in regard to both' (14, section 2). Aristotle represents the middle age of man's life as an ethically ideal state, the pinnacle of aspiration, but his *akmē* is a dead thing, nevertheless.

Apparently objective descriptions of the stepping-stone age, descriptions which are not obviously tied to underlying metaphors such as the seasons and ages metaphor which we shall consider in a moment, are typically found, as Aristotle's *akmē* is, in the context of advice to the rhetorician. As Ptolemy says with engaging pedantry in his *Tetrabiblos*, the rhetorician needs to 'predetermine the appropriate fitness of every age to such events as may be expected',[13] and the most influential rhetorician's guide to the ages, especially in the Renaissance, was that of Horace.[14] This 'excellent poet', says Thomas Milles, has

made devision of mans ages . . . into foure partes onely, according as Pythagoras did, to wit; child-hood, youth-hood, man-hood, and old age: all which he hath elegantly described in his Art of Poesie, with those conditions belonging to men, in all those severall times. (p. 338)

Admiring Horace's elegant pithiness, Milles (following Mexia) apparently does not perceive that his representation of the ages is satirical. Whereas the young man is proverbially compared to 'a piece of wax of the right consistency for the impress of a seal' (an image which Anselm used as his starting-point, Eadmer tells us, when he was explaining why he concentrated his efforts on the training of the young),[15] Horace's 'beardless youth' is 'wax to be moulded to evil' (163). The *aetas virilis* 'manhood' proverbially pursues honour; according to Horace, it *inservit* (is enslaved to) it (167).

Aetas virilis as a name for the middle age was originally associated with the constitutional status of Roman citizens and with the age of legal majority.[16] In the English Renaissance, however, it typically refers to the age which immediately precedes old age. For John Wodroephe, writing at the beginning of the seventeenth century, 'virilitie' is the fifth of man's six ages, the age when man is 'in his best force, understanding and disposition'.[17] For Thomas Sheafe (1639) 'mans-age', the fourth of man's five ages, is 'the most stable and the most commendable'.[18] But most of the names for the stepping-stone age metaphorically link the period between youth and old age with the third of the four seasons, the commonest English names for it being 'ripe age', from the end of the fourteenth century, and 'mature age', from the mid fifteenth century. 'After forty five, even to threescore', says Thomas Milles, 'the age of man is called *maturitas*, maturity, full of ripenesse' (p. 338). The

29

ninth of the eleven ages of man in Robert Farley's whimsical, grotesque *Kalendarium Humanae Vitae* (1638), the age corresponding to November, is *aetas provectior*, which he renders in English both as 'age farre spent' and as 'full ripe age'.[19]

The correspondence between the four seasons and the four ages of man's life, a doctrine associated with both Hippocrates and Pythagoras, has been the subject of a great deal of investigation; specifically, the correspondence between autumn, earth, the melancholy humour, Saturn and man's *maturitas* has been thoroughly examined by Raymond Klibansky, Erwin Panofsky and Fritz Saxl.[20] It was the concern of ancient Greek philosophers to establish mathematically-based correspondences between macrocosm and microcosm which led more or less directly to the conviction that man has an autumn-age, a stepping-stone age which is characterised by fruitfulness.[21] The Arabic scholars through whom ancient traditions about correspondences were made known to the later Middle Ages typically attempt to demonstrate that the Hippocratic and the Pythagorean traditions are reconcilable, that the division of the ages of man's life is founded upon both the hebdomad and the tetrad. The ninth-century medical writer Hunain ibn-Isḥāḳ (Al-ʿIbādī), editing the pseudo-Galenic commentary on the Hippocratic *De Septimanis*, concludes his division of the ages and corresponding seasons into childhood (corresponding to spring), youth (corresponding to summer), mature age (corresponding to autumn) and old age (corresponding to winter) with the confident assertion that 'it is now quite clear that Hippocrates is right when he compares the nature of man with the macrocosm'.[22] At the end of the chapter on the ages, after an examination of Hippocratic methodology, Al-ʿIbādī reaffirms that 'Hippocrates speaks about these four ages of man's life many times, and he devises three others, so that with them he may fulfil his promise concerning the hebdomads' (p. 61). The implicit message that the division of man's life into four ages which correspond to the four seasons is especially 'right', whatever other numerical divisions may be devised, comes very near to being explicit at this point.

Iconographic traditions undoubtedly reinforced metaphysical arguments about the correspondence between the seasons and the ages, and were themselves reinforced, in turn. Even as bare and bald a rendering of the idea as Anthony Sherley's (1604) succeeds in hinting at the familiar image of the four ages as a *series*, a procession:

> In a mans life there doth appeare
> The fowre strange faces of the yeare;
> Child-hood the Spring, Youth Sommer showes,
> Like Autumne Manhood, Age like Winter goes.[23]

1 'Volat Irrevocabile Tempus', Otto Van Veen, 1607.

Perhaps the finest Renaissance example of this image of the ages in procession is Otto Van Veen's magnificently-conceived emblem 'Volat Irrevocabile Tempus' (see plate 1),[24] which illustrates a passage from the seventh ode of the fourth book of Horace's *Carmina* ('Diffugere nives, redeunt iam gramina campis'):

The year warns you – the hour which forcibly carries off the kindly day warns you – 'Do not hope that anything will last for ever'. Severe coldness grows mild in the face of the westerly winds; summer tramples the ruins of spring underfoot, and it will be her turn when fruit-bearing autumn pours forth its abundance. Soon, too, the sluggish winter comes back again. (8–13)

The lesser cycle of the day and the greater cycle of the year are not overtly associated with the ages here, but Van Veen's *series* of the ages can be interpreted as a counter-response to the sudden and violent temporal transitions Horace suggests as he yokes together the predictable submission of the gentle to the harsh ('alum quae rapit hora diem') and the unexpected submission of the harsh to the gentle ('frigora mitescunt Zephyris'). Van Veen's ages are in procession, their backs half turned on us, led by the child who stretches his arms forwards in eager aspiration. Because the procession is moving away from us, the old man who is in the foreground is the largest of the four figures, in spite of the fact that he is bent crookedly over a staff: the ages are therefore in ascending order of size, and the near nakedness of the child turns by stages into the old man's almost complete envelopment in clothing. There is nothing abrupt; nothing which disturbs the perspective. The image inevitably calls to mind the best-known and certainly, in the Renaissance, best-loved of all representations of the sequence of the ages, Ovid's *Metamorphoses* 15:199–216, in which the transitions from age to age are very deliberately smoothed over:

> Then followeth Harvest when the heate of youth growes sumwhat cold,
> Rype, meeld, disposed meane betwixt a youngman and an old,
> And sumwhat sprent with grayish heare. Then ugly winter last
> Like age steales on   (209–12: Arthur Golding's translation)[25]

The linking of seasons and ages lent its considerable authority, then, to the idea of a stepping-stone age, 'maturus mitisque inter iuvenem senemque'. In the classical world and in the early Middle Ages the characteristic visual image both of the ages of man's life and of the seasons seems to have been the *series*, though images of the ages apart from their association with the seasons are rare.[26] In the Montecassino manuscript (dated 1022–3) of Rabanus Maurus' *De Universo*, an early ninth-century encyclopedia based on Isidore's *Etymologiae*, the chapter on the division of the ages is headed by an illustration of *infantia, pueritia, adolescentia, juventus, gravitas* and *senectus* (see plate 2).[27] Fritz Saxl has convincingly argued that this Montecassino manuscript is a copy of a lost, illustrated Carolingian original, and that this lost Carolingian manuscript in turn derived its illustrations from a manuscript of the *Etymologiae* produced in seventh-century Spain, in 'surroundings where classical imagery and the classical language of forms were still alive'.[28] Two details of the Montecassino miniature, *pueritia*'s head being nearly on a level with *adolescentia*'s (although

2   The six ages, Rabanus Maurus, *De Universo*, 1022/3.

his feet only reach to the hem of *adolescentia*'s tunic) and *senectus* being disproportionately large (*gravitas* only reaches to his shoulder), suggest that at some earlier stage of the transmission of this image the figures may have been in ascending order of size as well as ascending order of age. This series of the ages looks distinctly awkward.

The image of the ages as a series in ascending order of years (and perhaps of size), each age being more warmly clad than its predecessor, is probably in its origins, then, a classical image; non-naturalistic, but calculated to reassure the observer that the course of life is a steady and measured progress, predictable from beginning to end. But the very inevitability of this progress alarmingly reinforces the memento mori which is implicit in all representations of the sequence of the ages. When each step is known in advance, death seems uncomfortably close. The series of the ages invites the response 'how can man's movement from one age to the next be slowed down?', or even 'how can the progress be halted?'

In sixteenth- and seventeenth-century discussions of the Ages of Man, the characteristic counter-response to the reminder of mortality the ages bring with them is to exalt and protract man's autumn-age, the age which immediately precedes the onset of old age. More specifically, the protraction and exaltation of *maturitas* may be interpreted as a counter-response to the reminder of mortality implicit in the 'facts' of humoralism as they were received by the Renaissance; above all, the fact that the cold and dry humour, melancholy, is dominant in the autumn of man's life. 'There are four humours in man, which correspond to the various elements', says the anonymous author of *De Mundi Constitutione* (*c.*1100):

they increase in the various seasons and are dominant in the various ages. Blood corresponds to air, increases in spring and is dominant in *pueritia*. Choler corresponds to fire, increases in summer and is dominant in *adolescentia*. Melancholy corresponds to earth, increases in autumn and is dominant in *maturitas*. Phlegm corresponds to water, increases in winter and is dominant in *senectus*.[29]

Humours, elements, seasons and ages are here correlated in a sequence which goes back as far as the Pythagoreans and which is still common in the seventeenth century. The details of the humoral sequence vary to some extent (though blood, choler, melancholy and phlegm is the sequence most commonly found),[30] but melancholy scarcely ever corresponds to spring or summer, and by the later Middle Ages coldness and sluggishness had come to be associated with both melancholy and phlegm, to the extent that the melancholy and phlegmatic temperaments were no longer perceived to be distinct. The authors of *Saturn and Melancholy* argue that

this confusion lowered the status of the melancholy disposition until at length there was scarcely anything good to be said of it.   (p. 64)[31]

The ancient and medieval association between melancholy and the grim planet Saturn helped in this process of decline.[32] In the context of the doctrine of the temperaments, the negative attitude towards melancholy survived into the seventeenth century effectively unchanged, existing alongside the Renaissance concept of the gifted melancholic whose mind – according to Ficino – was 'truly withdrawn from the world', and whose soul was given over to contemplation inspired by Saturn.[33]

Cuffe, writing about *The Differences of the Ages of Mans Life* in 1600, presents an unrelievedly negative view of both Saturn and melancholy:

all the astrologians have observed Saturne to be a planet enemie unto life, as having a vertue of cold and drought, and accordingly (as some imagine) was he painted with a sithe in his hand, cutting down as it were and killing men with the operation and infusion of these two deadly qualities   (p. 91) melancholy resembling the earth and it qualities, cold and drought, both enemies to life, hasteneth the destruction of the body whereunto it is incident. (p. 98)

Here, the correspondence between planet and humour is inescapable, but Cuffe associates their hostile and destructive qualities only with the last of his seven ages, 'decrepit crooked age', which 'from the angrie aspect of drie Saturne sucketh the poisonous infirmities of crasie sicknesse and waiward pettishnesse' (p. 121). Only at the very end of life does the melancholy humour become dominant enough for its adverse effects to be inescapable; even during the sixth of the seven ages, 'old age' (from fifty to sixty-five years), 'there remaineth a will and readinesse to be doing', although 'our strength and heat are evidently impaired' (p. 120).

Cuffe's account of the correspondence between the ages and the seasons gives 'man-age', corresponding to autumn, positive attributes only. It is the age

when after the manifold turmoiles and dangers of our fore-spent life, the good giftes and indowments of our minde (as we see it fall out in the fruites of Nature) receive a kind of seasonable and timely ripenesse. (p. 116)

The Renaissance instinct to exalt the autumn-age triumphs, in Cuffe's engagingly forthright treatise, over the unpalatable aspects of the doctrine of the humours. Cold, dry melancholy is reserved for Saturn-influenced winter-age. And yet, the autumnal metaphor which seems to endow the mind of man in his *maturitas* with the plumpness of the 'fruites of Nature' and to replace melancholy with the moisture and warmth of the sanguine humour, in fact doubles back on itself. The very ripeness of the mind becomes the cause of melancholic reflection on 'the manifold turmoiles and dangers of our fore-spent life'. Oddly enough, the English Renaissance here joins hands with the Renaissance of the twelfth century, for Hugo de Folieto (died c.1174) provides the following moralisation of the correspondence between autumn and melancholy in his short treatise *De Medicina Animae*:

[Melancholy] is like autumn insofar as it resembles the maturity of ripe fruits . . . It increases in autumn, that is, in ripe understanding, for the further you advance in *maturitas*, both of age and of understanding, the greater should your grief grow when you think of the sins you have committed.[34]

The metaphorical age-name *maturitas* only has force in the context of an assumption that man's 'fruits' are the fruits of ripe understanding, and that these fruits are produced when a man is no longer young. Hugo de Folieto believes that increasing age ought to bring with it more mature wisdom, but he does not adopt the stance of a man in the autumn of his life in the treatise as a whole. Lotario dei Segni (Innocent III), the author of the most uncompromising and influential medieval account of the dangers and miseries inherent in each successive age of man's life, was thirty-five years old when he wrote *De Miseria Humane Conditionis* (1195), and in his preface he says that his aim is 'to suppress pride, which is chief of all the vices'.[35] Like Dante, he writes as one 'nel mezzo del cammin', 'in myddes of [his] lyfe', reminding others, as the poet of 'The Nightingale' does, that they 'of perfyt age. . . Aught to be war and wayte aftir þe wage / That Crist rewardeth'.[36] In the medieval period, it seemed natural that a man should be able to advocate mindfulness in his own *juventus*, that he should be able to transcend pride and the other dangers characteristic of youth.

In the Renaissance, by contrast, it did not seem appropriate that a man should portray the successive ages before he had reached *maturitas*. The *puer senex* 'old-man child' might be grave and wise beyond his years, as Fulke Greville says Philip Sidney was, but the fitting age for meditation on the course of man's life was after youth had passed.[37] That Jacques should discourse on the Ages of Man is of a piece, then, with the entire reversal of the natural order of life he is attempting. 'All the world's a stage' is a set-piece that naturally belongs to Duke Senior, who prompts the speech with his own reference to the world as a theatre (*As You Like It*, II,vii 136–9), and who is the only other person on stage as Jacques speaks. The 'old duke', however, is trying to keep reality at bay just as much as Jacques is – by surrounding himself with young men and disporting himself like Robin Hood.

> Young men are ayrie, and themselves not knowe;
> Old men more nearer earth more earthlie growe[38]

– this natural and inexorable opposition between the sanguine young man and the melancholic old man, between air and earth, is inverted in front of our eyes as Jacques characterises the Ages of Man. And yet, although the young man chooses to represent himself as old and the old man as young, the ages of man's life, according to Jacques, move steadily onwards from infancy to decrepitude, remorselessly pared of all positive characteristics.

5

'Secrete diminution'

Ageing is the process of maturation and decline   (1970)[1]

THE OPPOSITION between the 'ayrie' and 'earthlie' stages of man's life
reverberates through Renaissance writings on the ages. The exaltation of *maturitas* inevitably entailed the degradation of youth: only in
a totally negative account like 'All the world's a stage' could the two emerge
equal. Robert Farley even succeeds in making the sixth age of his kalendar of
man's life, 'mans youth' (the age corresponding to August) seem grotesque-
ly ugly:

> When youth is almost man, death may him take.
> Search you deaths lime pits, and you'le find therein
> As oft the young steeres as the oxes skinne;
> Oft time old gray-hair'd wrinkles swim in teares
> For youthes who dyed in their prime of yeares.[2]

The uglification of youth could scarcely be more thoroughgoing than it is in
this juxtaposition of wrinkled animal hides burned bald by lime and hairy,
wrinkled human hides washed by tears. A far less subtle, more characteristic
attack on youth is contained in Thomas Pie's assumption that the author of
Ecclesiastes, being wise, was in his *maturitas*:

Neither was it penned by Solomon in the unstaidnesse of youth, or in his wanton and
wilder years, but even in ripenesse of age, and maturitie of judgement, when wisedom
was grounded with experience, and experience had grown up with age.[3]

Thomas Pie's commentary on Ecclesiastes, based on the lectures of
Antonio de Coro (a hot-tempered Spanish Protestant who was always on the
verge of upsetting the delicate Anglican orthodoxy of Oxford in the 1580s),
runs smoothly along well-established exegetical lines. The young man
should

use a mean, folow measure, and hold in the outragious desires with the bridle of reason
. . . for else, nothing is more slippery than youth, nothing more readie to vice, nothing
more prone to vanity.   (pp. 205–6)

So many late sixteenth- and seventeenth-century moralists take their texts
from Ecclesiastes that it is tempting to diagnose a chronic spiritual fatigue
accompanying the deep but gradual changes which transformed medieval

into modern society, a weariness with the idea of man's prime. But Pie, de Coro and most other commentators fail to appreciate that if this weariness is to be given full imaginative expression it is not enough simply to assert 'childhood and youth are vanity' (Ecclesiastes 11:10). The author of Ecclesiastes understands that 'vanitas vanitatum et omnia vanitas' (1:2) only becomes a meaningful imaginative statement if those things which the reader misguidedly supposes to have some worth are given every chance to prove themselves before the ground is cut from under their feet. The joyful *carpe diem* of

> *Laetare ergo iuvenis* . . . Rejoice, O young man, in thy youth, and let thy heart cheer thee in the days of thy youth (11:9)

is not cancelled out by 'childhood and youth are vanity' (11:10).[4] The command and the conclusion hauntingly re-echo each other. This creative interaction is characteristically smoothed away in Renaissance commentaries; exultation and despair flatten into platitudes about the dangers of youth.

The *media aetas* originated as a stepping-stone age, easing the transition between youth and old age and, in Aristotle's *Rhetoric*, balancing out the opposition between them. As autumn-age, middle age moved further and further away from youth, until *maturitas* was no loger perceived as being followed by wintry decay. Instead, it was perceived as increasing with increasing age and becoming ever more opposed to youth's immaturity. One of the most disenchanted Renaissance representations of youth is found in 'senis cujusdam cygnea cantio', one old man's swan-song, as Thomas Sheafe histrionically describes his *Vindiciae Senectutis, or, a plea for Old-Age* (1639). Sheafe was 'past his great climactericall yeare' when he wrote it, and his book is patently an imitation of Cicero's *De Senectute*, the treatise on old age which Cicero wrote in his sixty-third year.[5] *Vindiciae Senectutis*, however, has none of the magnanimity of *De Senectute*. It belongs to what we may call the *vanitas vanitatum* or Jacques-type Ages of Man, the type which laments the miseries and infirmities of every age. In this kind of representation of the ages old age is usually the most miserable of all — 'mans malignant age', Farley calls it, thinking of the deadly influence of Saturn.[6] But for Sheafe old age is the time of renewal and restoration:

> The other ages are as violent winds and stormes that by often beating upon this house of clay (or as bad inhabitants that by their neglect) bring it out of reparations; and OLD-AGE is the carpenter to repaire it. (p. 124)

Sheafe's exaltation of old age involves him in saying more about youth than about any of the other pre-mature ages,

> for that it stands most in opposition to the age I treate of, and lookes at it commonly with an eye full of scorn and contempt. (p. 101)

He feels nothing but disgust for the young man at the age when 'like the untamed horse, newly broken from his rider' he can 'shise it abroad and runne the wild-goose-race without controle, up and down in the world' (p. 96). Such strong revulsion from the young man's energy, sexual potency and freedom tugs the reader's response in two different directions: there is certainly attraction mingled with Sheafe's contempt. For if the old man will not allow the young man to rejoice in his youth, the very vehemence of his protest may stand the negative on its head, and a *carpe diem* find expression after all. This is just what happens in Nathaniel Crouch's *Vanity of the Life of Man* (1688). For all Crouch's endeavours to keep the man in his prime within the didactic confines of a *vanitas vanitatum* Ages of Man – we are warned in advance that 'he is not serious' – youth bursts into life, even managing to invest the well-worn notion of correspondence between the ages and the seasons with freshness, by alighting on it as though it were a pleasant fancy of his own:

> He cryes: 'I'le still go on,
>> Let who will count me vain:
> If I these happy days neglect,
>> They'l never come again.
>
> Nothing but joy and mirth
>> And sweet delights appear,
> Methinks I represent the spring,
>> The best time of the year.
>
> I'le wallow in all pleasure,
>> For I am in my prime,
> And I in merriment and play
>> Resolve to spend my time . . .
>
> Ah, hah, what state of life
>> Can equal this of mine,
> Wherein the gallantry of youth
>> So gloriously doth shine.[7]

Crouch's young man is confident that the perfect age should be identified with youth's 'gallantry' (ostentation; vainglory); he is a charmingly naive Pride of Life. The violent collision between maturity and immaturity in the *vanitas vanitatum* Ages of Man tradition does away with the idea of the middle age, scorning gradual and gentle transitions between one age and another. In this respect, the *vanitas vanitatum* tradition is medieval rather than classical, for unambiguous references to an age intervening between youth and old age are distinctly uncommon in medieval England. Only in the context of schemes of the ages derived from Isidore of Seville do we sometimes find a middle age that is clearly an age of transition in the classical sense. Trevisa, translating Bartholomeus Anglicus' definition of this transitional age, carefully avoids possible ambiguities by distinguishing between *age = aetas* and *elde* = old age:

Isidir seiþ þat aftir þis age *iuventus* comeþ þe age þat hatte *senecta*, and is þe middel age bitwene þe age þat hatte *iuventus* and *senectus* . . . [men in this middle age] ben nouȝt in þe secounde elde, but here ȝouthe passith.[8]

In Isidore's own words, the intermediate age is the 'vergens aetas a iuventute in senium' (the age declining from youth into decrepitude).[9]

The recognition of the existence of this *vergens aetas* in medieval England ought logically, one would think, to have been accompanied by a blurring of the dividing-line between old age and youth. Yet Bartholomeus and his translator are quite clear that 'þe middel age' is 'þe first elde', the first part of old age. The survival of the classical concept of the *media aetas* as an age of transition does not seem to have resulted in a lessening of man's sense of the suddenness and completeness of the changes accompanying the transition from *youthe* to *elde*. Sometimes the phase of life preceding old age is protracted, so that it extends to sixty years rather than the more usual forty-five years, but the dividing-line is still firmly drawn.[10] This protraction of *juventus* obviously has affinities with the protraction of *maturitas* in the seventeenth century, but there is also an important difference. Whereas the protraction of the age of ripe understanding tended to increase the opposition between youth and man's mature adulthood, forcing youth into ingenuousness or blatant inanity, the medieval protraction of the part of life preceding old age made it possible for man's ripe age to be annexed to youth's territory. This development was inseparably bound up with the idea of the perfect age, and will be considered more fully in the second part of this book.

From Aristotle's idea of a forty-nine-year peak of perfection we have now moved to a medieval lack of recognition of any such stepping-stone age. This, then, seems the appropriate place to ask whether there is, anywhere in early Ages of Man writings, a middle age represented as being objectively verifiable, a middle age tied to the bodily facts of man's growth and decline.

Predictably enough, it is in Graeco-Arabic medieval writings that the sequence of the ages is represented as being most firmly attached to these physical 'facts'. Hali Abbas (d. 994) places his extremely influential discussion of the ages, in the *Liber Regius*, in the context of those things which affect the balance of complexions in the body, beginning: 'The complexions are also altered according to the ages [of man's life]' (fol. 7r).[11] The examination of the four ages that follows – the four being *pueritia* ('properly speaking' *pueritia* up to the fifteenth year and *adolescentia* up to the thirtieth year), *juventus* (up to the forty-fifth year), *grandiorum aetas* 'the age of those advanced in years' (up to the sixtieth year) and *senectus* – focuses on two problems, both directly arising from the Galenic account of the sequence of the complexions.

The first problem concerns the relative hotness of *pueritia* and *juventus*, for to say that youth is 'less hot' than childhood is tantamount to saying that man's life declines between those two ages, which is a manifest absurdity. Hali Abbas resolves this by demonstrating 'that the degree of heat in children and young men is the same, but the quality of the heat is different' (fol. 7v). The second problem concerns the complexion of old age. In spite of authoritative statements that old age is cold and moist, Hali Abbas is certain that 'the bodies of old men are as cold and dry as can be', for 'this age stands in opposition to childhood', which is 'as moist as can be, if it is compared with all the other ages'. The moisture of old age, he argues, is extrinsic, not intrinsic; it is the overflowing of the body's secretions, phlegm and mucus and tears. After full growth has been achieved, at the point when the limbs cannot become any firmer or more solid, the body becomes ever colder and drier until death intervenes.

This theory of a bodily growth and decline dependent at every stage on the balance of the humours, the dominant explanation of the process of ageing for more than two thousand years, would seem to provide the sequence of the ages with one, unmistakable pinnacle, although the age in years associated with the pinnacle-moment is often unclear.[12] Actually, although this theory of ageing depends upon the notion that at one specific moment growth ends and decline begins, what Arabic medical writers stress is not this summit itself but the gradualness of all the ageing processes. 'The age of those advanced in years is that in which a lessening and decline begins to be evident', says Hali Abbas, 'without, however, the body's power (*virtus*) being impaired' (fol. 7r). Avicenna's third age, the *aetas declinationis*, is 'a secrete diminution, and privie pathe unto olde age, whiche holdeth on fully the space of fiftiene yeeres' as Thomas Fortescue's picturesque translation (1571) of Pedro Mexia's account of Avicenna's division of the ages has it.[13] Avicenna goes further than Hali Abbas in the direction of levelling out all the ageing processes. For him, there is no one moment when growth is complete, but instead a plateau. 'To the second [age],' says Fortescue,

he geveth name, of a well stayde age [*aetas consistentiae*] or of an age, wherin bewtie in all menne perfecteth: this parte continueth until the five and fortie yeere, in which wee live seased of absolute perfection.

This levelling out from pinnacle to plateau, making the second age a 'consistent' age rather than an age of continuing growth, is not (it is hardly necessary to say) Avicenna's own idea. 'For as saith Aristotle', again in the words of Fortescue, what so is ingendred, in the beginninge augmenteth and increaseth, and afterwarde stayeth for a time, arrestinge in his perfection, but in the ende declineth and savereth of diminution.[14]

The idea of the age of perfection as a plateau, followed by an age sliding almost imperceptibly downhill, encouraged the belief that the decline into old age and death could be arrested, a belief which pre-dates Aristotle and survived at least as long as the Graeco-Arabic theory of the complexions and the ages. In 1683 Richard Browne translated Roger Bacon's *De Retardatione Accidentium Senectutis*, giving it the title *The Cure of Old Age, and Preservation of Youth*.[15] Browne puts the failure of Bacon himself to live to an uncommonly great age down to 'the gross ignorance and malice of those times', for he was imprisoned and put to death before he was able to make

the greatest of his experiments, *i.e.* in extending the period of his days as far beyond the common age of man as in knowledge he surpassed the common standard.

Translating Bacon's own statement of belief, Browne says:

Aristotle thinks it impossible that medicines so fading and so soon perishing should be able to preserve men's bodies in health, that they be not dissolved before the time, or that they should repel and restrain all the accidents of old age . . . But this medicine [Bacon's elixir] doth admirable things when it is well prepared (p. 74)[16]

Bacon's confidence that he can prepare a *medicina* which is not subject to the laws of corruption helps to explain why his reputation for more than common learning, not to say magical powers, lasted until well after the foundations of modern science had been laid down, and to explain why 'the defence (warding-off) of age' and even the 'recovery of youth' (to quote the title of Jonas Drummond's 1540 translation of Arnoldus de Villa Nova) seemed for so long a real possibility.[17] But few, perhaps, quite believed they would find the elixir which would restore the age of perfection, that *aqua* which, according to Bacon,

an old farm-worker in the kingdom of Sicily drank . . . and was so changed that he had the complexion and the physical appearance of a thirty-year-old, and became possessed of great judgment, memory and intellect.[18]

The belief in the possibility of arresting the ageing process was one of the earliest and one of the most long-lasting responses to the memento mori implicit in the representation of the sequence of the ages. The medieval concept of the perfect age was another such response, related to Avicenna's *aetas consistentiae* 'wherein bewtie in all menne perfecteth', but not identical with this age of perfection of the body. The next part of this book will explore the most characteristic aspects of the medieval Christian idea of the middle age of man's life.

PART II

The perfect age of man's life

6

The perfect age and the ages of the soul

in corpore non potest simul et juventus esse et senectus, in animo autem potest, illa propter alacritatem, ista propter gravitatem

(in the body there cannot be youth and old age at one and the same time, but in the soul there can; this is because of the soul's buoyancy, on the one hand, and the body's heaviness, on the other) Augustine, *Retractiones*[1]

THE BELIEF that the natural heat of the body can be preserved, prolonging the age of the body's beauty and strength and keeping old age at bay, was a creative response to the awareness of mutability thrust upon man when he is confronted with a representation of the series of the ages. The medieval concept of the perfect age was another such response. The idea that perfection is or may be obtainable here, in this world, is common to both these responses, but the medieval concept of the perfect age of man's life also draws on a range of ideas about the nature of perfection and the progress towards perfection which look beyond the changes the body experiences as it moves from age to age and which look towards the unchangeableness of eternity. Since our interest is in perfect age and not in perfection itself, the focus of our attention will be those writings about the nature of perfection which are associated more or less immediately with representations of the ages in sequence. (Besides, to work over the whole field of medieval ideas of perfection would require oxen of monstrous strength.)

In one of the most magnificent passages about the unchanging perfection of the intellect in all the writings of the Neoplatonists, Plotinus refuses to accept that there is any sense in which it is appropriate to talk about the *aetates* of the soul. He contrasts the perfection of the 'All', the unchanging absolute at the heart of the universe, the centre upon which the soul of every man turns, with the body's changeableness and tendency to corruption:

the All is beautiful, and there can be no obstacle to its inner goodness: where the nature of a thing does not comport perfection from the beginning, there may be a failure in complete expression; there may even be a fall to vileness, but the All never knew a childlike immaturity; it never experienced a progress bringing novelty into it; it never had bodily growth: there was nowhere from whence it could take any increment; it was always the All-Container.[2]

The soul, midway between the 'sensitive principle', which Plotinus likens to a scout, and the 'intellectual principle', which he likens to a king (p. 384), spends the lifetime of the body striving to adhere to its natural course, which 'may be likened to that in which a circle turns not upon some external but on its own centre, the point to which it owes its rise' (p. 621). Plotinus gives the soul within but apart from the body a complete as-it-were personal identity, a sense of its own past and its desired goal; the soul is aware that it can adhere to its natural course only if its movement is 'unthwarted'.

For Plotinus, the body's movement from age to age is merely an impediment to the natural progress of the soul, but other Neoplatonist writers prefer to trace the steps of the soul's progress towards its final goal of purification, or perfection, more schematically (though not necessarily less poetically) than Plotinus does. Often they choose to represent the stages of the progress of the soul as being analogous with the *gradus* which are the ages of the body. The Jewish philosopher Avicebiron (Ibn Gabirol) perceives *materia* rather than *forma* to be the instigator of the progress towards perfection. 'Matter seeks to become attached to form', he says in the *Fons Vitae*, written in Spain in the middle of the eleventh century; 'the movement matter makes towards form is the result of the love and yearning (amorem et desiderium) it has for it'.[3] Each particular *hyle* desires its own proper form, and the *anima rationalis* (which in its initial state is 'sicut hyle receptrix formae') desires *formas intelligibiles*. The earliest stages of this *anima sicut hyle*'s progress towards the goal of its journey, the *intelligentia universalis*, are indistinguishable from the earliest stages of bodily growth: 'matter is moved to take on itself the form of the *primae qualitates* (the four elements), and afterwards to take on mineral form, and then vegetative form, and then the form of the senses'. The next two stages Avicebiron enumerates, matter's assumption of rational form and then of the form of the intellect, are elsewhere (though not explicitly in the *Fons Vitae*) linked with the body's development up to the age of puberty, or up to the completion of growth.[4] The last stage of the journey, however, when matter 'conjungatur formae intelligentiae universalis' and achieves the longed-for state of unity, has nothing to do with the process by which the body ages.[5] Perfection cannot be associated with decay.

For Avicenna, as for Avicebiron, the *intellectus* is the ultimate form of the soul which is peculiar to human beings and sets them apart from the rest of animate creation. But according to Avicenna, as S. Van Riet says in his edition of *Liber de Anima* (*Al-Shifā*), it is the nature of the *anima* itself which 'is at the heart of the organisation of the body and its various functions' and which sets in motion the progress towards perfection.[6] In accordance with this Aristotelean view of the *anima*, bodily growth is seen as one of the three faculties (*vires*) of the *anima vegetabilis*. The *vis* to which this function is assigned enlarges the body 'by a proportional increase in all its dimensions, length and breadth and thickness, so that it brings the physical object (*rem*) to perfection'.[7] This *perfectio* is the perfection of the age which elsewhere, as we have seen, Avicenna calls the *aetas consistentiae*, or age of perfect beauty, as distinct from that ultimate, timeless perfection which consists in being able to judge what is true and what is false, the *intellectus contemplativus* (p. 78).

In the treatises of Avicebiron and Avicenna on the progress towards perfection, the *gradus* of physical and spiritual development stop running parallel to one another at the age of the perfection of the body. Beyond that point, the soul's progress towards its final goal, when it will no longer be subject to mutability, is spoken of in broadly metaphorical terms rather than measured in separate stages. Philosophers who were concerned to transmit and re-interpret Greek and Graeco-Arabic writings about the soul within a Christian context were inevitably made uneasy by this divergence. For them, it was not possible to regard the body and the soul as being accidentally or merely temporarily attached to one another; for them, ultimate, absolute perfection involved the joining together of the individual body and its soul in God's presence for all eternity.[8] It is the less surprising, then, that medieval Christian philosophers explored the idea of the relationship between the ages of the body and the ages of the soul with particular determination and imagination. Representations of the sequence of the ages were, as they understood them, more than just codifications of the body's growth and decline. If interpreted aright, they could be seen to contain within them truths about man's innermost nature and spiritual development. Here we have yet another kind of counter-response to the memento mori implicit in representations of the ages.

Neoplatonist and Aristotelean (and mixed) accounts of the steps of the progress of the soul assume that the maturity of the material body, physical perfection, has to be achieved before any more true and lasting perfection may be – if it ever is to be - achieved. Thomas Aquinas, discussing the sacrament of confirmation in *Summa Theologiae*, allows (as we saw in chapter 3) that it is nature's intention 'ut omnis qui corporaliter nascitur, ad perfectam aetatem perveniat' (that everyone who is born physically should reach the perfect age), but:

multo autem magis de intentione Dei est omnia ad perfectionem perducere, ex cujus imitatione hoc natura participat
(much more is it God's intention to bring all things to perfection, nature sharing in this intention by way of imitation).[9]

Although in terms of the bodily ages perfect age is incompatible with childhood, and therefore it would seem inappropriate that the sacrament conferring the spiritual *perfecta aetas* should be received *in aetate puerili*, the soul has its own times and seasons:

Anima . . . potest, sicut tempore senectutis spiritualem nativitatem consequi, ita tempore juventutis et pueritiae consequi perfectam aetatem; quia hujusmodi corporales aetates animae non praejudicant.

(The soul is able to undergo spiritual birth during old age and is able to attain to perfect age during youth and even boyhood, because the ages of the body are not detrimental to the ages of the soul; p.212.)

The sacrament bestowing the spiritual perfect age is appropriate at any age of the body whatsoever.

But Aquinas' argument works in another, less explicit way, as well. Although the soul's nativity may take place when the body belonging to it has already reached old age, Aquinas reminds us that the soul has its own sequence of ages, its 'birth and age of spiritual perfection'. Our knowledge that the sequence of bodily ages cannot be varied encourages us to believe that the soul's development to its culmination in *perfecta aetas*, according to God's intention for it, will likewise be an inevitable process, once it has begun. Aquinas directs our attention to spiritual perfection as the proper end of the process initiated by physical birth.

By the time Aquinas came to make use of the topos of the distinction between the ages of the soul and the ages of the body to argue for the universal applicability of the sacrament of confirmation, the topos already had a long and rich history within the Christian tradition.[10] Augustine's writings are especially well-provided with elaborate analogies between the ages of the body and what in sermon CCXVI he calls the 'articul[i] vel gradus aetatis' (divisions or stages of age) of the soul.[11] In sermon CCXVI, Augustine only briefly maps out what these *gradus* are, his concern being to ascribe a specific spiritual virtue to each bodily age, one that is appropriate enough to seem its proper and natural companion:

Infantia vestra innocentia erit, pueritia reverentia, adolescentia patientia, juventus virtus, senium meritum, senectus nihil aliud quam canus et sapiensque intellectus. Per hos articulos vel gradus aetatis, non tu evolveris, sed permanens innovaris.

(Innocence will be your childhood, reverence your boyhood, patience your adolescence, strength in well-doing your youth, deserving the first part of your old age and nothing other than wise and white-haired intellect your extreme old age. By means of these divisions or stages of age you will not change from one state to another but, staying the same, you will always know newness.)

This sequence of spiritual virtues so closely parallels the sequence of virtues characteristically associated with the ages, from childhood's innocence down to the wisdom proverbially associated with white hairs, that it seems for a moment that Augustine is not going to distinguish the soul's ages from the ages of the body at all. This makes it all the more effective when he suddenly engages our full attention again with his paradoxical assertion that *these* ages will bring perpetual permanence and, at the same time, everlasting newness. Our interest captured, he offers a series of variations on the particular aspect of the contrast between the ages of the body and the ages of the soul he wants to stress in this sermon:

Non enim ut decidat prior secunda succedet, aut tertiae ortus secundae erit interitus, aut quarta jam nascitur ut tertia moriatur; non quinta quartae invidebit ut maneat, nec quintam sexta sepeliet. Cum simul aetates istae non veniant, tamen in anima pia et justificata pariter et concorditer perseverant. Hae te ad septimam perennem quietem pacemque perducent.

(For the second age will not follow so that an end may be put to the first; nor will the rise of the third mean the ruin of the second; nor will the fourth be born so that the third may die; nor will the fifth envy the staying-power of the fourth; nor will the sixth suppress the fifth. Although these ages do not all come into being at one and the same time, they continue together in harmony with one another in the soul whose relationship with God is right, and they will conduct you to the everlasting peace and tranquillity of the seventh age.)

Augustine's evocation of a peaceful and orderly succession of ages of the soul, conducting the faithful Christian to the seventh age 'in resurrectione finali', recalls the image of the ages of man's life as a procession, one knowable step followed by another. As always, the procession of the ages has a memento mori associated with it, and Augustine, with a characteristic leap of the imagination, deflects the harsh and threatening aspects of the representation of the sequence of the ages on to the ages of the body as opposed to the ages of the soul, so that the peacefulness of the seventh age shines forth the more serenely and temptingly for following after five images of ruin and destruction. Augustine is imaginatively aware that the *gradus* making up the procession of the ages and ensuring a smooth and unbroken progress from birth to death have a way of turning inwards and dissociating themselves from one another; of becoming, in effect, a series of smaller, separate lives.[12] As a result of this, representations of the sequence may be seen to involve not just a warning of the death awaiting the body in the end but as many warnings as there are ages represented. The threat is multiplied and the need for a counter-response is intensified.

Here, in sermon CCXVI, Augustine uses the anxiety generated by the five-fold threat to rouse the reader to spiritual exertion: 'Vitam quaeritis? Currite ad eum qui est fons vitae' (Are you looking for life? Run to the one who is the fountain of life). Augustine's best-known analogy between the ages of the *vetus homo* and the ages of the *novus homo*, in *De Vera Religione*, is a more mechanical affair altogether.[13] It appealed to later writers because it is schematic and detailed; it is interesting to us in our quest for perfect age because of the disproportionate attention given to the vices of youth in its account of the ages of the unredeemed man. During *juventus*, 'prohibitio peccatorum . . . carnalibus animis atrociores impetus libidinis gignit et omnia commissa congeminat' (the act of preventing the transgressions of others begets even more violent urges of desire in carnal spirits, redoubling everything already done). Augustine does not simply turn away from these vices with disgust; rather, he writes as one who has himself been subjected to these *labores*, and who has himself sighed with relief on reaching the measure of peace (*pax nonnulla*) which is granted to the older man – though he was only between 35 and 37 years old, in fact, when he wrote this. His sense of the sinfulness of his own *juventus* is made explicit in the *Confessiones* (here in Tobie Matthew's recusant translation):

Now was the profane and wicked time of my adolescence dead, and I went into the state of more confirmed youth. So much as I was more growne in years, so much more was I defiled with vanity; not being able to apprehend any other substance, but such as I could see by these eyes of myne.[14]

In complete and very deliberate contrast, the fourth age of the 'new' man, the redeemed equivalent of *juventus*, is the age 'emicantem in virum perfectum' (breaking forth into perfected manhood), the age which can stand firm in the face of persecutions and of the storms and tempests of this world. By implication, those who call the fourth age of the 'old' man the *perfecta aetas* are confusing the ages of the 'old' man with the ages of the 'new'; *juventus* is the least perfect of all the 'old' man's imperfect ages.

The fourth age is again represented as being especially significant in the chapter on the seven degrees of greatness (*magnitudinis gradus*) of the soul in the treatise *De Quantitate Animae*.[15] Augustine expresses his beliefs about the relationship between the soul and the body by way of the topos of the ages of the soul more fully and coherently in this chapter than in sermon CCXVI or *De Vera Religione*, though perhaps less imaginatively than in the former and less personally than in the latter. As we have seen, there are particular points Augustine wants to make by contrasting the ages of the soul and the ages of the body as sharply as he does in the two passages already looked at, but the contrast tends to have the effect of blunting what R.A.Markus sees as being one of the most important anti-Manichean and anti-Platonist perspectives in his works, the belief that

the soul itself is liable to all the vicissitudes of change and living, to sin and repentance, and is ever in need of God's grace. Man only has one self, which is the subject and the agent of his empirical career; there is not a recondite real self remote and exempt from the turmoils of life.[16]

In *De Quantitate Animae* Augustine gives a Christianised version of the Neoplatonist concept of the soul's journey from inception to perfection, towards the seventh *gradus*, 'not now a stage, but as it were a resting-place' (neque jam gradus, sed quaedam mansio; section 76). In this resting-place there will be 'so much pleasure in contemplating the truth . . . so much purity, so much sincerity, such undoubting faith in things' that mors quae antea metuebatur, id est ab hoc corpore omnimoda fuga et elapsio, pro summo munere desideretur

(death, which was feared before, will be desired as the supreme reward, as a complete and absolute escape from this body)

At first sight this looks more like a rejection of the body than an acceptance of it. And yet, however much an escape from this temporal world may be desired, this seventh stage is still a stage of the existence of the soul in the body; it is not the state non-Christian Neoplatonists look to as their goal, the state in which the contemplative intellect is finally freed from *materia*. While still in this body, not, like Troilus, looking down from the heavens, 'vere videbimus quam sint omnia sub sole vanitas vanitantium' (we shall see, indeed we shall, that all things under the sun are nothing but vanity). But this chapter of *De Quantitate Animae* involves an even more radical re-interpretation of the journey of the *anima* towards perfection. Augustine's account of the first three stages of the soul's development, the vegetative (section 70), the '*vis* of the soul in the senses' (section 71) and the '*vis* of reasoning and working things out' (section 72), the first common to all living things, the second common to all the animal creation and the third common to all men, good and bad, educated and uneducated, contains nothing that is not repeated again and again in treatises on the nature of the soul. It is when he comes to the fourth *gradus*, 'in which everything good and praiseworthy begins', that he begins to re-interpret the soul's journey. The fourth stage is the stage of crisis, the stage in which the new man will be born, if he is to be born at all.

Neoplatonists outside the Christian tradition frequently assume, as Augustine does, that there is a hierarchy among human souls: sometimes they recall and dilate upon Plato's division of men into three groups, in *The Republic*, according to whether their souls are governed by delight in money, or honour, or knowledge.[17] Only the noblest souls are capable of reaching the purity of *intellectus*. The soul-hierarchy is described in an unusual amount of detail in the *Rasā'il*, the encyclopedia (compiled in the second half of the tenth century) of the Mohammedan sect who called themselves the *Iḥwan al-ṣafa* 'the sincere brethren'.[18] The first stage, from four to fifteen years, is governed by the *anima sensibilis*; souls on this level have not entered the mystic hierarchy. The second stage, from fifteen to thirty years, is the artisan level, governed by the *virtus* of instinctive reason. Wise men and rulers reach the third level, from thirty to forty years, governed by the *virtus* of acquired reason. From forty to fifty years, kings and accomplished philosophers enjoy the *virtus regitiva* of the fourth level, in which inspiration may lead to revelation. Finally, from fifty onwards, the law-making *virtus* belongs to prophets and divine beings; and if, at death, the spirit is perfect, there then follows the *virtus* which lifts it to the supreme assembly. Obviously there is a paradox here: all men may expect to live through the sequence of the ages, but they may not all expect to enjoy the *virtutes* which are the natural companions of those ages, unless they are specially blessed. (The learned readers of the *Rasā-il* would know themselves to be so; they would have at least reached the third level.)

Although Augustine does not associate numbers of years with the seven stages of the soul, his account of them contains this same paradox. If a man wants to reach the fourth stage of the ascent, to progress beyond the level which all men reach by virtue of being human, he is told 'suspice . . atque insili', he must look up and take a leap at it (section 73). Yet this fourth stage is clearly related to *juventus*, with its characteristic, for Augustine, *labor* (I quote here from J.M. Colleran's appropriately dramatic translation):

The goods of the world it does not account its own, and comparing them with its own power and beauty, it keeps aloof from them and despises them [but this] requires strenuous effort, and the annoyances and allurements of this world engage it in a mighty struggle, bitterly contested.[19]

The soul in the fourth stage also has to battle against the fear of death, understanding for the first time the width of the gulf between purity and corruption.

The age which in bodily terms and in worldly parlance is the *perfecta aetas* can only properly be called the perfect age if its characteristic strength and insight are used to foster a newly-born soul. Where this happens, the middle age of man's life becomes the mirror in which we see, albeit darkly, the true age of perfection, the age which despises the things of this world peacefully, not strenuously, and· desires death instead of fearing it. Rather than following one after the other in a linear sequence, the ages in *De Quantitate Animae* all gravitate towards one central point, the perfect age.

7

The perfect age and the perfect man

Et tunc [in .15^{m0}. anno] adest vis intellectiva . . . et adquirit aliud regimen usque ad complementum .30. annorum
[nota:] quia tunc plena fortitudine mentis et corpore viget homo secundum sapienciam sacram, et beatum Hieronimum et alios; et ipsa philosophia et experiencia propria certificat

(And then in the fifteenth year the faculty of intellection is present, and the soul attains to another regimen until the thirtieth year is completed – because then man flourishes in the full strength of mind and body, according to divine wisdom, the blessed Jerome and others; and philosophy and personal experience bear witness that this is so.)

THIS *nota*, with its all-embracing appeal to the authority of sacred writers, pagan philosophers and personal experience, comes from Roger Bacon's edition of the pseudo-Aristotelean *Secretum Secretorum* (*Kitāb Sirr al-asrār*), purporting to be a letter from Aristotle to Alexander. Bacon calls the work *Liber Decem Scienciarum*.[1] The chapter in which this note on the thirty-year-old is found concerns the knowledge of one's own soul and the 'divisions of the *virtutes* of the soul and of the soul's ruling states and conditions in this life and in the life to come'. By no means all versions of the *Secretum Secretorum* contain this chapter; it derives, by way of Philippus Tripoletanus' Latin translation of the 'Long Form' of the Arabic treatise, from the Mohammedan *Rasā-il*.[2]

The thirteenth-century Franciscan reproduces the *Rasā-il*'s essentially Neoplatonistic account of the hierarchy of the human soul, but gives it a Christian veneer by way of his notes and glosses. *Intellegencia*, for instance, is glossed 'id est, angeli'. As Bacon sees it, there is nothing incompatible with Christianity in the hierarchy of the faculties of the soul, linked at every stage with the ages of the body.[3] Only at one point does he acknowledge that physical decay may be an impediment to the growing perfection of the soul (something that the *Rasā-il* never recognises): 'the last age is the age when the law-making *virtus* is present, because of the perfection of wisdom which flourishes during it – during the first part of it, at least'. In a concluding note on the ages of the embodied soul, he declares that

distinccio jam facta etatum sive parcium vite colligitur principaliter ex Sacra Scriptura et doctrina scienciarum et similiter ex philosophia, sed nimis longum esset auctoritatibus et racionibus explicare

(the division of the ages or parts of life made here is gathered chiefly from Holy Scripture and from what the liberal arts and philosophy teach us – but it would take too long to go into detail about authorities and reasons.)

Bacon's no more than superficially Christianised edition of the *Rasā-il*'s account of the increasing perfection of the ageing soul raises many questions about scholasticism and the philosophical tradition, but from the point of view of this study it is interesting most of all for the tension Bacon introduces into the Neoplatonist scheme with his note on the flourishing of mind and body in full strength in the thirty-year-old. The fundamental notion of the division of the *virtutes* of the soul is of an uninterrupted ascent from one regimen to the next, until the elect soul, having completed its time in the body, is led to *superna perfeccio*. In this scheme, which ignores the body's decline, an acme at thirty years of age makes no sense at all. Bacon, however, believes there is overwhelming authority for it, and so the note is added. It is worth noting that he considers it relevant to appeal to personal experience, such an appeal being rare in schemes of the ages – in the *Compendium Studii Philosophiae* he again makes it clear that he regards thirty as a particularly significant age.[4] As for his appeal to *philosophia*, we know that pagan authorities testify that the mind enjoys a later flowering-time than the body, and that they typically associate the acme-age, whatever it be called, with a wide time-span rather than with a specific moment. It is Bacon's appeal to *sapiencia sacra*, then, that points us in the direction of authoritative statements about a *perfecta aetas* which is not a step in the procession of the ages but the consummation of the life of man – a consummation achieved in the life of Christ, and thus potentially to be achieved in all men's lives.

Bacon is right about Jerome: he is especially eloquent on the subject of the link between the thirtieth year and the perfect age, a link which was forged for all time by the perfect man. The idea of the perfect-aged perfect man offering the perfect sacrifice sustains his ingenious explication of Mark 14:5, in the *Tractatus in Marci Evangelium*.[5] The woman who has anointed Jesus is reproached by the bystanders, who say 'that ointment could have been sold for three hundred denarii'. According to Jerome, these words are the culmination of the story of the woman's sacrificial act, not an indignant misinterpretation: they said this because 'the one who was anointed with this ointment was crucified'. Having announced the answer to the mystery, Jerome shows us how we may arrive at it. 'Consider the *sacramenta* of numbers'; specifically, the measurements of Noah's ark. The fifty cubits of the ark's width is the number of penitence, the fiftieth psalm being David's penitential prayer; the three hundred cubits of the ark's length is the number which reveals to us the cross – for its letter-sign is T, the sign which, borne on the forehead, wards off the devil. These two numbers are perfected in the third, the thirty cubits of the ark's height, and the three then become one:

The perfect age and the perfect man

Primum agimus paenitentiam in quinquaginta: deinde per paenitentiam venimus ad crucis mysterium: ad crucis mysterium venimus per perfectum verbum, qui Xpistus est

(first we do penance according to the number fifty: then by way of repentance we come to the mystery of the cross: we come to the mystery of the cross by way of the perfect word, which is 'the anointed one'.)

What has the number thirty to do with *perfectio*? Jerome proceeds to explain the missing step in his argument. Jesus was thirty years old when he was baptised, and he was sold for thirty pieces of silver. Nicely ironic as it would have been if Judas had asked for three hundred pieces, it should not surprise us, Jerome says, that he asked for thirty, for

scriptum est in Levitico, scriptum est in Exodo, quod sacerdotes a triginta annis esse incipiant. Ante triginta annos non licet sacerdotibus ingredi templum Dei: quomodo et in jumentis et animalibus tertius annus perfecta aetas est . . . et hominibus perfecta aetas triginta anni sunt

(it is written in Leviticus and Exodus [and Numbers 4:3] that priests may exercise priestly functions from the age of thirty. No priest may enter God's temple to offer up a sacrifice before he has reached this age, and this is because the third year is the perfect age in cattle and other animals . . . and thirty years is the perfect age in men).[6]

With calculated ingenuousness Jerome then asks on the reader's behalf whether Jesus could have been baptised at, say, twenty-five, or twenty-six, or twenty-eight . . . he could have been, yes, but 'perfectam hominis expectabat aetatem, ut nobis tribueret exemplum' (he was waiting for the perfect age of man's life, so that he could provide us with a pattern). Moreover, in the opening verse of Ezechiel we read 'it came to pass in the thirtieth year': all these things have been said, Jerome grandly concludes 'ut tricentarii numeri sacramenta panderemus' (in order to make known the mysteries of the number thirty).

Christ's baptism and crucifixion are inextricably interwoven in this passage; the ointment worth three hundred denarii becomes both chrism and cross. The Jewish priest cannot offer up the sacrifice which reconciles man with God before he reaches the age of thirty, the perfect age of man's life; Christ bides his time until he is thirty years old, and is then baptised in preparation for the sacrifice in which he is both priest and victim. Jerome binds together the perfect word, the perfect sacrifice and the perfect age, and firmly attaches to them the number thirty, in a performance beautifully blending painstaking exegesis and unexplained allusion. When he quotes the beginning of Ezekiel, he presumes that the same reader whom he has just imagined asking ludicrously uninformed questions about Christ's baptismal age will at once recall that the Jews did not permit anyone beneath the age of thirty to read the beginning and end of that book, the beginning of Genesis, or any part of the Song of Songs – because these portions of Scripture demand a width of knowledge and depth of spiritual understanding which only the perfect age can give. So, too, the friends who accompany Christ the Bridegroom in the Song of Songs are to be understood, according to Gregory of Elvira, as being angels and those 'qui pervenerunt in virum perfectum'.[7]

The reasons why Christian priests should wait until the age of thirty before being ordained were very generally known, since the issue was one that immediately affected Church order and discipline. Gregory the Great gives the impetuous young a solemn warning in his *Cura Pastoralis*, taking as his text Ecclesiastes 32:7 ('Young man, do not say too much, even when your own interests are involved'; *NEB*):

idem Redemptor noster, cum in coelis sit conditor, et ostensione suae potentiae semper doctor angelorum, ante tricennale tempus in terra magister noluit fieri hominum; ut videlicet praecipitatis vim saluberrimi timoris infunderet, cum ipse etiam, qui labi non posset, perfectae vitae gratiam non nisi perfecta aetate praedicaret

(although our Redeemer is in heaven as heaven's creator, and as the everlasting teacher of the angels by the manifestation of his might, he did not desire to become a teacher of men before his thirtieth year on this earth. This was because he wanted to instil into rash and hasty men the faculty of most wholesome fear, considering that he who was incapable of stumbling did not himself preach the gracious gift of perfect life until he had reached the perfect age.)[8]

With a pressing personal interest in the issue of the appropriate age for ordination, Jerome, in a letter to Theophilus, Bishop of Alexandria, lists among his complaints about John of Jerusalem's ecclesiastical chicanery that John has maliciously spread it abroad among the Western bishops that Jerome's brother, Paulinian, has been ordained a priest in spite of being an *adolescentulus*, scarcely more than a boy. Relieved, no doubt, by the certainty that the lapse of time has given him an unassailable argument, Jerome counters John of Jerusalem with:

cum ad triginta annorum spatia jam pervenerit, puto eam in hoc non esse reprehendendam, quae juxta mysterium adsumpti hominis in Christo perfecta est

(now that Paulinian's life-span has reached thirty years, I cannot see how that can be grounds for rebuke in this matter, for the age of thirty has been made perfect by means of the mystery of Christ's adopted manhood.)[9]

Reminders that the priest should have reached thirty years of age before ordination are not found solely in admonitory or apologetic contexts. The devout King Edgar, who guided and supported the tenth-century revival of monasticism in England, came to the throne in 959, but was not crowned until 973, his thirtieth year. Edgar's Archbishop of Canterbury, Dunstan, 'like many Frankish churchmen of his age', F.M. Stenton says:

was strongly influenced by the parallel between the anointing of a king and the consecration of a priest, and there is every probability that the king, his pupil in religion, was moved by the same conception.[10]

The perfect age and the perfect man

Below the age of thirty he might carry out the duties of kingship, but he should not receive the sacramental oils until he had reached the perfect age.

The time of the body's flowering is not, within the medieval Christian tradition, dissociated from the time of the ripening of the mind and the maturity of the spirit. All are comprehended in what Abelard, quoting Origen in the preface to his *Expositio in Hexaemeron,* calls the *aetas perfecta maturaque,* perfection containing maturity within it, and the number thirty is stamped indelibly upon this fully-grown, ripe age, because of its association with Christ's baptism, preaching ministry and crucifixion.[11] But the relationship between Christ's perfect age and man's *aetas perfecta maturaque* is not simply one of example, on Christ's part, and emulation, on man's part. Christ died at the perfect age, 'tempus implens corporis' (completing the body's growth-span and fulfilling his time in the body), but he also rose from death at the perfect age.[12] Those who live in him by faith and by recognition of his lordship will also, Jerome argues, be resurrected at the perfect age, and they will know 'unius aetatis consummata perfectio' (the fulfilled perfection of the one and only resurrected age).[13]

Jerome is prepared, however, to concede that this is not an easy concept to grasp. During his consideration of the 'very-much debated' (*famosissima*) question concerning the resurrection of the body, Jerome asks John of Jerusalem:

Miraris si de infantibus et senibus in perfecti viri aetatem resurrectio fiat, cum de limo terrae absque ullis aetatum incrementis, consummatus homo factus sit?

(Do you find it a cause for wonder that the resurrection should bring into being the perfect age of man in infants and in the very old, when man was made from the mire and clay, complete and perfect, without any of the stages of growth associated with the ages?)[14]

Nevertheless, it *is* easier, Jerome's readers might well have countered, to believe that Adam was created at the perfect age than to imagine a baby or an old man, who already have their fixed places in the sequence of the ages of man's life, all of a sudden leaping forwards or backwards in the sequence, to be resurrected at the *perfecti viri aetas.*

The difficulties of coming imaginatively to terms with the idea were aggravated by the ambiguities of the text most often cited and expounded in justification of it, Ephesians 4:13:

So shall we all at last attain to the unity inherent in our faith and our knowledge of the son of God – to mature manhood, measured by nothing less than the full stature of Christ
(NEB)

More literally, the second half of the verse reads 'to a *teleios* (perfect, or, fully-grown) man, to the measure of the *elikia* (age, or, stature) of the fullness of Christ'.[15] Tertullian alludes to Ephesians 4:13 in his treatise *De Anima,* written at the beginning of the third century, in the context of his argument that the soul will preserve whatever age it has reached at the time of death (since without a body a change of age is impossible), until the day in which 'perfectum illud repromittitur ad angelicae plenitudinis mensuram temperatum' (it is promised perfection tempered to the measure of angelic plenitude).[16] The context demands that *perfectum* (an adjective used here as a substantive) should be understood to include *perfecta aetas* (the point being that the soul will indeed change its age at the Last Judgment), but perfection in the wider sense is evidently intended, too. Tertullian, who shows us a soul which is as nothing without its accompanying body, prefers to understand *teleios* both as 'perfect-aged' and as 'perfect' absolutely, and most later Christian commentators choose to follow him.

Augustine, discussing Ephesians 4:13 in *De Civitate Dei*, corrects one of the misinterpretations of it which had arisen from its confusing juxtaposition of *metron* (measure), *elikia* and *plēnoma* (fullness):

nec fas est dicere cum resurrectionis omnium tempus venerit accessuram corpori [Christi] eam magnitudinem, quam non habuit quando in ea discipulis in qua illis erat notus apparuit . . . suam recipiat quisque mensuram quam vel habuit in juventute etiamsi senex est mortuus, vel fuerat habiturus si est ante defunctus

(it is wrong to say that when the time of the general resurrection comes Christ's bodily size will increase, so that he will be equal to the tallest, though he had no such size in the body when he appeared to the disciples . . . each one is to receive his own measure, either the size that he had in youth, if he died an old man, of if he died in childhood, the size he would have reached.)[17]

Augustine admits that he is not sure whether 'the measure of the age/stature of the fullness of Christ' refers to the perfecting of Christ's body, when all his people, as limbs of his body, will be added to him, its head; or whether the phrase refers to men's bodies, in which case 'we should understand that the dead do not rise with bodies either older or younger than the state of youth (*juvenalis forma*), but have bodies of the age and strength that we know Christ reached here'.

Whereas Jerome, as we have seen, chooses to define this age from scriptural references, Augustine chooses to defer to 'saeculi hujus doctissimi homines', the authorities of this world, who say that thirty years is the limit of *juventus*.[18] Authorities for the completion of bodily growth at about this age are not far to seek, but Augustine goes on to claim that the 'doctissimi homines' also say that 'cum fuerit spatio proprio terminata, inde jam hominem in detrimenta vergere gravioris et senilis aetatis' (when that limit is reached, then man begins to decline into staid age and decrepitude).[19] The philosophers whom Augustine reveres, and whose authority he regards as absolute in matters not directly relating to man's redemption, do indeed say that man begins to decline after he has lived through *juventus*, but the imaginative awareness Augustine shows here of extreme old age following hard on the heels of the age of perfection is peculiarly medieval and Christian.

If non-Christian Neoplatonists preferred to ignore the decay of the body and focus on the progress of the soul towards an incorporeal perfection, the idea of a perfect age which might be achieved at the end of a full life-span as a natural consummation, not as a miraculous Day of Judgment metamorphosis, attracted Patristic writers, too. Jerome, who has a more abstractly intellectual love of numbers and number-linked concepts than Augustine does, occasionally claims that the number which is the pinnacle of the triad of perfection (30:60:100) is the age at which man will be resurrected.[20] Dante, in the *Convivio*, reminds us that the pagan *vir perfectus*, Plato, is said to have lived for eighty-one years:

e io credo che se Cristo fosse stato non crucifisso, e fosse vivuto lo spazio che la sua vita poteva secondo natura trapassere, elli sarebbe a li ottantuno anno di mortale corpo in etternale transmutato

(and I believe that if Christ had not been crucified and had lived out his natural life-span, he would have been transformed from an earthly into a heavenly being when he was eighty-one years old.)[21]

But a perfect age which ignores bodily reality could not compel the mind or imagination for more than an occasional, whimsical moment. The accepted fact that Christ died at the perfect age and did not experience physical decay focused the attention of the medieval centuries on the age of man's life in which Christ redeemed and perfected human nature. The ages following the perfect age were left to labour beneath the double disadvantage of bodily infirmity and Christlessness.

8

The perfect age and the ages of the world

Haec aetas [quarta] similis juventutis est. Et revera inter omnes aetates regnat juventus, et ipsa est firmum ornamentum omnium aetatum: et ideo bene comparatur quarto diei, quo facto sunt sidera in firmamento coeli. Quid enim evidentius significat splendorem regni, quam solis excellentia?

(This fourth age of the world can be compared with *juventus*. Youth is held in reverence as king of all the ages; of all the ages it is the unchanging embellishment. And so it is appropriate to liken it to the fourth day of creation, in which the stars were established in the firmament of heaven: for what is more manifestly a sign of the splendour of royal rule than the radiance of the sun?)

THIS CELEBRATION of *juventus* as the king of the ages comes from the twenty-third chapter of the first book of *De Genesi contra Manichaeos*, in which Augustine likens the days of creation to the ages of the world and to the ages of man's life.[1] The fourth age of man's life is like the fourth *aetas mundi*, in which David ruled over the kingdom of Israel. The third age of the world, which was brought to a close by the 'ill-will of Saul, the worst of kings', God wants us to understand as corresponding to adolescence, the earliest age capable of bearing children. In that age, explains Augustine, a race singled out for God's purposes was brought to birth and separated by its progenitor, Abraham, from the vain and labile beliefs of all other nations, just as God separated the sea, 'ruffled by every wind', from the dry land 'thirsting for the celestial rain of the divine commandments', on the third day of creation (section 37). On the fourth day of creation God made the sun, the moon and the stars. The sun's radiance is a sign of *splendor regni*;

plebem obtemperantem regno splendor lunae ostendit, tanquam synagogam ipsam, et stellae principes ejus, et omnia tanquam in firmamento in regni stabilitate fundata

(the moon's brightness represents a people obedient to royal authority, as it were the synagogue herself; the stars, the rulers of the synagogue – with all things rooted and grounded in the stability of kingly power, as if in the firmament; section 38.)

The fixedness of the kingdom of David, the stars in the firmament and man's youth, the '*firmum* ornamentum omnium aetatum', contrasts markedly with the poetically-evoked waverings and wanderings of the gentile kingdoms, from which God saves his chosen people at the beginning of the third age of the world; but the stability of that kingdom did not, in historical fact, last. The 'evening, as it were' ushering in the fifth age of the world was the sin which resulted in the exile of the Jews in Babylon, the age in which the strength of their kingdom was 'bent and broken', as the strength of a man is bent and broken during the fifth age of his life, the '*declinatio* from youth to old age'. On the fifth day of creation God made fish that swim and birds that fly, and in the fifth age of the world the Jewish people 'inter gentes, tanquam in mare, vivere coeperunt, et habere incertam sedem et instabilem, sicut volentes aves' (began to live among the Gentiles as if in the sea, and began to have an unsure and unfixed habitat, like the birds of the air; section 39). When Augustine comes to the sixth day (section 40), he scarcely draws any distinction any longer between the corresponding age of the world and age of man's life:

Hac enim aetate illud carnale regnum vehementer attritum est, quando et templum dejectum est et sacrificia ipsa cessaverunt; et nunc ea gens quantum ad regni sui vires attinet, quasi extremam vitam trahit

(in the sixth age that fleshly kingdom was destroyed by violence, when the temple was overthrown and the sacrifices ceased; now the Jewish people, so far as the might of their kingdom is concerned, labour, as it were, in extreme old age.)

The poignancy of Augustine's contrast between the *vires* of the fourth age and the decrepitude of the sixth, impossible to convey adequately in translation, is no mere rhetorical flourish; Augustine wants us to be thinking about the utter unlikeness of mighty youth and worn-out old age as we go on to read 'in ista tamen aetate tanquam in senectute veteris hominis, homo novus nascitur, qui jam spiritualiter vivit' (yet in that same age, as in the *senectus* of the old man, a new man is born, a man who now lives according to the spirit).

The body of the man in the sixth age may be worn away almost to nothing, but the new, spiritual man is, in Christ, a *parvulus* – a little child. Also in the sixth age, Christ is the new David who 'rules over the souls of those who obey him', his Church – no longer Jews alone, like David's subjects, but Gentiles as well. As the new Adam, Christ rules over and tames those vices figured forth in the mammals, reptiles and birds of the earthly paradise, man's *concupiscentia* (lust of the flesh), *curiositas* (lust of the eyes) and pride (1 John 2:16).[2] David's reign in the fourth age of the world is fulfilled in the reign of Christ; the reign of youth, the fourth age of man's life, is fulfilled in the reign of Christ in his perfect age. The decay of the sixth age will become the seventh age's perfection, for, as God rested from his labours on the seventh day, 'requiescant cum Christo ab omnibus operibus suis ii quibus dictum est, *Estote perfecti, sicut Pater vester qui in coelis est*' (Matthew 5:48) (those to whom it has been said "Be ye, therefore, perfect, even as your Father, who is in heaven, is perfect" will rest with Christ from all their labours; section 41).

The perfect age of man's life

Augustine's full and rich investigation into the correspondence between the sequence of the ages of the world and the sequence of the ages of man's life in *De Genesi contra Manichaeos* was the most influential and remains the best-known of the many treatments of this theme. It is a commonplace that the medieval world was seen by its inhabitants to be (in Otto of Freising's words, echoing Augustine) 'already deserting us, as if drawing the very last breath of extreme old age'.[3] Historians of all kinds have produced evidence that the belief that a transitory world was labouring in its sixth and final age affected every aspect of medieval life – though such evidence needs to be seen in a broad perspective, given that many historical ages have produced equivalent myths of decay. The excuse, if one be needed, for looking again at this well-known passage of Augustine here is that commentators both medieval and modern have focused on its sequential aspects rather than on its polarities.[4] To be sure, Augustine presents his comparison 'by way of the sequence of the days', starting from the creation of light on the morning of the first day and ending with the seventh day 'which has no evening', and he emphasises its historicity: 'ista expositio per ordinem dierum sic indicat tanquam historiam rerum factarum' (this exposition by way of the sequence of the days points to the fact that it is as it were a history of events which have happened; section 41). The days of creation and the ages of the world are presented *per ordinem* to reveal what will certainly happen in the future and to enable us to prepare for it. In effect, Augustine makes the days of creation and ages of the world sequence bear the memento mori burden which the sequence of the ages of man's life normally bears, and thus he frees himself from the chronological series in order that he may explore the ages of man's life in terms of patterns and paradoxes.

At the heart of the chapter is the paradox of rejuvenation: youth is given back to the man who has already had and lost his youth. This paradox (or, rather, mystery) is rooted in Jewish belief about the workings of God in human history as a whole and in the life of the individual man:

> Even the youths shall faint and be weary, and
> the young men shall utterly fall,
> But they that wait upon the Lord shall renew
> their strength; they shall mount up with wings
> like eagles; they shall run, and not be weary;
> and they shall walk, and not faint. (Isaiah 40:30–1)[5]

The Jewish prophet's vision of his people, their dragging weight of lassitude thrown off, entering into an eternity of buoyancy and power, magnificently expresses a felt relationship between strength and *alacritas*, frailty and *gravitas*. Decay drags man downwards; perfection impels man upwards: these are the two directions in which the ages are felt to move.

Augustine habitually impels his reader's mind towards the consummation of these two opposed states, perfection and decay, even where, as in *De Genesi contra Manichaeos*, he is apparently treating the ages sequentially and processionally. In the fullness of time, when the world was full of years, Christ, the perfect man at the perfect age, restored to perfection man broken and bowed by decrepitude, and established for ever the kingdom of *juventus*, fulfilling the resplendent reign of David in the flower of the world's age. The reign of Christ the king, the new David, is likewise the culminating point of a series of hymns based on Augustine's comparison between the ages of the world, the ages of man's life and the days of creation: Abelard's series of hymns beginning 'Aetates temporum nostrique corporis' (the series is also based on Abelard's own, abbreviated version of *De Genesi contra Manichaeos* 1, 23).[6]

In that evening-less seventh day celebrated in the last hymn of the series, 'O quanta, qualia sunt illa Sabbata' (no. 29), the true Jerusalem is interpreted as the city of peace and joy:

> Ubi non praevenit
> rem desiderium,
> Nec desiderio
> minus est praemium   (13–16)

(where 'wish and fulfilment can severed be ne'er/ nor the thing prayed for come short of the prayer').[7]

But this everlasting correspondence between longing and reward can only be fully grasped if the hymn is encountered, as Abelard assumed it would be, in its proper context. What might otherwise seem to be inappropriately commercial language depends upon the concept of *caritas* explored in the two hymns in the middle of the series, 'Quarta lux decorat coelum sideribus' (no. 22), the hymn for Wednesday lauds, and 'Aetates saeculi quartae primordium' (no. 23), the hymn for Wednesday vespers. In these two hymns Abelard reveals the correspondence between the fourth day of creation, the fourth age of man's life and the reign of David.

The lauds hymn for the fourth day of the week associates love with permanence and with perfection. *Caritas* burns with undying energy, like the stars placed in the heavens on the fourth day of creation; moreover, it arrogates to itself the realm of the stars, 'sibi vindicat / sedes aethereas'. Love pertains especially to the number four because of the stability associated with that number:

> Quadrati corporis
> est magna firmitas,
> Et cuncta sustinet
> invicta caritas

(a body built four-square has great stability, and love supports all things without being overcome; 13–16.)

The perfect age of man's life

Abelard puts spiritual perfection and bodily perfection in apposition:

> Virtutum caritas
> est consummatio,
> Virilis virium
> aetas perfectio

(love is the consummation of the virtues; the *aetas virilis*[8] is the perfection of bodily strength; 17–20.)

and he then proceeds to invoke the consummation of the likeness between the fourth age and the number four:

> Ut corpus hominis
> hoc implet viribus,
> Sic mentem caritas
> consummat moribus

(as the fourth age fills man's body with strength, so may love perfect the mind with moral power; 21–4.)

This love made perfect is figured forth in David, king in the morning of the fourth age of the world, as Abelard says in the Wednesday vespers hymn:

> In David caritas
> perfecta noscitur
> Quae saevos domat et
> hostes amplectitur

(. . . that love which tames savage spirits and cherishes enemies; 9–12.)

For a moment, in the clear light which the Wednesday lauds hymn sheds on the perfect king of the vespers hymn, *caritas perfecta* seems readily apprehensible, perhaps even attainable, but the purity of the ideal dissolves in a complex pattern of images of love and enmity, bondage and release, as David's reign gives way to the Babylonian captivity in the evening of the fourth age:

> Hostilem religat
> praedonem caritas,
> Nec erit animae
> cum hoc captivitas,
> Ubi defuerit
> salus amittitur,
> Et nostri pectoris
> urbs hosti traditur

(love binds the hostile despoiler, nor where love is present will the soul be made captive; where it is lacking, salvation is forfeited and the city of our breast is given over to the enemy; 17–24.)[9]

Abelard's poetic recreation of Augustine's sequence of the ages of the world and the ages of man's life raises *juventus* to an even loftier prominence than Augustine accords it. For Augustine, the fourth age is the king and the unfading flower of the ages; full of strength, full of beauty, but only redeemed after Christ's coming. For Abelard, the entire sequence of the ages can only be understood in terms of the perfection properly pertaining to the fourth age. Although the seventh age, eternity, is the consummation to which Abelard's (and any medieval Christian) sequence of the ages of the world is tending, the middle age of man's life is the point at which he sees perfection manifesting itself. The poetry of the *Hymnarius Paraclitensis* ultimately resists explanation in any terms other than its own, but the perfect age Abelard creates in the 'Aetates temporum nostrique corporis' hymns is a consummately medieval one, depending upon a conviction that physical perfection is inseparable from mental and spiritual perfection, the all-too-evident realities of sin and decay notwithstanding.

Nor was this conviction merely a matter of theory, an idea which did not in practice affect the way in which men perceived their own and other people's lives. Odo of Cluny, in his life of St Gerald, Count of Aurillac (d. 909), presents Gerald's adolescence as a simultaneous and mutually interdependent growth of body and spirit. The image of blossoming which is habitually used of bodily growth, Odo uses of Gerald's spiritual growth:

cerneres lilium inter spinas crevisse, et quo vicinior maturitate fiebat, eo repansos virtutum flores diffusius expandisse. Ergo sicut in rerum vertice situs, in illa beatitudine superna mentis affectum defixerat

(a lily could be seen growing among thorns, and the nearer at hand his *maturitas* was, the more fully could the blossoming flowers of his virtues be seen to open. And so, when he was on the summit, as it were, of earthly things, he fixed the desire of his heart on heavenly blessedness.)[10]

Physical maturity, spiritual wisdom and earthly domination all coalesce in Odo's representation of the perfect age of a saint. The Graeco-Arabic concept of the middle of man's life as a plateau scarcely impinges upon Odo's way of thinking about the ages of Gerald's life at all. In his view, the middle of man's life is a *vertex*, where he sits like a king – or, if he is a saint, with his eyes raised towards the heavenly king.

The medieval summit-age, the perfect age, arrogates to itself the characteristics of all the ages except the age of decay; it is budding age, blossoming age and ripe age. Youthful prime, manhood and maturity are all absorbed into it and reappear as aspects of the same age of perfection, man's 'excellence and flour', to use one of Chaucer's terms for it (The Knight's Tale; *CT* 1:3048). It was the Jewish rather than the Greek roots of Christianity which fed the Christian Middle Ages with the idea of an age including within itself all the processes of growth, an age which is the consummation of vitality rather than one of the stages of man's life. Hezekiah the King became 'sick unto death' (Isaiah 38:1) in this age of his life, and the opening of his hymn of thanksgiving for his recovery expresses the full poignancy of a situation in which a thoroughly self-aware perfect age is faced with its own end:

I thought I shulde have gone to the gates of hell in my best age, and have wanted the residue of my yeares   (Isaiah 38:10; Coverdale's trans., 1535)

The Jewish poet found Hezekiah's situation a peculiarly apt one for the expression of the perfect age's characteristic life-hungriness. Coverdale's age-name *best age*, rarely encountered in English, is the only early translation to come close to the force of the Hebrew *bidmi yamai*, which means literally 'in the blood / sap of my days', and contains the idea of the vigour of youth and of the strength of the middle of life.[11] The Septuagint's 'in the summit of my days' makes explicit what is implicit in the Hebrew, a violent movement downwards from the pinnacle of life 'to the gates of hell'. As in Odo of Cluny's account of Gerald of Aurillac's perfect age, the visual image of the king at the top of the wheel here seems very close: let us now, then, turn our attention to that image, the typical medieval icon of the perfect age.

9

The perfect age and the image of the wheel

> On knes I kyþed þat kyng:
> He seyde, 'sestou, swetyng,
> How I regne wiþ ring,
>   Richest in ryȝth –
>   *versus*
> Richest in ryȝth, quen and knyth
> Kyng conne me calle;
> Mest men of myȝth,
> Fair folk to fote me falle.
> Lordlich lif led I,
> No lord lyvynde me ilich.
> No duk ne dred I,
> For I regne in ryȝth as a riche.'   (96–107)

kyþed acknowledged;   *Mest men of myȝth* men of greatest strength

HUS speaks the king sitting 'on a semeli sete' on top of Lady Fortune's 'rennyng ryng' (rotating wheel), in the fourteenth-century poem *Somer Soneday*.[1] 'Sestou, swetyng,' and the following two lines are addressed to the huntsman–poet who tells us about his Sunday *aventure*, his vision of the Wheel of Fortune and the four figures sitting on it. The social distinction between king and poet is so great that the casual second-person-singular 'sestou' seems appropriate; together with the condescending endearment 'swetyng' it suggests that the king knows full well how magnanimous he is being in speaking to the poet at all. The poet's (or scribe's) pointer, *versus*, draws the reader's attention to the separate verse-unit containing the words spoken to the world at large by this haughty-hearted, readily-roused monarch, sitting with one leg insolently athwart the other (91–2). The poet is altogether too accomplished to allow the *versus* to become detached from the narrative of the poem as a whole and stand out in awkward isolation: a triple *concatenatio* binds together the stanza and the *versus*, the beginning and end of the *versus* ('Richest in ryȝth' . . . 'ryȝth as a riche'), and the *versus* and the stanza following it ('Of riche þenkeþ rouþe is to rede and to roune', 108).

By chance, though, the poet's very virtuosity has played its part in marring understanding and appreciation of his poem. So well does he integrate the speeches of the figures on Fortune's wheel with the stanzas of narrative that in the absence of the indication *versus* before the lament of the third figure, the king who has lost his crown, the poem's editors have felt justified in attaching these eight lines (121–8) to the five long lines surviving at the end of the only copy of the poem we have. T.M. Smallwood has shown that these five lines are certainly the opening lines of a new stanza, but, since *Somer Soneday* is composed in thirteen-line stanzas, the temptation of editors of the poem to make a complete, final stanza by joining these five long lines and the eight-line lament was perfectly understandable, though unfortunate. Smallwood also implies, and he is surely right about this, that the poem must originally have contained not only the concluding lines of the stanza which introduces the fourth figure on the wheel, the 'bare body in a bed' (132), but also a fourth *versus*, the dying words of the 'duk' with his bier close by (131–2) – and one or more concluding stanzas, in all probability, as well.[2] For *Somer Soneday*, as Smallwood's article argues, is a poetic recreation of the 'formula of four' Wheel of Fortune:

He þat gos upward saies 'I regne shalle';	[*regnabo*]
He þat gos dounward saies 'I falle';	[*regnavi*]
He þat is heghest saies 'I regne nobly';	[*regno*]
Þo lowest saies 'withouten regne am I'.	[*sum sine regno*]

These lines, taken from the flatly expository fourteenth-century Northern poem 'Þo Whele of Fortune' (53–6),[3] clearly describe the kind of Wheel of Fortune christened the 'formula of four' by H.R. Patch.[4] A good English example of a wheel of this kind, *c.* 1320–30, is found in the Holkham Bible Picture Book (see plate 3).[5] The English translation of the fourfold formula would be without particular interest but for the words put in the mouth of the king at the top of the wheel, 'I regne nobly'. The exigencies of rhyme are no doubt chiefly to thank for this slight elaboration of the *regno* written alongside the crowned king in those representations of the Wheel of Fortune which make use of this, by far the commonest 'formula of four'. Minimal and adventitious as the poet's elaboration of the formula is in 'Þo Whele of Fortune', it nevertheless serves to suggest that the four components of the formula are unequally weighted. For two divergent impulses lie behind the formula (taking 'formula' to include both the images of the four kings and the words assigned to them). One is the narrative impulse implicit in the sequence of tenses and in the movement up and down the wheel. F.P. Pickering explains the origin of the formula entirely in terms of this impulse: 'some artist of the (early?) twelfth century determined that the kings should be four in number, to represent dynastic history in its full cycle'.[6] The more deterministic and more convincing explanation Alexander Murray gives is still an essentially narrative one; he attributes the appearance of the image of the Wheel of Fortune to 'the growing prevalence and vigour, in the eleventh and twelfth centuries, of up-and-down social movement'. Men 'forged an image' for what they saw going on around them.[7]

3 The 'formula of four' Wheel of Fortune from the Holkham Bible Picture
Book, 1320/30.

The narrative impulse behind the 'formula of four' has received plenty of recognition; a second impulse, working against the sequence of the narrative, has not. And yet, when we look at a 'formula of four' Wheel of Fortune, our eyes are immediately drawn to the figure of the king at the top of the wheel; seeing that he is saying 'I reign', we then make our way round the wheel to find the would-be and have-been kings accompanying him. That is the way the image works. The figure of the crowned king, fascinating all who look at him, draws into himself all the energy generated by the image's narrative impulse; then, this force being redirected into his assertion of his pre-eminent identity, the narrative sequence defines itself anew around him. This is a fanciful way of putting it, perhaps, but there is a real sense in which the reigning king's self-proclamation – by means of what he wears, how he comports himself and what he says – is the 'action' that the image of the Wheel of Fortune exists in order to represent. There is little room for any recognition of this in a poem like 'Þo Whele of Fortune', where the image is boiled down to its bare didactic bones:

> For a whele, when hit turnes invirowne,
> Þat turned is up is titt turned downe,
> And þat is heghest is lowest turned sone:
> Þus fares hit by þo whele of fortune. (31–4)

>> *invirowne* around; *titt* quickly

Yet even here, though nothing is said about what 'he who is highest' looks like, the poet's choice of 'I regne nobly' to translate the *regno* in the image he is describing suggests he is aware that the crowned king's utterance has the liveliness of self-revelation, not the deadness of a formula.

This king's feeble effort to assert his pre-eminence seems muted to the point where it can scarcely be heard when we compare it with the 'action' at the heart of *Somer Soneday*, the *kete* (bold; brave) king's manifestation of himself to the poet and the world. 'I saw [one] sitting . . . crowned like a king' says the poet, and kneels to acknowledge him. The king, duly recognised, invites the poet to 'see' him reigning at the top of the wheel, incomparable and impregnable:

> Lordlich lif led I,
> No lord lyvynde me iliche.
> No duk ne dred I,
> For I regne in ryȝth as a riche.

There are obvious similarities between assertions like these and the boasts kings are in the habit of making in all manner of narrative and dramatic contexts in late medieval English literature. But there is an important distinction to be made, too. Kingly boastings have a characteristically frenzied note; the language in which they are clothed is a language which all the time hurls itself against language's limitations, and seems for ever on the point of relapsing into the incoherence of acute hysteria. After the Massacre of the Innocents in the *Ludus Coventriae*, King Herod at last feels that his kingship is secure, and he seats himself on his throne 'as kynge of myghtys most'. Nevertheless, the calm confidence of the *Somer Soneday* king completely eludes him:

> If any brybour do bragge or blowe aȝens my bost,
> I xal rappe þo rebawdys and rake þem on rought
> With my bryght bronde;
> Þer xal be neyther kayser nere kynge
> But þat I xal hem down dynge[8]
>
> *brybour* rogue;   *rake þem on rought* make them huddle together

The jigging and prancing Absolon of The Miller's Tale is responding to this aggressiveness and incipient hysteria when he resorts (inter alia) to 'playing Herod' in an attempt to woo the carpenter's wife. It is a grotesque thing for him to choose to do with a body like his, but, like all his other grotesque actions in the tale, it suggests how ill-matched his physical being and his habits of mind are. He is in character as Herod, but when he tries to demonstrate this he makes himself a laughing-stock; hysterically aggressive words are funny rather than frightening, unless the speaker has a magnificent presence.

About the magnificence of the reigning king's presence in *Somer Soneday* there can be no doubt, in spite of the fact that, as far as the trappings of royalty are concerned, the poet limits himself to colourlessly conventional details – he sits on a 'semeli' seat and is 'comely' clad in a cope. A marginal gloss saying 'here the poet sees the king sitting at the top of the wheel' would have fulfilled the same function; we are assured that this is the king who says *regno*, and can concentrate undistractedly on the 'action'. This is quite unlike what happens in the previous stanza. There, the poet does not make it clear who the 'gome gameliche gay' introduced at the beginning of the stanza (67) is, until, at the end of the stanza, he identifies himself as the would-be king:

> Þe crowne of þat comely kyng
> I cleyme be kynde.   (77–8)

Fortune's wheel is turning for the would-be king, and the movement delights him, making him laugh and bestow 'loveliche lokyngges' on the poet. For the has-been king, too, the wheel is turning, though this time the poet shows us his wretchedness before indicating that it is the wheel's downward movement that has caused the emotion:

> Al blok was his ble in bitere bales browth,
> His diademe of dyamans dropped adoun,
> His weyes were aweyward wroþliche wrout   (111–13)
>
> *blok* wan;   *His weyes* . . . i.e. he was sprawling pitifully, like the *regnavi* king in plate 3

Again, using the same narrative device as he does in the stanza devoted to the would-be king, the poet does not allow us to be sure that this 'nedful and nawthi' (necessitous and destitute) wretch is the king who says *regnavi* until, at the end of the stanza, his low-key greeting evokes the information, interrupted by the has-been king's tears, that 'he was crouned kyng in kiþ / and caytif (wretched) become' (119–20).

Regnabo; *regno*; *regnavi* . . . the narrative structure of *Somer Soneday* evidently reflects the implicit narrative of the 'formula of four', and because the whole narrative does not have to be experienced simultaneously in a poem (as it does in the visual image) the poet is able to add the narrative dimensions of movement through time and of gradual, rather than instantaneous, perception. And yet, at the heart of the poem, in the stanza and *versus* devoted to the king at the top of the wheel, the poet deliberately dispenses with these 'realistic' dimensions of narrative. Though the wheel is 'rennyng', the king remains enthroned at its highest point; that he is the king who says *regno* is obvious at once. Sitting 'ryȝth on þe rounde', with the eyes of the would-be king and has-been king fixed on him, there is no need for him to resort to the hysterically aggressive behaviour and language of a boasting king like Herod. The other kings on the wheel, the poet and the reader all acknowledge him. Not that there is any doubt that he would act impetuously if there were the slightest threat to his dominion – 'that lord would be exceedingly loath to abandon his lordship' (93) – but, meanwhile, the certainty that he is recognised as the crowned king enables him to restructure the poem effortlessly around him, with the same perfectly relaxed control with which he 'caste kne over kne' and 'leyde his leg opon liþ'.

His *versus* shows the same control and the same relaxation. Like the formulaic *regno* of the reigning king in the Wheel of Fortune image, it is not a boast but a statement: unlike the formulaic *regno*, the *Somer Soneday* king's *versus* requires us to make a distinction between boast and statement as we read. Language which in other contexts would certainly be self-glorifying –

> Lordlich lif led I,
> No lord lyvynde me iliche –

is self-revealing language, here. The transformation of the one kind of language into the other is the most significant thing that happens in the poem, the linguistic equivalent of the impulse that draws our eyes inevitably to the king saying *regno* when we look at a 'formula of four' Wheel of Fortune. In *Somer Soneday*, as in the visual image, the narrative energy of the 'formula of four' is diverted into the reigning king's revelation of himself, and this 'action' transforms our response to the narrative. Even the unexciting poet of 'Þo Whele of Fortune' makes a token attempt to reproduce this process; the infinitely more gifted poet of *Somer Soneday* creates a *regno* that informs our understanding of how the 'formula of four' works, but in the last resort it baffles our attempts at analysis, and goes on haunting the mind.

The image of the Wheel of Fortune is characterised by the relationship shown to exist between the reigning king and the would-be and have-been kings. In Wheel of Fortune images with the *regno*-formula, in Wheel of Fortune images with what Pickering calls the 'one regular variant on the formula' – *glorior elatus; descendo minorificatus; infimus axe premor; rursus ad alta vehor*[9] – and in poems and plays elaborating on either formula, or both,[10] the figures not yet on top of the wheel and the figures no longer on top of the wheel all look towards the reigning king, and define their state in relation to him. 'Wynd wel, worþliche wyȝth!' (turn the wheel well, my dear lady) the would-be king begs Fortune in *Somer Soneday* (83), as he eagerly anticipates sitting on the king's throne; the *caytif* looks back and laments that he, who was once called king by kings, is now 'fallen from friends' (123).

A similar tradition is represented in the verbal formulae which the eighteenth-century Byzantine painter Dionysius of Fourna instructs the artist consulting his manual of iconography to give to each of the seven ages in the wheel-picture representing 'the vain life of this world'.[11] Dionysius tells us in his manual that in his youth he learned the art of painting by carefully copying the works of one of the greatest of all the Byzantine masters, Manuel Panselinos. Tradition has it that this fourteenth-century master wrote his own painter's manual, and it is possible that Dionysius may have had access to it: in any case, Dionysius' manual is a repository of centuries-old conventions of Byzantine iconography.[12] The seven ages of man's life, says Dionysius, are to be depicted around the circumference of the third and largest of the three concentric circles which make up the picture of 'the vain life of this world'. The other, inner circles carry the signs of the zodiac and the four seasons – spring represented as a man sitting in a flowery meadow, wearing a chaplet of flowers and playing a *kithara*, summer as a harvester, autumn (at the bottom of the wheel) as a man threshing trees to harvest the fruit and winter as a man in furs in front of the fire. 'Next to the mouth' of each of the ages, to represent them speaking, must be written:

> Child, aged 7: When shall I go up higher?
> Boy, aged 14: O time, hurry up and turn, so that
>   I can go up quickly.
> Adolescent, aged 21: Here I am now, close to
>   sitting on the throne.
> Young man (*neos*), aged 28: Who exists like me,
>   and who is higher than I am?

Man (*aner*), aged 48: O time, now I see youth go by.
Older man, aged 56: O how you have deceived me,
   wretched one, O world.
Old man, aged 75: Alack-a-day! O death, who can
   escape you?

'High up, on top of the wheel' sits the 28-year-old, whose kingly attitude and regalia Dionysius describes with great care:

draw [a] man, with the beginnings of a beard, sitting on a throne, with his feet on a cushion and his hands stretched out on either side. He holds a sceptre in his right hand and a bag of money in his left hand, and he wears a crown and is dressed as a king.

King *Neos*' words are cast in the form of a question, but they are as bold an assertion of pre-eminence as the *Somer Soneday* king's 'no lord lyvynde me iliche'. At the bottom of the wheel the painter is instructed to depict a tomb in which Death stands, armed with a large sickle which he hooks around the old man's neck, while nearby a dragon is swallowing his blood. The blood-gulping dragon perhaps represents an attempt on the part of the creator of the image to divert attention from the crowned king at the top, or at least to create a visual balance between the top and bottom of the wheel. Be that as it may, the precise details Dionysius provides about the appearance of the young man at the top of the wheel, from his crown to the cushion on which he rests his feet, remain the outstanding feature of his account of the wheel of the ages of man's life.

As in the Wheel of Fortune poem *Somer Soneday*, the narrative impulse implicit in the sequence of verbal formulae is countered by an anti-narrative impulse, the king's self-revealing 'action'. The other ages respond to the king's assertion of pre-eminence by showing what it is that they lack; for them, the kingly state of youth is a hope in the future or a reality that the movement of the wheel has robbed them of. Though the *moralitas* of Dionysius' wheel-picture is expressed through the figure at its centre, the 'vain and seductive and wily' King World, the image just as clearly celebrates King Youth. In this Byzantine Wheel of Life there is the same balance between narrative and anti-narrative impulses that characterises the Wheel of Fortune, a balance which depends on the figures on the upward-turning wheel and the figures on the downward-turning wheel making it apparent by their attitudes and by their words (where the image has a verbal component) that they define their position on the wheel in terms of their relationship with the ruling king.

No surviving representation of 'the vain life of this world' is altogether like the one prescribed by Dionysius, but the French art-historian Adolphe Didron, travelling in Greece in 1839, saw a wall-painting closely related to it in the church at Sofádhes in the plain of Thessaly. At this stage of his journey Didron did not know of the existence of Dionysius' manual, and for a long time he had been puzzled about the iconographic significance of two French Romanesque wheels bearing a succession of human figures, the rose-window half-wheel in Amiens Cathedral and the full-wheel window in the church of St Etienne, Beauvais. Then, on Mount Athos, he was given access to Dionysius' manual, and relating the details of 'the vain life of this world' to the wall-painting he had seen at Sofádhes he became convinced that the Amiens and Beauvais wheels should also be interpereted as wheels representing the course of the individual man's life, and not, as had been thought until then, wheels representing the activities of a fortune who presides over the universal destiny of man.[13] The publication of Dionysius' manual in a French translation in 1845, containing Didron's commentary on the image he called the 'échelle circulaire de la vie' or 'roue de la vie humaine', firmly established the independent existence of the image of the Wheel of Life.[14]

Whether the separate identity of the Wheel of (individual) Life and the Wheel of (universal) Fortune was apparent to the medieval eye is another matter. In wheels of fortune, the opposition between the reigning king and the other figures on the wheel is often made explicit by the ages of the clambering-up and falling-down figures being differentiated, as in the Holkham Bible Picture Book (see plate 3) and *Somer Soneday*.[15] The poet of 'Þo Whele of Fortune' understands that the four kings on fortune's wheel may be taken to signify man's changing state:

> Fro wayknesse to strengthe þat upward es,
> And fro strengthe dounward to wayknes;
> Fro childeheed to monheed unto strength be maste,
> Þat þen withdrawes hit, as olde men may taste (93–6)
>
> *unto strength be maste* until strength is greatest

Here childhood and old age are perceived solely in terms of the power they do not have, and the stress-pattern reinforces the centrality of 'monheed'. A proverb about the transience of the central age, 'labilis ut ventus sic transit leta juventus' (joyful youth goes by, fleeting as the wind), accompanies the Wheel of Fortune Herrad of Hohenbourg included in the *Hortus Deliciarum* she prepared for her 'little throng of *adolescentulae*', after she had been elected abbess in 1167. The proverb about youth is immediately followed by verses referring to fortune's wheel:

> Quod fortuna fidem non servat circulus idem
> Plane testatur, qui more rote variatur

(that circle, which is rotated like a wheel, clearly testifies that fortune does not keep faith).[16]

The juxtaposition was noticed by G.McN. Rushforth, who realised that it suggested a connection between the king at the top of the Wheel of Fortune and the king at the top of the Wheel of Life.[17] Less tentatively, one could very well argue that all wheels of fortune are also wheels of life, whether explicitly or only potentially, because the king at the top of the wheel represents the acme of royalty and the acme of age.

There seems little point in trying to create an artificial distinction between the two kinds of wheel, based on whether or not the ages are differentiated. Such differentiation is merely one of the optional features of the image, as the two fifteenth-century examples entitled 'Rota Vite Alias Fortune' and 'Rota Vite Que Fortuna Vocatur' make sufficiently clear.[18] The meaning of the image is contained in the relationship between the king who reigns in the flower of his age, motionless at the top of a moving wheel, and the figures on either side of him, who enjoy neither majesty nor youth. The *regno*-king is a perfect-aged man; *juventus* reigns among the ages: the mirroring begins with the earliest Wheel of Fortune images and becomes a commonplace. There is a touching example of it in an early sixteenth-century French kalendar, where May is represented not by the usual gilded youth but by a crowned king (see plate 4). With his sceptre in his right hand and a flower in his left, he wanders through a forest, an incongruous and rather anxious-looking figure, accompanied by a cheerful hound.

The idea of the flower of man's age as a reigning king, enthroned at the top of a Wheel of Fortune/Wheel of Life, profoundly influences the way in which English writers in the late medieval period conceive of man's journey through the series of the ages. But we are likely to misunderstand the nature of this influence or underestimate it unless we recognise that there are two quite distinct traditions of verbal formulae associated with the ages of the Wheel of Life. Until this point, we have been concerned with the tradition that has the ages talking about where they are placed on the wheel in relation to the reigning king, and since the words of the ages give voice to the attitudes in which they are depicted this can be seen to be an essentially iconographic tradition. There is another tradition, however, which can be seen to be essentially literary – a tradition that has the ages speaking in turn about their own characteristics, without reference to the king at the top of the wheel. Within this tradition, the image of the Wheel of Life is more often implicit than pictorially realised, so that often it is only the nature of the words spoken by the kingly age in the middle of life that makes the underlying wheel-image apparent.

In the thirteenth-century poetic miscellany Corpus Christi College Cambridge MS 481, there are four poems grouped together in which the ages speak in sequence.[19] Only the last of the four makes explicit reference to the Wheel of Life:

4 Crowned king representing May, early 1500s.

The perfect age of man's life

Hanc, homo, cerne rotam: seriem circumspice totam,
Quomodo res prima circumvertitur ad ima

(man, look at this wheel: follow the whole sequence round and see how the first state of man is turned round to become the last and lowest.)

There is, in fact, no wheel-figure in the manuscript and no space left for one, but the words of *Juvenis* remind us of it:

Ad sedes letas juvenilis me vocat etas;
Elatus regno, puto numquam sum sine regno

(*juventus* calls me to a joyful seat; I reign on high, and do not expect ever to be deprived of kingly rule.)

This regal youth's 'puto' may remind us of the verb the poet uses on the king's behalf in *Somer Soneday*, 'he *wende* al þe world were at his weldyng' (94). The function of the verb in both poems is to remind us of the unstoppable movement of the wheel ('he supposed', but he supposed wrongly), and yet the expectation of everlasting pre-eminence itself becomes an essential aspect of the self-revelatory action of the *regno*-figure. So *Juvenis* in the first of the four age-poems in the same manuscript, which otherwise has no reason to be associated with the Wheel of Life, says

Nunc potenti et decenti juventute floreo;
Celsus regno sum et regno credo numquam careo;
Prudens, fortis sum, non mortis adventum pertimeo

(now I flourish in mighty and beautiful youth; I am exalted in kingly rule and expect never to lack lordship; I am wise and strong and have no fear of the approach of death).

More tersely, *Juventus* in the third poem says 'regnans, regnabo, puto semper in omnine leto' (I rule and shall rule for ever; I expect to be entirely happy always).

In none of these four poems is there any expressed relationship between the regnal figure and the other ages. In 'Hanc, homo, cerne rotam', *Adolescens*, presumably immediately below *Juvenis* on the upward-turning wheel, is 'growing little by little' and praising the present age; *Vir*, immediately below *Juvenis* on the downward-turning wheel, congratulates himself on his discriminating worldliness, deliberately directing his mind to 'res terrenas'. The balance between narrative and anti-narrative impulses which characterises the Wheel of Fortune is therefore entirely lacking in these wheel-poems of the ages, and the main function of the underlying wheel-image would seem to be to provide a context within which the perfect-aged king can express his kingship without seeming to be either boastful or deluded. He waits his turn to speak, just as though he were one of the steps in the sequence of the ages, but as soon as he speaks he separates himself from the ages in procession and declares himself immune from change. The image created to express the inevitability of death recreates within itself a representation of the invulnerability of life. It is to the best-known English example of a Wheel of Life, accompanied by a poem belonging to this second, essentially literary tradition, that we now turn.

10

The perfect age and the De Lisle Psalter

[*Infans:*]	Mitis sum et humilis; lacte vivo puro.
[*Puer:*]	Numquam ero labilis; etatem mensuro.
[*Adolescens:*]	Vita decens seculi speculo probatur.
[*Juvenis:*]	Non imago speculi sed vita letatur.
[*Vir perfectus:*]	Rex sum; rego seculum; mundus meus totus.
[*Senex:*]	Sumo michi baculum, morti fere notus.
[*Decrepitus:*]	Decrepitati deditus, mors erit michi esse.
[*Infirmus:*]	Infirmitati deditus, incipio deesse.
[*Moriens:*]	Putavi quod viverem; vita me decepit.
[*Mortuus:*]	Versus sum in cinerem; vita me decepit.

Text from British Library MS Arundel 83 (II), fo. 126v:[1]

[*Infant:*]	I am tender and lowly; I live on milk alone.
[*Boy:*]	I shall never know transience; I weigh up the present age.
[*Adolescent:*]	The glorious life of this world is examined in a mirror.
[*Young man:*]	No image in a mirror but life itself delights me.
[*Perfect-aged man:*]	I am a king; I rule the world; everything in the world is mine.
[*Old man:*]	I take up my staff, almost acquainted with death.
[*Decrepit man:*]	Given over to decrepitude, death will be my condition.
[*Sick man:*]	Given over to sickness, I begin to fail.
[*Dying man:*]	I thought I should live for ever; life has cheated me.
[*Dead man:*]	I have become dust and ashes, life has indeed cheated me.

THESE lines are written around the medallions at the end of the ten spokes of the wheel of the ages of man's life in the De Lisle Psalter (see plate 5). The 'psalter', which has lost its psalter text, is called after its first known owner, Robert de Lisle (d. 1343), who left it to his daughters Auderé and Alborou, intending that it should finally become the property of the Gilbertine nuns of Chicksands Priory, in Bedfordshire. Now sadly incomplete and with its leaves probably bound in the wrong order, but secure in its reputation as one of the greatest treasures of medieval English art, it forms the second part (fos. 117–35) of MS Arundel 83 in the British Library. It has most recently been described by Lucy Freeman Sandler, who argues for a date of around 1310 for the work of the first of the two main artists who produced it, the 'Madonna Master', and a date after 1330 for the work of the second, the 'Majesty Master'.[2] She associates the Madonna Master, who painted the Wheel of Life, with Westminster and with the court school.

5   The Wheel of Life from the De Lisle Psalter, *c.*1310.

The De Lisle Psalter, like the Howard Psalter and Hours with which it is now coupled, contains several of the moral and theological diagrams associated with the late thirteenth-century Franciscan John of Metz and known collectively as the *Speculum Theologie*: the *lignum vite afferens fructus duodecim* (fo. 125v), the *turris sapiencie* (fo. 135r) and seven others. Moral and theological schemes of this kind both precede and follow the three pages of this manuscript (fos. 126r–127r) which interest us particularly here.[3] Written

81

ich am afert· Il olbher ich fe·De puukey hit ley deucles yu· Ich besibel faur· uth schelton lr·Flor godes lo

6   The three living and the three dead from the De Lisle Psalter.

inside a wheel on fo. 126r is the poem 'Parvule, cur ploras', in which *Racio* questions each of the twelve ages in turn: we shall consider this poem after we have looked in detail at the Wheel of Life on fo. 126v (which is described by Sandler, p. 40), and, for the sake of the illuminating comparison it provides, the picture of the three living and the three dead and the poems accompanying it on fo. 127r (see plate 6; described by Sandler, p. 42).

As works of art, the Madonna Master's Wheel of Life and picture of the three living and the three dead are far more exciting than the diagrammatic schemes accompanying them. Even so, it is worth bearing their context in mind. The Franciscan spirituality which created and was sustained by trees of life and towers of wisdom may seem to us to have been obsessively concerned with pattern, number and correspondence, but at least as important within the *Speculum Theologie* tradition is the perception that the 'altercation of opposites' underlies all things. In the *rota altercacionis oppositorum* (see plate 7), at the top of the wheel *Superbus* (the proud man) proclaims 'Despicio miseros, quia dicor maximus heros' (I look down on the lowly, for I am called the greatest of heroes) and immediately afterwards (the wheel reads from left to right) *Humilis* counters the proud man with 'Non curo dici dominus, quia fortia vici' (I do not wish to be called 'lord', for I have overcome the mighty). The miserly man and the magnanimous man then speak their opposing verses, and so on all round the wheel; opposites

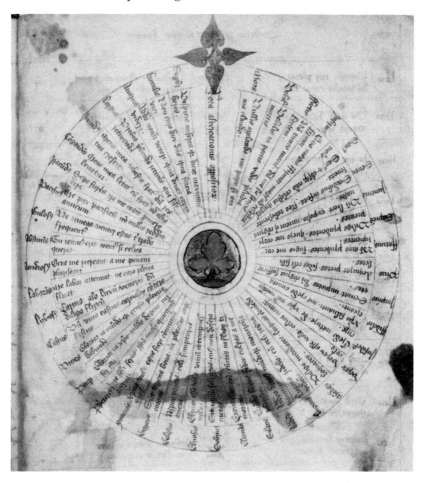

7 The *rota altercacionis oppositorum*, early 1400s.

confront each other, visually yoked together, until Death, back at the top of the wheel, concludes the altercation with 'I praise nothing; I spare nothing; I bring all things to an end'. In the De Lisle Psalter the tree of the vices and the tree of the virtues oppose each other on facing pages (fos. 128v and 129r), and eternally opposed realities are cogently represented beneath 'the life everlasting', the last of the Twelve Articles of Faith (fo. 128r), when Christ is shown sitting in glory with Lazarus in his bosom and Dives is shown entering the mouth of Hell. Undramatic as the *Speculum Theologie* schemes may at first appear to be, there is nothing comfortable about them, and they may well have influenced the artist(s) who designed the images of life and death on fos. 126v and 127r of the De Lisle Psalter, the Wheel of Life and the three living and the three dead.

The De Lisle Wheel of Life has been reproduced and described many times,[4] and everyone who sees it must be impressed by the magnificence of the elaborately-patterned background, and by the contrast between the mazes of interwoven lines within the segments of the wheel and the simple, clear lines of the figure-drawing inside the medallions. Because this picture is so widely known, any mention of wheels of the ages of man's life is likely to bring it to mind, so that what may be a distorted sense of the currency of the Wheel of Life image in late medieval England is perhaps fairly general. Very few English wheels of life survive. On the north wall of the former chapel of St Anthony in Leominster Priory church in Herefordshire, a ten-spoked wheel, with ten medallions on the circumference and one central medallion, is all that can now be seen, but at the beginning of this century, when Rushforth examined it, there were still enough details remaining for him to be sure that this was a Wheel of Life, and that it was very like the De Lisle wheel, even to the extent of including the same Latin verses.[5] Just over twenty miles away, on the Herefordshire/Gloucestershire border, a ten-spoked wheel, with ten medallions on the circumference and one central medallion, is visible on the north wall of the nave of St Mary's church, Kempley, a church famous for the twelfth-century frescoes in its chancel.[6] This wheel is the same size as the wheel at Leominster, and, like the Leominster wheel, has a surrounding rim. No traces of any inscriptions have been recorded, but it is probable that the Leominster and Kempley wheels were copies of the same design.

Only a minute proportion of the medieval paintings once covering the interiors of many churches and secular buildings as well are now visible at all, and even those paintings which have not vanished altogether are ghosts of their former selves, so that it is impossible to base an estimate of how many wheels of life once existed, and what they looked like, on the fragmentary remains in the South-West Midlands. A few tentative things can, nevertheless, be said. Neither the Leominster nor the Kempley wheel is likely to post-date the De Lisle wheel by many years (they are more likely to pre-date it), and if the Wheel of Life image remained popular during the fourteenth and fifteenth centuries it is surprising that no later example is known. Again (this may be putting the same thing another way) no surviving detail of any English wall-painting which has been even tentatively identified as a complete wheel of the ages of man's life is incompatible with the Wheel of Life design known to us from the De Lisle Psalter, a design which includes the poem 'Mitis sum et humilis' as an integral part of the whole.

Valuable evidence of the closeness of the link between visual and verbal elements in this Wheel of Life design was provided by the Leominister Wheel, in its former state. Even without this external evidence, though, there could be no question of the De Lisle medallion-pictures standing alone, without their accompanying texts: at least two of the representations of the ages are conceived as illustrations of their encircling verses, and would be puzzling without them. The figures of the boy using a pair of scales and the adolescent looking into a mirror need to be interpreted in the light of the words supposed to go with them: 'I shall never know transience; I weigh up the present age' (recalling the proverb about the transience of youth in the *Hortus Deliciarum*) and 'the glorious life of this world is examined in a mirror'. The Madonna Master unfortunately transposed the two pictures, though the Latin verses read in the right sequence. This blemish is irritating to the eye, but (as Rushforth says, p. 49) it does serve to establish the fact that the artist was reproducing a design, not inventing it.

If the intimacy of the relationship between verse and picture in the *puer* and *adolescens* medallions of what may be called the 'De Lisle-type' Wheel of Life confused the Madonna Master, it also appears to have been too subtle for the poet who wrote '3ing and tender child I am', probably in the late fourteenth century:

[*Infans:*]	3ing and tender child I am, and souke my moder tete.
[*Puer:*]	Qwat is to com hald I no tale; my play ne wyll I lete.
[*Adolescens:*]	My fayre lokkys þet I keme, my vice in meror I se.
[*Juvenis:*]	With hors, falcon and wit hound, I lyve in jolite.
[*Vir perfectus:*]	Alle thyng wit my strengnt overcom well I may.
[*Senex:*]	Myn eyn be dymmer þan þei wer; clere sight is gon away.
[*Decrepitus:*]	On my cruche I lene me; I begyn to heelde.
[*Infirmus:*]	Ded me has doun dryven; þet makes my mykell elde.
[*Moriens:*]	Wele I wend to have lyved ay; lorn is my lyffe, my wyt.
[*Mortuus:*]	Fro erth I come to erth; I shall be closyd in a pyt.

TEXT from Lincoln Cathedral Library MS.66, fo. 84r/p. 167[7]

vice visage;   *heelde* stoop

Preserved only in this northern copy, along with another (Latin) poem in which the ten ages speak in turn, this poem looks at first sight like an English translation of 'Mitis sum et humilis'.[8] As in the Latin poem, the ten ages are divided into five pairs, and some of the verbal parallels are unmistakable: the infant's opening words; the decrepit man's 'sumo michi baculum' and 'on my cruche I lene me', and the dying man's 'putavi quod viverem' and 'wele I wend to have lyved ay'. On the other hand, the words the English poet puts in the mouths of the boy, the adolescent, the young man and the *vir perfectus* would seem to suggest that he has in front of him (or in his memory) a De Lisle-type Wheel of Life, not just the Latin poem, for these verses apparently describe the pictures of *Puer*, *Adolescens*, *Juvenis* and the man in the flower of his age rather than reproducing the meaning of the Latin text. This does not really matter in the case of the boy, the young man and the full-aged man; what they say in the English poem echoes many other ages of man poems, though the *regno* is a somewhat enfeebled proclamation. (His kingship must be in doubt: he could be a soldier, like the *vir perfectus* in the accompanying Latin poem.) The English poet's literal reading of the De Lisle picture of the adolescent results in nonsense, however, for narcissistic self-admiration is neither what the artist is actually representing nor an accepted characteristic of this age. His poem, which is otherwise at least workmanlike and at best genuinely eloquent (the final couplet, particularly), is of course the poorer for this misunderstanding, but it is a lucky misunderstanding for us in that it provides us with one piece of evidence that the De Lisle-type Wheel of Life may have been known in the later fourteenth century, and in the north of England (all our other evidence being southern).

Whether or not '3ing and tender child I am' was written to take the place of 'Mitis sum et humilis' in a Wheel of Life image, the nature of the English poem, part translation of the Latin, part description of the medallion-pictures, tends to confirm that the De Lisle pictures and the Latin poem were regarded as being ineluctably twinned. Conceivably those same subtleties which the English poet was unable either to reproduce or to eliminate altogether satisfactorily stood in the way of the popularity of this kind of Wheel of Life image, but the difficulties associated with specific details of the image should probably be seen not as a cause of the scarcity of extant examples but rather as a symptom of the image's overall failure to do the two things a memento mori image needs to do, to shock the observer into a new awareness of the reality of his own end and at the same time to acknowledge and express his instinctive reaction against the reminder.

Needless to say, where there is so little evidence and where the evidence there is is so indefinite, this judgement that the De Lisle-type Wheel of Life was 'unsuccessful' can only be a comparative one, and it may therefore be possible to cast some light on the kinds of ways in which it is disappointing if we turn now to the page facing the Wheel of Life in the De Lisle Psalter and look at the picture of the Three Living and the Three Dead (see plate 6) and the poems accompanying it. This memento mori image was extraordinarily popular in the fourteenth and fifteenth centuries. In wall-paintings in English churches the three kings and the three corpses they encounter are often larger than life-size (considerably larger at, for instance, Wickhampton in Norfolk), so that the exquisitely fine picture in the De Lisle Psalter inevitably fails to suggest one of the things which contributed towards the image's success, the impact made by sheer hugeness.[9] The Leominster and Kempley wheels are surprisingly small, between four and five feet in diameter, and the details in the medallion-pictures can never have been easy to pick out: perhaps this helped to prevent the Wheel of Life image from becoming, or remaining, a favourite subject for wall-paintings.

Above the kings and the corpses in the De Lisle picture of the Three Living and the Three Dead are written the words assigned to them in the English quatrain often found together with the image:

[*King 1*:]   Ich am afert [*King 2*:] Lo, whet ich se!
[*King 3*:]   Me þinkeþ hit beþ devels þre.
[*Corpse 1*:]   Ich wes wel fair. (*Corpse 2*:) Such scheltou be.
[*Corpse 3*:]   For godes love be wer by me.[10]

These verses are only meaningful in the context of the image, but they are by no means just a formula. They underline the suddenness of the encounter between the living and the dead kings (a vital aspect of the image's meaning, not at all easy to represent visually); they express the uncomprehending terror of the living kings, confronted by an ugliness right outside their experience, and they define the moral to be drawn from the dead kings' hideousness, again drawing attention to the urgency of the situation – 'for God's love take heed'.

Underneath the picture of the Three Living and the Three Dead in the De Lisle Psalter is written another poem consisting almost entirely of the words spoken by the kings and the corpses when they confront each other, kings' words written beneath kings and corpses' words beneath corpses. This poem, here entitled *De Vivis Regibus et de Mortuis Regibus*, is a short form of one of five French poems on the same subject.[11] It begins, without any explanation, 'Compaynouns, veez ceo ke jeo voy!' ('lo, whet ich se!'), so that we need the image in front of our eyes, or in our minds, to make sense of what is being said and who is speaking. Urgency turns to fear ('I'm about to lose my wits'), but fear and urgency are then dissipated in the mechanics of explanation, as the poet drops back into the narrative mode:

> Veez la treis mors ensemble,
> Cum ils sunt hidous et divers,
> Purriz et mangez des vers

(see the three dead bodies in a row there; see how hideous and grotesque they are, putrefied and worm-eaten.)

The second king tells the first he wishes to repent and be reconciled with God; the third king 'wrings his hands' and asks why man was created when life and joy last so short a time – 'God never did anything as pointless as this'.

The words of the kings, then, anticipate what the corpses will have to say about pride, about transience and about amendment of life; the poet has deconstructed the image, making explicit the question 'why?': 'Why must earthly splendour end in putrefaction?' Without evolving into a fully autonomous poem, 'Compaynouns, veez ceo ke jeo voy!' significantly changes the nature of the image to which it is attached, whereas the 'Ich am afert . . .' quatrain both takes meaning from the image and gives it back heightened meaning. Nevertheless, the rendering of the image in the De Lisle Psalter, particularly of the living kings, shows the influence of the French poem rather than the English. Although 'Ich am afert' is written above the king on the far left, the inventor of the design clearly did *not* intend the king's attitude to signify fear; he stands apart from his companions, mournfully wringing his hands, well knowing what he sees and what it betokens.[12] The designer is unable and perhaps unwilling to represent the blasphemous nature of the detached king's meditation in the French poem; whether consciously or not, he has in fact incorporated into the image the sorrowful and pensive reaction that the ideal observer of the image is supposed to have. This works in the picture in a way that is not possible in the poem. The picture conveys the suddenness and the terror of the confrontation by way of the attitudes of the other two kings, and by the mocking reflection of their attitudes in those of the first and second corpses. We see the ugliness, take in the moral lesson, react to it and watch the king standing apart meditating on it, all at one and the same time – or, rather, with our awareness of chronological time suspended. The continuous interaction between the unexpected meeting and the composed meditation stands in place of an answer to the question implicit in the image's structure, the 'why?'. Our instinctive reaction against the memento mori is accepted into the image and made part of it.

The two memento mori pictures facing each other in the De Lisle Psalter are both, then, related to the poems accompanying them in intimate and complicated ways, and both involve a confrontation between life and death. The picture of the Three Living and the Three Dead, illustrating a poem which itself derived from the image, expresses this confrontation dramatically and satisfyingly; the horror of death and the instinctive reaction against the horror of death are perfectly balanced within the image, and the balance depends on the artist's being able to represent the narrative content of the image synchronically. Represented diachronically, the narrative is robbed of its force. In the case of the Wheel of Life image, though, the reverse is true: the impact of the poem is greater when it is read apart from its visual context, because the narrative, the sequence of the ages of man's life, needs to be represented and experienced as moving through time.

The designer of the De Lisle Wheel of Life instinctively understood this, and has done his best to suggest the movement of the wheel from left to right by making the figures in each of the medallions (or, where there are two, the outer figure) all face inwards, towards the circumference of the wheel. Nevertheless, the medallions with their encircling verses give emphatic visual expression to the separateness and self-enclosedness of each age. At the top of the wheel, the king enthroned within his own medallion asserts that he rules the world and everything in it, but, in order that our instinctive reaction against the memento mori implicit in the representation of the sequence of the ages might find adequate expression in King *Vir perfectus*' assertion, the artist would need to find a way of making it visually evident that the words he speaks are different in kind from the words spoken by the other ages.

The poet is able to make us feel that the king's words are different by leading us through the sequence of the ages one by one. Indeed, the 'Mitis sum et humilis' poet underlines the fact that the sequence of the ages is a sequence of separate little lives and deaths by pairing them, and also by making them imitate each other's words (a device which the English 'translator' does not attempt to copy). The couplet-form, the internal rhyme and the verbal repetition all lead us to expect that the paired ages are talking *to* each other, but the expectation the poet creates in us only serves to increase our awareness that there is no communication between the ages at all. The adolescent looks at life's splendour as in a mirror; the young man rejoices in life itself, not in shadows. Each age lives and experiences in the present tense. Reading the poem, then, we move from present tense to present tense, from one step in the sequence to the next, and only when we discover what *Vir perfectus* says do we have the satisfaction of suddenly realising that the image we ought to be thinking of is the image of a wheel of the ages of man's life, with *Vir perfectus* enthroned as a king at the top.

The tension between the sequence-structure and the wheel-image in the poem generates the energy that makes the perfect-aged man's assertion different from the statements made by the other ages. The artist cannot reproduce this tension, because when we look at the Wheel of Life image our eyes are at once drawn (as when we look at a Wheel of Fortune) to the king at the top. Afterwards we look at the ages on either side of him and, realising that they do not relate to him at all, understand that what is in front of us is nothing but a sequence of the ages which happens to be represented in the form of a wheel. This act of perception may produce a certain amount of pleasure, but once the mind has deconstructed the image in this way there is no tension left.

Much of what has been said here about the poem 'Mitis sum et humilis' and the De Lisle Wheel of Life is highly speculative, but it is a fact that there is very little evidence to suggest that the De Lisle-type Wheel of Life was widely known at the end of the Middle Ages in England. Certainly it is most improbable that it was widely-enough known for it to have had any marked influence on the dissemination of ages of man poems in which the flower of man's life is represented as a king among the ages. This concept of the acme-age is first and foremost a literary concept, not an iconographical concept, in spite of its Wheel of Fortune origins. King Perfect Age's assertion of his own pre-eminence always has to be seen against the background of the movement of time. We now turn back to the poem on the page preceding the Wheel of Life in the De Lisle Psalter, in order to consider the relationship between the perfect age and the movement of time more fully.

> Hic Racio loquitur homini, sic ut videatur,
> Quid sit, quid fuerit, quidque futurus erit.
>
> *Racio*: Parvule, cur ploras, dum vitales capis horas?
> *Nascens*: Nudus ut est moris, terram flens intro laboris.
>
> *Racio*: Dic quid disponis, infans, expers racionis.
> *Infans*: Insons absque dolo, matris fruor ubere solo.   4
>
> *Racio*: In quo letaris, puer, aut in quo gratularis?
> *Puer*: Ambulo securus dum vivo crimine purus.
>
> *Racio*: O flos, o fenum, que te dat causa serenum?
> *Adolescens*: Informans mores, in me flos promit odores.   8
>
> *Racio*: O siccis herbis ens vilior, num superbis?
> *Juvenis*: Nature decore, juvenili gaudeo flore.
>
> *Racio*: Tu sublimatus, in quo sis, quaero, beatus?
> *Vir*: Viribus ornatus, in mundo vivo beatus.   12
>
> *Racio*: Quid, senior, sentis? Affectum decito mentis.
> *Senex*: Terreno censu ditatus, polleo sensu.
>
> *Racio*: Quid de te loqueris, verbis edissere veris?
> *Decrepitus*: Transcendo metas vite, mea sic probat etas.   16
>
> *Racio*: Quid percepisti de mundo quem coluisti?
> *Imbecillis*: Artus sustento baculo gradiens pede lento.
>
> *Racio*: Mundane sortis meritum vir, dicito, fortis.
> *Infirmus*: Febribus arreptus, jaceo jam factus ineptus.   20
>
> *Racio*: Dic licet, invite, sumenda stipendia vite.
> *Moriens*: Terminus est in quo mundum moriendo relinquo.
>
> *Racio*: Dic ubi sunt gentes, ubi cari, quove parentes?
> *Mortuus*: Vermibus esca datus, oleo nulli modo gratus.   24

Text based on British Library MS Arundel 83 (II), fo. 126r (see plate 8)
Hic . . . erit *only in* L (where it is written in the first segment of the wheel) *and* O (line) 4 insons C Lc O] infans L T; 9 *and* 11 *are reversed in* C Lc; 14 ditatus C Lc T] contempto L O; 17 percepisti C Lc O T] suscepisti L; 19 mundane C L] humane Lc (*but* mundane *written above*) O T; meritum L Lc O] finem C casum T 21 licet C Lc O] hoc L T 23 sunt C Lc O T] nunc L; cari C Lc O T] mundus L
See note 13 for details of MSS

> (Here Reason speaks to man, in order that what is, what has been and what will be may all be apparent now.
> *Reason*: Little one, why do you weep while your life is just beginning?

8   The poem *Duodecim proprietates condicionis humane, inc.* 'Parvule, cur ploras'.

New-born child: Bare as a berry I come crying into this workaday world.

Reason: Tell me what you do, child, devoid of reason.

Infant: Innocent, guileless, I enjoy nothing but my mother's breast.

Reason: What do you delight in, boy, what gives you pleasure?

Boy: While I live without wrongdoing I walk without fear.

Reason: O flower, soon to wither away, what gives you grounds for being cheerful?

Adolescent: The flower of life, bringing virtuous habits into being in me, promises sweet scents.

Reason: You are more contemptible than withered grass – surely *you* are not proud of yourself?

91

Young man:	I rejoice in the flower of youth, in the beauty of my appearance.
Reason:	I ask you, raised up on high, what it is that makes you blessed.
Man:	Adorned with all manner of strength, my life in this world is a blessed one.
Reason:	What are you experiencing, old man? Tell me about your cast of mind.
Old man:	Enriched with worldly wisdom, I am influential in my judgments.
Reason:	What have you to say about yourself? Tell me the truth.
Decrepit man:	I am overstepping the boundaries of life; my age shows this to be so.
Reason:	What have you come to understand about the world to which you devoted yourself?
Enfeebled man:	I support my limbs and step slowly with the help of a staff.
Reason:	Strong man, declare the outcome of worldly fortune.
Sick man:	Assailed by fevers, I now lie reduced to helplessness.
Reason:	Reluctant one, speak, you have permission – now that you are about to receive life's rewards.
Dying man:	The end has come; dying, I leave go of the world.
Reason:	Tell me, where are your kinsmen, your relatives and your friends?
Dead man:	Food for worms, I don't smell nice at all.)

In the medallion at the centre of the wheel in which 'Parvule, cur ploras' is written, in the De Lisle Psalter, there is represented a nimbed head identified as *sancta trinitas* in the surrounding couplet. On the *verso* of the leaf, at the centre of the De Lisle Wheel of Life, a similar representation of the godhead is surrounded by the words 'I see all things at one and the same time; I govern everything according to *racio*'. The questions *Racio* puts to the twelve ages, and the answers they give, are written inside a wheel only in the De Lisle copy of the poem, although in two other copies (mss *C* and *O*) the poem occurs in the context of *Speculum Theologie* diagrams.[13] The poem's title (in the De Lisle Psalter and in mss *O* and *T*) *The Twelve Characteristics of the Human Condition*, suggests the concern with number that pervades the Franciscan schemes, but, more importantly, the fact that the questions and answers are presented in tabular form (see plate 9) in all four of the other copies clearly indicates that the pattern the poem makes on the page was felt to be one of the aspects of its meaning. The visual yoking of demand and reply isolates the ages from each other and emphasises their separateness, just as the enclosing of each age within a medallion cuts the ages off from each other in the De Lisle Wheel of Life; moreover, within each step of the sequence there is also a visual hint of that confrontation between unlike things which is the essence of the *rota altercacionis oppositorum*, the scheme which in mss *C* and *O* immediately precedes 'Parvule, cur ploras'. *Racio* asks the questions, but the answers elicited – the visual pattern implies – do not conform to reason.

9 The poem *Speculum etatis hominis, inc.* 'Parvule, quid ploras', fourteenth century.

The pattern the poem makes on the page in the De Lisle Psalter gives less emphasis to the separateness of each step of the sequence of the ages, but the confrontation between *Racio* and each age in turn, reading around the wheel counter-clockwise, again brings to mind the Wheel of the Altercation of Opposites. Perhaps the juxtaposition of 'Parvule, cur ploras' and this *rota* in some sequences of *Speculum Theologie* schemes was of itself sufficient to suggest that the poem could well be written in wheel-form, too. Nonetheless, it is tempting to suppose that the design of the poem was influenced by the wheel of the ages of man's life on the following page, for it is surely not accidental that what 'Man' says about himself in reply to Reason's question 'I ask you, raised up on high, what it may be that makes you blessed?' – 'Adorned with all manner of strength, my life in this world is a blessed one' – comes at the bottom of the wheel. At the top of the wheel, where the Wheel of Life king asserts that he rules this world and owns everything in it, a rubric informs us that 'here Reason speaks to man, in order that what is, what has been and what will be may all be apparent now'. *Sublimatus* according to his own perception of time, *Vir* is at the lowest point of his journey through the ages to death and judgment according to Reason's perception of time, which is God's all-seeing now.

A similar point about the difference between man's perception and God's perception is made visually in the mid thirteenth-century De Brailes Wheel of Fortune (see plate 10).[14] The outer series of segmental medallions make up a 'formula of four' Wheel of Fortune, with a variant of the *glorior elatus* formula and with twelve ages of man's life interspersed between the four figures (again, differentiated according to age) who speak the formulaic verses. The attitudes of most of the figures represented around the wheel are determined by their relation to the king at the top of the wheel, so that rather than being a Wheel of Fortune combined with a Wheel of Life it is a Wheel of Fortune with the ages differentiated somewhat more elaborately than usual. In the inner series of eight segmental medallions the life of Theophilus is represented. Having sold his soul to the devil with a bond written in his own blood, Theophilus sits at the bottom of the wheel as a king on a throne, with two devils worshipping him. Though he may seem to be emulating the reigning king who is saying 'raised up in glory' (*glorie alatus*) at the top of the outer wheel, his own fortunes are all too evidently at their lowest point. After he has repented and called upon the Virgin, and she has redeemed his bond with a charter containing her own name, two angels lift his soul to Heaven, at the top of the wheel. De Brailes is comparing the words of the Wheel of Fortune formula, which represent earthly glory as the most desirable goal, with the words which, but for a miracle, would have condemned Theophilus to Hell. Only the words which represent the person of the Mother of God interceding for him are powerful enough to release

10   The wheel of fortune of W. de Brailes, mid thirteenth century.

him from his grotesque mockery of kingship, and bring him to the glory not of this world.

The power of the written word is at the heart of the meaning of this Wheel of Fortune (and anti-wheel of fortune), but the impact it makes is all due to De Brailes' genius as artist and designer. The impact 'Parvule, cur ploras' makes, on the other hand, is essentially literary rather than visual: Reason's delicately ironic questioning of *Vir*'s assumption that he is 'raised up' and 'blessed' does not need the blatant visual underlining the wheel-design gives it in the De Lisle Psalter. The concealed mockery of Reason's 'what is it that makes you blessed?' allows perfect age to reply with a *regno* rather than with self-justification. All the ages, not just perfect age, speak in character, and it is because we know what the ages are going to say about themselves that we can appreciate the questions Reason puts to them. What looks like demand and reply really works the other way round; the self-enclosedness and predictability of each age is so absolute that questions can safely be modelled

95

on anticipated answers. The young man rejoices in the flower of his youth, apparently oblivious to the harshness of Reason's words: 'You are more contemptible than withered grass – surely *you* are not proud of yourself?' The man in extreme old age can think of nothing but his physical frailty – 'I hold up my limbs and step slowly with the help of a staff' – while Reason requires of him an intellectual response to his predicament: 'What have you come to understand about the world to which you devoted yourself?' The twelfth characteristic of the human condition is death itself, and the dead man's whimsical meiosis, 'I don't smell nice at all', ignores Reason's taunt (which echoes through medieval literature about death and dying): 'Tell me, where are your kinsmen, your relatives and your friends?'

The series of strangely oblique conversations which make up 'Parvule, cur ploras' causes us to think about the sequence of the ages of man's life as movement through time. The idea of the sequence itself suggests diachronic movement, even without the wheel or the separate 'steps' of the poem written in tabular form as visual reminders, and Reason expects that the ages will be able to recognise that they exist in a world containing past, present and future time. 'Flos' must turn into 'fenum', and actions performed 'now' will be appropriately rewarded when the sequence of ages has run its course. 'Racio loquitur homini', *one* man at twelve ages according to the rubric, but what the ages themselves say gives no hint of a continuum of experience; indeed, the fact that the same questioner moves from one age to the next only reinforces the reader's awareness that questioner and questioned are experiencing time quite differently.

The dissociation between question and answer in 'Parvule, cur ploras' heightens this awareness, but even where the words of the questioner and the questioned relate directly to each other the very fact of there being a questioner moving through the sequence of the ages chronologically, while the ages all speak from their present-tense-experience, underlines the essential discontinuity of the sequence. In 'Enfes, que demande tu?', the poem which accompanied the frescoes of the seven ages in the corridor linking the left transept of the cathedral at Foligno to the Palazzo Trinci (*c.*1400), an angel puts questions to each of the seven ages in turn (see plate 11).[15] The poem was no longer completely legible when Salmi described it at the beginning of this century, but it is clear that the ages and the angel were actually talking to each other. The *valeton* (15 years old), on being asked what he wishes for, replies, 'Lonc esté; court jueinoir' (a long summer; a short Lent); the *vielliart* (on the point of death), asked 'pour choy es si desfais?' (why are you so dejected?), replies 'Tout va a fin forque bien fais' (everything comes to an end except good deeds).[16] Demand and reply fit together in this poem to the extent that the words of the ages cannot stand alone, as they can in 'Parvule, cur ploras', but, as in the Latin poem, the questions asked are

11   Three of the Ages of Man from
the frescoes in the Palazzo Trinci,
Foligno, *c.*1400.
(a)   The 21-year-old.
(b)   The 40-year-old.
(c)   The 84-year-old.

97

modelled on the ages' predicted answers, not the other way round. Again, the fact that the questioner remains the same (and is moving through the sequence of the ages as we readers are) while the ages are fixed in their own presentness, makes us conscious of chronological disjunction; but because the angel is conceived as an entirely sympathetic observer of the ages, utterly unlike *Racio*, his questions mirror the sense of time the ages themselves have, instead of reminding us that man's life is a progress through the ages of this world to eternity. All the ages in 'Enfes, que demande tu?' live in an eternal present, and yet there is a distinction between the presentness experienced by the forty-year-old (*jovenes?*)[17] and the presentness experienced by the other ages. The angel asks the first three ages, the *enfes*, the *valeton* and the *jovencaus*, what it is they are wanting; he asks the sixth age (eighty-four years old) how he has lived '(Vieus dous, coment as tu vesqut?'),[18] and the seventh age, the *vielliart*, what it is that is oppressing him.[19] Only the question the angel puts to the fourth age, 'que note tele flours?', is devoid of any explicit or implicit reference to time future or time past – as is his reply, 'joie de quir (heart), deduit d'amour'.

The looking forward and looking back from an unchanging present, which is much more evident in this poem than in 'Parvule, cur ploras', is completely at odds with the awareness of past, present and future time Reason wants to inspire in man, according to the rubric accompanying the Latin poem. Reason associates awareness of the movement of time with awareness of mortality and of God's transcendent timelessness; for the ages themselves, awareness of the movement of time is associated with an instinctive turning towards the age which asserts its pre-eminence for ever in the present tense, 'I reign', 'vivo beatus', '(I have) joy and delight'.

Everything we have found out about the relationship between King Perfect Age and the other ages suggests that the idea of the perfect age depends upon the sequence of the ages being represented as a sequence of present-tense experiences, so that the flower of life may be seen to be the consummation of the *now*. The perfect age is given kingly status because it is not an age in the way in which the other ages are ages: it turns the sequence of the ages into a wheel, and changes our understanding of the movement of time. Perfect age reigns among the other ages insofar as it does this; otherwise it is simply one of the steps in the sequence. It may be useful, however, to pause here for a moment over a Wheel of Life which does not have a king at the top, the Longthorpe Wheel of Life (see plate 12) in order to remind ourselves that it is not the kingship metaphor *per se* which breathes life into the idea of the perfect age.

The 'great chamber' of the tower built to fortify the manor house at Longthorpe, two miles from the centre of Peterborough, contains what E.C. Rouse and A. Baker describe as 'the most important domestic mural

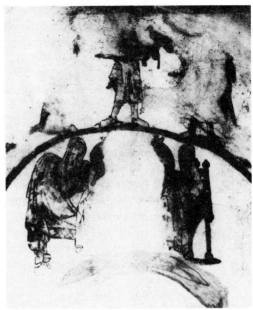

12 (a) The half-wheel of the Seven Ages of the north wall of the 'great chamber' of Longthorpe Tower, near Peterborough, 1330/40.
    (b) Detail of *juvenis*.

paintings of the medieval period in England', and there are certainly amazing visual riches in this rather small room.[20] The wall-paintings, which were executed between 1330 and 1340, have stylistic affinities both with the Queen Mary Psalter and with the De Lisle Psalter, with work produced in London-based ateliers and with work produced in East Anglian centres, notably Peterborough.[21] The wheel, actually a half-wheel of the ages of man's life at Longthorpe is not, then, very far removed from the De Lisle Wheel of Life either in time or in artistic milieu, but the two are completely different. At Longthorpe, the seven ages of man, *infans, pue[r], adolescens, [juvenis], [seni]or, se[nex]* and *decrepitus*, are represented around the arched window-recess of the north wall.[22] At the top of the arc the young man, with falcon and lure, stands facing forwards, looking directly at the observer. *Puer* and *adolescens* are positioned facing inwards towards the arc; *senior*, who carries a falcon, like the young man, and wears a sword, is turning slightly away from the arc, and *senex* and *decrepitus* are both definitely turned away from the arc, so that they face the east wall.

What we have at Longthorpe, in other words, is essentially a procession of the ages which is modified by the presentation of *juventus* at the top of the arc.

99

The difference between *juventus* and the other ages is suggested visually by the young man's stance; he alone is standing still and looking straight at us, while all the others are portrayed in attitudes indicating frozen movement. Although the age at the top of the wheel is not a king, the Longthorpe design makes the visual point that the age in the middle of the ages is unlike the others as effectively as does the De Lisle design, and without either arousing or disappointing expectations about the relationship between the figure at the top of the wheel and the figures on either side of him. The tension between the movement of the ages through a sequence of present tenses and the perpetual present tense enjoyed by *juventus* is here very simply and satisfactorily expressed.

The Longthorpe Ages of Man image makes it clear that the perfect age can be effectively differentiated from the other ages without being represented as a king. The array of age-names given to the figure at the top of the wheel – *juvenis, vir, vir perfectus* and so on – also makes it clear that it is not the age-name itself which differentiates the age at the top of the wheel from the other ages of man's life. Refusing to acknowledge past time, or future time, or the existence of any good thing that it does not already enjoy, the age at the top of the wheel brings the procession of the ages to a standstill. 'I reign' challenges 'what has been and what will be'. And yet, in spite of the freedom from the laws of God and Nature which perfect age arrogates to itself in these poems associated with the image of the Wheel of Life, its transforming power can only operate in the context of a schematic representation of the ages. Representations of the ages are perfect age's natural and proper environment.

While all other ages mirror man's experience of the progress of his life from birth to death, and are conditions of being which each and every man can look forward to experiencing at a particular time in his life, only perfect age is an unrealisable stage of existence. The newborn child in the poem 'Parvule, cur ploras' who answers Reason's question, 'why are you weeping?' with a traditional lament deftly turned – 'Bare as a berry I come crying into this workaday world' – is both earliest infancy, in the abstract, and a human being at the beginning of his movement through the ages. The particular instance and the general condition are inseparably joined. In the same poem, the general condition and the particular instance are again indivisible when *Vir* says that he is 'viribus ornatus', the strongest age. His assertion 'in mundo vivo beatus', on the other hand, signals a shift from manhood to the age which is different in kind from the other ages, from a realisable to an unrealisable stage of life. The present tense and the unparticularised voice are essential aspects of perfect age's identity; man's longing for a state of unchanging beatitude here in this world receives a recognisable identity, language and context as King Perfect Age.

PART III

The perfect age in Ricardian poetry

II

Myddel age in *Piers Plowman*

POEMS associated with the image of the Wheel of Life provide a context
within which perfect age can readily identify himself as king in an
eternal present tense. But as soon as our quest for perfect age takes us
outside this very confined generic context we realise that the idea of the
kingship of perfect age can actually stand in the way of the medieval poet's
attempt to shape a poetic structure around the Ages of Man. The ages of the
Wheel of Life poems are cut off from one another, with perfect age standing
both inside and outside the series. How, then, may a poet who does not want
to represent the Ages of Man in the abstract, and wishes instead to write
about man's experience of his own past and present and feared or hoped-for
future, adapt or transform the idea of an age which exists in a blessed and
never-ending present?

The presence of the outward trappings of King Perfect Age in a poem,
even the presence of his characteristic vocabulary, is no guarantee that the
inner significance of the idea has been absorbed into the poem's shape and
structure. The lyric 'As I gan wandre in my walkinge' is a good case in point:
it belongs to that species of late Middle English memento mori lyric in which
the speaker, who is about to die or already dead, narrates his own experience
of each of the ages in turn. Mourning and sighing, the man at the end of his
life in 'As I gan wandre' compares his successive ages to the hours of the day,
summing up each stage in the refrain 'þis world is but a vanyté'. At mid-day,
he says, he was a knight and a warrior, and then

> At hiȝ noon y was crowned king,
> Þis world was oonli at my wille;
> Evere to lyve was my liking,
> And alle my lustis to fulfille. (41–4)[1]

'I *was* crowned king': a *regnavi* demands to be placed in relation to a *regno*, but
here we have the past tense without the present tense which gives it meaning.
Forced by the constraints of genre to conform to the other ages – regarded as
a step once taken and now left behind – King Perfect Age becomes an
absurdity, inviting the response 'you, a king?'

The four Ricardian narrative poems which are the subject of the rest of this book, *Piers Plowman*, *Confessio Amantis*, *Sir Gawain and the Green Knight* and the *Book of the Duchess*, are all concerned to a significant extent with the individual's journey through the ages. In all of them, I shall argue, the idea of perfect age is an essential aspect of the meaning of the whole; in all of them, perfect age is offered as a tantalising possibility, as a stage of life which might, were it to be reached, undo the bonds binding the individual to the Wheel of Life.

Identifying perfect age within short, compact poems associated with the image of the Wheel of Life is a very different matter from recognising and interpreting perfect age within the huge, eclectic and labile poetic world of *Piers Plowman*. Not only is *Piers Plowman* utterly unlike Wheel of Life lyrics in kind, in scope and in imaginative range, but it is also a peculiarly personal poem; in Derek Pearsall's words, 'a highly individual response to the world of the late fourteenth century . . . cast in a highly idiosyncratic form'.[2] Since perfect age characteristically speaks in an impersonal voice and in the present tense, we should not expect to find perfect age represented in *Piers Plowman*, or in any narrative poem, as a stage of life which any of the persons or personifications have left behind in their individual pasts or expect to reach in their individual futures. More specifically, we should not expect to find perfect age in *Piers Plowman* bound to the cycle of the Dreamer's life: whatever Langland wants us to understand about Will's movement through the ages, it is surely not that any one stage of his life is blessed and raised above all the others.

The conclusions this study has so far suggested about the relationship between perfect age and the sequence of the ages of man's life would nevertheless lead us to expect to find perfect age in close association with representations of the sequence of the ages. Our investigation into Langland's perfect age will therefore focus on those parts of *Piers Plowman* in which the ages are brought into conjunction with one another, and, first of all, on the ways in which the Dreamer experiences the sequence of the ages in the Third Vision. An understanding of the ways in which Langland transforms the idea of the perfect age has to go hand-in-hand with an understanding of his idiosyncratic view of the ages of man's life. Perhaps because *Piers Plowman* is singularly deficient in the comfortable and the commonplace, those passages which apparently schematise the ages of man in well-worn ways and assign the Dreamer, and perhaps even Langland himself, to a definite stage of life, notably the dream of Fortune and Elde (B11: 6–62 and C11: 165–12:14), the beginning of the Ymaginatif passus in the B-text (B12: 1–11) and Elde's attack on the Dreamer in the final passus, have generally been regarded as little islands of clarity, where the reader can step more confidently than Langland usually allows. 'These precise references, both circumstantial and "biographical" . . . help to establish the Dreamer as "real" and enable him to fulfil the function of dreamer', says David Mills,[3] and words like 'precise' and 'fixed' occur again and again in discussions of these passages, as though it can be taken for granted that Langland refers to the ages of the Dreamer in order to make him a less enigmatic figure than those ageless beings who come and go without warning.

This assumption, though, seems to me to stem from a misunderstanding of the nature of Langland's mysteriousness. He is not a writer who expresses himself obliquely and enigmatically by choice, taking care to leave his readers a few strategically-placed clues to encourage them to persevere. Rather, the habits of his mind and the logic of his poetry are idiosyncratic through and through. He has a unique instinct for making the familiar unfamiliar, for upsetting the reader's sense of where he stands in relation to the text and for changing from one figurative mode or one linguistic register to another in a quite unprepared-for way. His poetry is essentially unpredictable, not quixotically unpredictable. The ways in which he talks about the ages of the Dreamer's life are as peculiarly his own as the ways in which he talks about winning and wasting, or about patient poverty, or about any other matter which had already been deeply imprinted with traditional patterns of thought before it entered his consciousness.

Nowhere in the representation of the Dreamer's life in *Piers Plowman* do we see the steady and measured progress suggested by traditional representations of the ages and by the assigning of each individual man to his proper place within the scheme, as one age succeeds another. So unpredictable and so extreme are the changes the Dreamer undergoes as he moves from youth to decrepit old age that reassurance is the last thing the reader can reasonably feel when Langland brings the ages into conjunction with one another. In a poem in which youth can so suddenly and completely turn into *elde*, perfect age does not need to stand right outside the series of the ages as an intrinsically unobtainable stage of man's life, related to manhood but yet distinct from it. For Langland, the stage of life called *manhod* and the concept of blessedness here in this world called perfect age are indivisible. On the one hand, the perfect age of manhood is a condition which man might naturally hope, or even expect, to achieve; on the other hand, the poem suggests, the only man who has assuredly achieved the perfect age of manhood is Christ himself.

The last word Ymaginatif utters before he suddenly vanishes at the end of passus 12 of the B-text is the age-name *manhod*:

> "And wit and wisdom", quod þat wye, "was som tyme tresor
> To kepe wiþ a commune; no catel was holde bettre,
> And muche murþe and manhod;" and riȝt wiþ þat he vanysshed. (295–7)[4]

'Courteous behaviour, good manners, gentility' are the glosses the *MED* suggests for *manhod* in this specific context (*manhēd*, 2c), taking it to mean that kind of humaneness appropriate in a social context (compare *menske*, 2a). But *manhod* may also mean the behaviour appropriate to the age of maturity, or the age of maturity itself, and the connection Ymaginatif is making here between *manhod* and 'wit and wisdom', innate and acquired understanding, does not allow us to understand *manhod* as the equivalent of *gentilesse*. Rather, it is the state or stage of life which man's natural faculties naturally bring him to, if sin does not prevent them. Perfected maturity, as Ymaginatif perceives it, is the state of man's life in which *clergie* and *kynde wit* complement each other and are more highly regarded than any other possessions – but this state of life is pushed back into the indeterminate past, 'som tyme', and is associated with the whole community rather than with any particular person. Besides, Ymaginatif has no sooner named the perfect age than he disappears.

Ymaginatif's enigmatic departure matches his enigmatic arrival. All Langland gives us by way of introduction to him in the C-text is 'and thenne was there a wyhte, what he was y neste' (what kind of creature he was I did not know; 13:218).[4] On the face of it, it seems only reasonable to draw a distinction between figures such as Ymaginatif, who come and go without warning, and the figure of the Dreamer, who is in some sense a continuing presence throughout the poem and around whose life at least the bare bones of a narrative are apparently constructed. There can be no doubt that the Dreamer has reached decrepit old age at the end of the poem, for Elde marks him with the signs of approaching death (B20:183–98; C22:183–98), and since the end of the sequence of the Dreamer's ages is predictable it has generally been taken for granted that his progress through the ages is predictable, too.[5] John Burrow, in his recent study of 'Langland *Nel Mezzo Del Cammin*', forcefully argues that the Dream of Fortune and Elde, and Ymaginatif's warning to the Dreamer that he should amend his life, 'present a portrait of spiritual crisis in middle age'.[6] The more radically 'autobiographical' stance Burrow proceeds to adopt, and his conclusion that B11:6–62 and B12:1–11 are 'a precise and somewhat painful rendering of Langland's own thoughts and fears' at the end of middle age (p. 41), may receive less general assent, perhaps: middle age, nevertheless, is the stage of life in which the Dreamer is commonly taken to be during the greater part of the Vita. A chronologically rational narrative would therefore seem to emerge. The middle-aged Dreamer briefly recalls his youth in the Dream of Fortune and Elde, and becomes an old man as the poem ends.

At this point, the reader who is alive to the fact that chronological narrative and sequential structure are by no means characteristic of Langland's poetry is likely to become uneasy about this commonsensical approach to the ages of the Dreamer's life. Uneasiness sharpens into the urge to cry *contra* with the realisation that at every point where the ages of man's life are brought into conjunction with each other in *Piers Plowman* Langland compels his reader to recognise that the progress of man's life is neither gradual nor predictable. Awareness of the series of the ages is associated for him with anxiety and uncertainty. Langland's interest in the representation of the ages is not, in fact, a narrative interest at all, but an interest in the moment of crisis when one age confronts another, for at such crisis-moments a man may be urged into salutary action.

Even at such moments the Dreamer can only very briefly sustain a sense of urgency. This is especially evident in the final passus, which is in part (as Pearsall points out in his note on C22:154) an apocalyptic recreation of the Dream of Fortune and Elde. In spite of the violence and viciousness of Elde's assault –

> [Elde] over myn heed yede
> And made me balled bifore and bare on þe croune;
> So harde he yede over myn heed it wole be sene evere
>
> (B20:183–5; cf. C22:183–5, unrevised)

yede went

– Will responds to the element of game rather than the physical force. After cursing Elde for his atrocious manners, he asks the rueful but relaxed question 'Since when has there been a footpath over men's heads?' (187). Although the grotesque inadequacies of decrepit old age are unmistakable and although, following Kynde's counsel, the Dreamer sets about making satisfactory preparations for his last journey (200–13), the advice Kynde gives that he should 'lerne to love . . . and leef alle oþere' (208), while he waits in the barn Unitee until he is sent for, evokes from him a question which makes it clear that he is still thinking of his life in the world as continuing for an extended and indefinite period of time: 'How shal I come to catel so to cloþe me and to feede?' (209). Even on the threshold of death, Will cannot sustain a sense of crisis or an awareness of the memento mori implicit in the series of the ages.

Ymaginatif's solemn warning also needs to be understood in the context of the Dreamer's natural and habitual inclination to conceive of his lifetime as having neither definite nor knowable boundaries. In the B-text (but not in the C-text), Ymaginatif offers the Dreamer both a schematic representation of the ages and a definition of his own position within the scheme:

> I have folwed þee, in feiþ, þise fyve and fourty wynter,
> And manye tymes have meved þee to mynne on þyn ende,
> And how fele fernyeres are faren and so few to come;
> And of þi wilde wantownesse whiles þow yong were
> To amende it in þi myddel age, lest myȝt þe faille

107

In þyn old elde, þat yvele kan suffre
Poverte or penaunce, or preyeres bidde:
Si non in prima vigilia nec in secunda etc.   (12:3–9)

mynne think;   *fernyeres* far-off years

'If neither in the first watch nor in the second . . .' refers to the interpretation of the three watches kept by the servants awaiting their lord's return from the wedding feast (Luke 12:36–8) as the three ages of man's life, a traditional interpretation which Burrow fully documents.[7]

Ymaginatif's representation of the ages is in fact based on a peculiarly threatening memento mori fiction. Built into the analogy between the three watches and the three ages is the fiction that the person receiving the warning has passed through the first age without amending his life, is at present in the second age and can by no means be certain that he will have the strength to amend his life in the third age, even if he is willing to do so. The cogency of this memento mori derives from the fact that within it two traditional attitudes towards the ages are held in tension. On the one hand, the ages are simply mathematical divisions of a man's lifetime, just as the watches divide up the hours of the night: in the words of Ælfric, in his 'Sermo in Natale Unius Confessoris', 'seo forme wæcce is witodlice in cildhade, and seo oðer wæcce is on weaxendum cnihthade, and seo þridde wæcce is on forweredre ylde' (the first watch, to be sure, is in childhood, the second in adolescence and the third in decreptitude; 67–9).[8] On the other hand, the ages are not simply divisions of time but are separate stages of life with their own characteristics and concerns. So, after enumerating the three watches and the three ages, Ælfric continues with the warning: 'Let the man who has not chosen to be vigilant in the first watch be sure to be vigilant in the second watch, turning his heart away from earthly follies' (70–2). In effect, Ælfric annuls the first chance to be watchful by relegating it to the past and the negative, 'se ðe nolde wacian'. The characteristics of youth make it most unlikely that a man will be watchful then. Gregory the Great in his version of the ages and watches analogy had made this quite explicit, referring to the *pravitates* of *pueritia*.[9] The 'wilde wantownesse' Ymaginatif attributes to the Dreamer in his youth should not, therefore, be taken as an indication that Will has been signally depraved. 'Men chaungeʒ thurgh dyverse ages', declares the *Prose Life of Alexander*, 'for wha will luke efter wysdome in a childe, in a ʒunge man stabillnes, or in an alde man wildenes?'[10]

For Ymaginatyf, as for the writer of *The Prose Life of Alexander*, the sequence of the ages and the characteristics of the ages are predetermined and perfectly predictable. Man's lifetime has definite and knowable boundaries. Moreover the memento mori fiction of the watches and the ages is exploited by Ymaginatif in such a way as to arouse the greatest possible anxiety in the Dreamer, for the passage threateningly suggests that the second age, man's only clear chance to repent, is almost over. Langland and his contemporaries, as Burrow demonstrates, would have associated 'fyve and fourty wynter' with the dividing-line between *juventus* and *senectus* and, indeed, the tradition that *juventus* ends at forty-five persisted until the end of the eighteenth century. The 45-year-old in a ballad entitled 'The Age and the Life of Man' (1805) is described as follows:

> When he looks on how youth is gone,
>   and shall it no more see;
> Then may he say, both night and day,
>   have mercy, Lord, on me.   (p. 5)[11]

I strongly suspect, however, that the mention of a specific number of years (outside the context of encyclopedic schemes of the ages) would have been considerably less telling for Langland's contemporaries than any kind of defining statement about age. To us, 'þise fyve and fourty wynter' is a precise age-indication and 'fele fernyeres are faren and so few to come' is an imprecise one, but I think that Langland intends both to be menacingly enigmatic. Both suggest, but do not state, that the third age is about to begin. Ymaginatif's representation of the ages is placed where it is in the poem in order to induce a sense of crisis, not in order to let the reader know that the Dreamer is forty-five years old; still less, that Langland himself is forty-five years old.

The age-name Ymaginatif uses for the second of the three ages, *myddel age*, has fortuitously turned out to be an obstacle to twentieth-century readers of *Piers Plowman*, suggesting that Langland is inviting us to see the Dreamer, at this stage of the poem, as a 'middle-aged' man in something like the modern sense, a man who has left youth behind him but who has not yet entered old age, a man wise in the affairs of the world and inclined to hold himself aloof from emotional display. Burrow warns us against reading into the text the 'melancholy implications' (p. 33) of the modern age-name, reminding us that *juventus* is both the strongest age and 'the age at which man is furthest away from God and most likely to be spiritually lost' (p. 34). But we should also bear in mind how uncommon the age-name *myddel age* is. Any apparently unambiguous reference in Middle English to an age of transition between youth and *old elde*, outside the encyclopedias, ought to alert us to the likelihood that the writer has some particular reason for distinguishing between 'young' youth and *juventus*.

The age of transition is personified as Medill Elde in the fourteenth-century debate the *Parlement of the Thre Ages*. In this poem, as in the B-text of *Piers Plowman*, man in the second of the three ages receives an urgent warning to be mindful of his end, but the warning Medill Elde is given comes from his 'sire' Elde, the three ages being represented as three generations:

> Thou man in thi medill elde, hafe mynde whate I saye!
> I am thi sire and thou my sone, the sothe for to telle,
> And he the sone of thi-selfe, þat sittis on the stede   (649–51)[12]

Medill Elde is a 60-year-old, Youthe a 30-year-old and Elde a 100-year-old, numbers which derive, as Beryl Rowland has shown, from the patristic triad of perfection with its origin in the variant yields of the good seed in the parable of the sower (Matthew 13:18–23).[13] The traditional exegesis of this parable associates 30, 60 and 100 with a hierarchy of holiness or of chastity; in this context they are not usually associated with the ages of man's life (as Rowland points out, p. 346). We should hardly expect them to be, given that thirty years and one hundred years are both, as we have seen, associated with the perfect age, while sixty years brings to mind the onset of old age and the end of the period of male fertility.[14] The idea of a hierarchy of perfection is very much at odds with medieval understanding of the series of the ages. In fact, we cannot know that the numbers of the triad of perfection will be the ages of the three 'thro men' in the *Parlement of the Thre Ages* until we come to the end of the description of Medill Elde. Until then, there is every reason to suppose that in the persons of the first and second contestants the poet is offering us a conventional contrast between youth and age. The 'renke alle in rosette' (137) is weighed down with 'golde' and 'gude' and old age and covetousness proverbially go together.[15] Only when we reach the last two lines of the portrait—

> Hym semyde for to see to of sexty ȝere elde,
> And þer-fore men in his marche Medill Elde hym callede   (150–1)

– do we realise that the third party in the debate will have to be a very old *elde* indeed.

During the 'flytyng' of Medill Elde and Youthe, the older man is apparently speaking as one who is separated from and opposed to *juventus*, but once Elde has described how old age 'undir-ȝode' (went beneath; 283) him and left him decrepit, Medill Elde and Youthe are perceived as standing together on the other side of the dividing-line, while they both receive Elde's offer of himself as a memento mori, 'Make ȝoure mirrours bi me, men, bi ȝoure trouthe' (290). The two-tiered debate between three ages works poetically precisely because of the ambiguous status and nature of Medill Elde. Were we to interpret him as a 'middle-aged' man manifesting the classical vices of the stepping-stone age, we might find ourselves tempted to ask, as Thorlac Turville-Petre does, whether a character 'as obviously in the wrong' as Medill Elde is made out to be 'is not altogether superfluous to the poem'.[16] Turville-Petre goes on to argue that Medill Elde does, neverthe-less, fulfil a poetic function insofar as he 'acts as a foil to Youthe', but surely his function is rather to transform a 'threpe' between two opposed ages of perfection into a quite different genre. The idea of the transience of life is especially linked (as Turville-Petre demonstrates, pp. 66–9) with the division of the ages into three. The *myddel age* attributed to the Dreamer at the beginning of the Ymaginatif passus and the Medill Elde of the *Parlement of the Thre Ages* share, I believe, a functional, genre-bound existence: named explicitly as ages of transition, enjoying none of the characteristics we have come to associate with the perfect age, they belong to that kind of representation of the ages which is specifically designed to make man think on his last end.[17]

From within that genre, Langland selects the analogy between the three ages and the three watches for Ymaginatif to lay before the Dreamer in the hope of provoking him into an awareness of his perilous condition. This analogy postulates that man is situated in the *myddel age*, the age most timely for amendment of life, lacking the characteristic disadvantages of the first age and the third age. According to this same analogy, the most positive characteristic of the *myddel age* is that it is an age of transition. Any time now, the third age may take its place. This labile *myddel age*, which Ymaginatif assigns to the Dreamer at the beginning of the passus devoted to him, is assuredly not the *manhod* he recalls from the past as he vanishes at the end of the passus. The perfect age of full maturity, as Ymaginatif represents it, is characteristically accompanied by *murþe* (B12:297), not by fearful anxiety. There is no place for perfect age in Ymaginatif's predetermined and ruthlessly predictable sequence of the ages.

Those readers of *Piers Plowman* who have interpreted Ymaginatif's opening gambit as Langland's signal to them that the Dreamer should be perceived as a middle-aged man have been hard put to it to account for the fact that Langland, in the process of revising the B-text, chose to omit Ymaginatif's warning altogether. In accordance with his 'autobiographical' reading of the Third Vision, Burrow suggests that Langland omitted B12:4–9, and altered 'fyve and fourty wynter' to 'mo then fourty wynter' (C14:3), because the anxieties peculiar to the end of middle age were no longer of any immediate interest to him at the time of his last revision of the poem (pp. 40–1). If Langland was on the threshold of old age when he was composing the Third Vision of the B-text, however, he was undoubtedly an old man by the time he came to revise it: nevertheless, in the Third Vision of the C-text the Dreamer is still menaced by Elde. The Dreamer does not move through the ages with the poet. Langland is not interested in his own past or in the earlier states of his poem, as Burrow rightly says, but the revised opening of the Ymaginatif passus cannot be explained in terms of

Langland's having left a certain stage of life behind him. It may be, as Pearsall suggests in his note on C14:11–12, that he was impatient to 'tackle squarely' the issues which take up the body of the passus, but a more weighty reason, I think, was that the analogy between the ages and the watches, though a most effective memento mori, incidentally entailed the introduction of a threefold scheme of the ages. When he came back to this part of the B-text, Langland may very well have felt that this isolated allusion to the three ages blurred the twofold scheme underlying the Third Vision as a whole.

Now, if Langland had been content to assign the Dreamer to any one stage of life, or to indicate his progress through a series of ages in a straightforwardly chronological way, he would have been free to make use of twofold, threefold or manifold schemes of the ages without there being any risk of confusing his readers. The most commonplace of commonplaces about man's life was that it could be divided into any number of different stages. In the Third Vision it is certainly the case that Langland encourages his readers to ask themselves what stage of life the Dreamer is situated in, but he does not provide a clear-cut answer. While we are doing our best to understand what Langland is saying about the position of the Dreamer in relation to Fortune and Elde, who are perceived as overlords of their respective age-territories, the complicating notion of there being a third, intervening age is unhelpful and unwelcome. And yet, Langland's decision to omit Ymaginatif's sequence of the ages from the C-text may well be a matter for regret. The juxtaposition of the sequence of the ages as the Dreamer experiences it and the sequence of the ages as Ymaginatif lays it before him has a strangely disturbing and disorienting effect. According to Ymaginatif, the sequence of the ages is rooted in the need for man to be convinced that immediate regenerative action is demanded of him, but in the 'inner dream', an elusive and indeterminate interlude – it is, after all, a dream within a dream, seen reflected in a mirror – the sequence of the ages appears to be shifty, full of surprises and devoid of moral imperatives.[18] Ymaginatif puts the ages firmly into the Dreamer's own hands, '*þi myddel age . . . þyn old elde*', whereas the ages in the 'inner dream' are in no sense in the Dreamer's possession. Fortune 'ravysshe[s]' the Dreamer (B11:7), carries him off into her own country and offers him marvels; Ymaginatif patiently follows the Dreamer as he moves steadily through *juventus*, teaching him time and time again to remember that he will die (B12:4).

Two very different experiences of living through the sequence of the ages are presented in the Third Vision of the B-text, then, and the two guardians of the Dreamer's youth could scarcely have less in common, but Fortune and Ymaginatif desert the Dreamer with equal suddenness, and in both sequences the poetic emphasis falls on the moment of transition from *juventus* to old age. Because he believes that both sequences represent Langland's own experience of living through the ages, Burrow argues that the two sequences should be understood as being the same sequence viewed from different perspectives.[19] Quite rightly, he points out that the period when the Dreamer is '3ong and 3ep' (C11:177)[20] and allies himself with the elder of Fortune's maidens, *Concupiscencia Carnis* (the first of the godless triad of 1 John 2:15–16), and the period when he takes his pleasure in the younger maiden, Covetyse-of-yes (Lust of the Eyes, traditionally a figure of avarice) should be understood as being two distinct stages of life.[21] Moreover, when Langland came to revise the B-text version of the dream of Fortune and Elde he sharpened the distinction between the lustful and avaricious phases of the Dreamer's subservience to Fortune. He separated them from one another by Rechelesnesse's discourse on the futility of learning (C11:201–311);[22] he placed the second intervention of Elde, which serves as prologue to the period of the Dreamer's association with Covetyse-of-yes, at the beginning of a new passus (C12), and he provided an echo of Rechelesnesse's own response to Elde's solemn warning 'by Marie of hevene' against Fortune and her three attendants (C11:187–92) – ' "3e? reche þe nevere", quod Rechelesnesse' (C11:193) – in Covetyse-of-yes' response to Elde's anguished, riddling lament:

> [Elde]: 'That wit shal turne to wrechednesse for wil hath al his wille!'
> Covetyse-of-yes conforted me anon aftur and saide,
> 'Rechelesnesse, reche the nevere'   (C12:2–4)

Even more clearly in the C-text than in the B-text, then, the Dreamer's godless and hopeless existence as Rechelesnesse, in the 'lond of longyng and love' which is Fortune's territory (C11:167), is divided into two phases.[23] The characteristic vices by which these two stages of life are identified would tend to make one associate them with the Youthe and Medill Elde of the *Parlement of the Thre Ages* rather than with the youth and *myddel age* of Ymaginatif's three-age scheme, according to which the second age is defined, as we have seen, slowly in terms of its salvific potential. The ruling vice both of Medill Elde and of the second part of the Dreamer's sojourn with Fortune is plainly covetousness (B11:53; C12:4–5),[24] while Youthe in the *Parlement of the Thre Ages*, like the Dreamer during the first part of his stay, is wholly absorbed in physical delight. The sharp contrast between early and late *juventus* is, however, an important aspect of the meaning of the *Parlement of the Thre Ages*, whereas, in *Piers Plowman*, the contrast operates only within a very limited and confined area. Although Langland concedes that Fortune's territory is experienced as two separate age-spaces, he nevertheless brings all his poetic resources to bear on the task of persuading us that the earlier and the later stages of *juventus*, the age of *fauntelete* (C11:309), adolescent bravura,[25] and the age of shameless worldliness, are situated on the same side of a very evident boundary, the sharp dividing-line between youth and old age.

The allure of lust in earlier youth and of avarice in later youth is figured forth as erotic attraction in both stages; Fortune's fair maidens take it in turns to *confort* the Dreamer, and in turn supply him with what he desires. Their mistress, Fortune, herself reveals the *wondres* of worldly yearning and satisfaction to the Dreamer, in the mirror which contains the image of the world she rules (C11:168–70), and she crowns her maidens' offers of themselves with her own more discreet but no less amorous promise that she will be his *frende* (C11:184). Her *lykyng* is law throughout the age-territory she possesses, but from the moment the Dreamer encounters her it is evident to the reader that her favours will not last for ever, for, in Boethius' words, translated by Chaucer, 'yif Fortune bygan to duelle stable, she cessede thanne to ben Fortune'.[26] Two more dissimilar rulers of age-territories than Fortune and King Perfect Age can scarcely be imagined; perfect age embodying the certainty that worldly joy is not subject to the laws of change, Fortune embodying the certainty that the opposite is true. Langland refuses to admit the idea of the perfect age into the Dreamer's experience of the series of the ages in the 'inner dream'.

As though deposing King Perfect Age and setting up Fortune as ruler of *juventus* in his stead might not in itself be a sufficient indication of his attitude towards perfect age's claims, Langland transforms personified perfect age into the Pride of Life, Fortune's minion. He is the first of Fortune's attendants to intrude himself upon the Dreamer, and Langland gives him the effete accent of the professional courtier, a breed he wholeheartedly despises:

> Pruyde-of-parfit-lyvynge pursuede me faste
> And bade me for my continaunce counte clergie lihte. (C11:174–5)[27]
>
> *continaunce* physical appearance

Unlike *Concupiscencia carnis* and Coveytise-of-yes, he is the Dreamer's constant companion while Will remains in Fortune's realm, for whereas lust is associated with one phase of youth and covetousness with another, Langland wants the third vice of 1 John 2:16 to be associated with the whole of the Dreamer's youth. His translation of the Vulgate's *superbia vitae* as Pruyde-of-parfit-lyvynge strongly suggests that he interpreted *vita* (βίος) here as 'period of life' rather than 'means of life',[28] and that the name of Fortune's courtier is intended to yoke together the vice of pride and *juventus*, the very name thus making a mockery of the idea of the perfect age. That pride and youth are linked in Langland's mind in the relationship of inhabitant and habitation is again suggested in the discourse of *Anima* (C-text: *Liberum Arbitrium*) on the nature of charity. When Charité has visited the poor and the imprisoned he will become a laundry worker:

> And yerne into youþe and yepeliche seche
> Pride wiþ al þe appurtenaunces, and pakken hem togideres,
> And bouken hem at his brest . . . (B15:188–90)
>
> *yerne* run; *bouken* cleanse

As long as the Dreamer is a young man, Fortune is his friend and Pruyde-of-parfit-lyvynge is his companion. The differences between the first and the second stage of youth, according to the 'inner dream', are insignificant; heedlessness is man's characteristic state throughout. On the other hand, three total oppositions mark the Dreamer's sudden entry into the second age-territory of the dream:

> . . .y forȝet ȝouth and ȝorn into elde.[29]
> And thenne was fortune my foo for al her fayre biheste
> And poverte pursuede me and potte me to be lowe.   (C12:12–14)
>
> *forȝet* gave up, abandoned;   *ȝorn* ran

On one side of the dividing-line is youth, and on the other old age. On one side is Fortune, and on the other Elde, whose prophecy is at once proved true:

> "Man", quod he, "yf y mete with the, by Marie of hevene,
> Thou shalt fynde fortune þe fayle at thy most nede."   (C11:187–8)

On one side of the boundary is Pruyde-of-parfit-lyvynge, and on the other poverty, for, as Pacience later makes explicit in the first *sentence* of his definition of poverty, 'Poverte is the furst poynte þat pruyde moest hateth' (C16:120). Langland represents the movement from one age to another, or rather from one age to the other age, as a moment when the world the Dreamer knows is bewilderingly reversed and his former friends desert him.

When the Dreamer wakes up on the verge of lunacy after Ymaginatif's sudden disappearance, and turns his dream over in his mind, the first thing he thinks of is the moment of Fortune's defection:

> And many tyme of this meteles moche thouhte y hadde:
> Furste how Fortune me faylede at my most nede,
> And how Elde manaced me, so myhte happe
> That y lyvede longe, leve me byhynde
> And vansche alle my vertues and my fayre lotus   (C15:4–8)
>
> *meteles* dream;   *lotus* outward appearance

Langland has already put our minds in readiness for the Dreamer's recapitulation and reorientation of the events of his sleeping life, with the startling analogy (which puzzled most B-text scribes) 'as a freke þat fay were forth can y walken' (C15:2).[30] Though the Dreamer may appear to be offering nothing more significant than, in Pearsall's words, 'a summary of scattered episodes' from the Third Vision, to be musing as aimlessly as he is wandering in the guise of a beggar–friar, he now knows that as a bodily creature he is *fay*, doomed to die.[31] Langland's reconstruction of Will's dream points it inexorably in the direction of what is yet to come. Told again, the dream begins with Will's recollection of how Fortune deserted him and Elde threatened him, compelling him to recognise that his physical being is doomed; the dream continues with his realisation that 'lewede men' who are left in their ignorance are doomed 'thorw unkunynge curatours to incurable peynes' (C15:16), unless Christ intervene to help them, and it ends with his wondering reconsideration of what Ymaginatif said about the righteous man, 'that *justus* bifore *Jesu in die judicij non saluabitur* bote *vix* helpe' (C15:22). Even the man who lives the life which pertains to Dowel will not be saved, except by special grace.[32] What Ymaginatif did actually say, in the context of the more specific question of the ultimate fate of the righteous heathen, was defiantly optimistic: 'He will scarcely be saved; therefore he *will* be saved' (C14:203–4). Here, the Dreamer interprets the text (derived from 1 Peter 4:18) more pessimistically.

The re-interpreted and newly-ordered dream is in fact a meditation on The Four Last Things, with the joys of heaven an almost inconceivably remote possibility. The dominant emotional note of the passage is the friendlessness of man, a condition which is mitigated only by the helping virtue of Christ. All other creatures 'a londe and o watere' (C15:19) live secure in the constant presence of Kynde's love and guidance; only man experiences the progress of his life as a series of losses and vanishings. This idea is perhaps commonplace enough, but Langland animates it with an extraordinary intensity in this, one of the most highly concentrated episodes in the poem. The Dreamer's understanding of the series of the ages has absorbed the sense of dereliction he and the reader feel at the end of the previous passus; Elde's threat is left unspecified in the B-text, but the fear he has inspired in the Dreamer in the C-text is a fear of being left alone, suddenly deprived of his most intimate companions, his *vertues* and his *lotus*, his inner faculties and his outward attractiveness.

In his sleeping life, he crossed the dividing-line between youth and old age; there was no territory which did not belong to Elde or Fortune. Looking back, he remembers Fortune leaving him and he remembers Elde menacing him, but he no longer envisages himself as being in or travelling through either Elde's or Fortune's territory. As the waking Dreamer understands it, he has left the one and cannot be sure that he will ever enter the other; he no longer inhabits *any* age-space. For men who spend their lives awake, and who perceive their movement through life as a series of predictable steps, this is a logical impossibility, but Langland chooses to set the Dreamer free from the wheel of the ages of man's life in order that he may be able – neither as a young man, nor as an old man, nor yet as a man in the *myddel age* between the two – to begin to understand that there is an age which stands outside the imperfect sequence of the ages he has lived through in the 'lond of longyng and love'.

This is the age which is completed and fulfilled in the manhood of Christ, the age we have come to know as the perfect age. Manhood and perfection are indeed so closely linked in Langland's poetic consciousness that to explore manhood in *Piers Plowman* at all adequately we should have to consider the poem as a figuring forth of the perfect life, and to retrace the steps of M.W. Bloomfield, who has left us in no doubt of the significance of this aspect of the poem.[33] Our concern here, however, is not with the idea of perfection or the search for perfection as such, but rather with the nature of the connection Langland makes between the stage of life he calls manhood and the condition of being perfect, as he understands perfection. We have followed through the poetic processes by which Langland very carefully and deliberately excludes the perfect age from the sequence of the ages lived through by the Dreamer in the course of the Third Vision, so that he can be certain, after the recapitulation at the beginning of B13 and C15, that his readers will not be led astray; that they will not associate manhood with any stage of life the Dreamer has experienced, or is experiencing. Nevertheless, manhood as Langland understands it is in the first place a stage of life, the name of an age rather than an abstract notion, and until it is allowed to take its place in the series of the ages it remains an unrealised and unrealisable state. After the experiences the Dreamer lives through in the 'inner dream' of the Third Vision, the complete absence of the perfect age is felt as a gap which cannot be tolerated for long.

I2

Hy tyme in *Piers Plowman*

JUST BEFORE the perfect age is at last made present in *Piers Plowman*, Langland puts our minds in readiness for a new representation of the ages by reminding us of the imperfection of man's youth. The allegory of the growing fruit which is not left to ripen but is assailed at one stage by the world, at another by the flesh and at a third by the devil (B16:31–52; C18:31–52) is part of the larger, immensely complex allegory of the Tree of Charity.[1] The exposition of the imperfections of the different stages of *juventus* is followed in the C-text (18:53–102) by a discussion between the Dreamer and *Liberum Arbitrium* concerning the three grades of chastity, traditionally linked with the triad of perfection.[2] *Liberum Arbitrium*'s explanation of why the fruit grows in three differing degrees culminates in exalted praise of virginity (88–99), the most perfect state attainable by mankind:

> Maydones and martres ministrede hym here on erthe
> And in hevene is priveoste and next hym by resoun
> And for þe fayrest fruyte byfore hym, as of erthe,
> And swete withoute swellynge; sour worth hit nevere. (96–9)

Within the allegory as a whole, imperfection gives way to its opposite, and both imperfection and perfection are closely linked with the processes of growing and ripening.

At the end of the Tree of Charity allegory in the C-text, there are three totally unprepared-for shocks: the devil gathers the fruit Elde shakes down from the tree, the fair vision is succeeded by 'derkenesse and drede' (116) and the rhetorical register descends abruptly from high to low:

> [Elde] waggede wedewhed and hit wepte aftur;
> A meved matrimonye, hit made a foule noyse. (108–9)

These three shocks herald the first representation of the ages of Christ's life, which begins, enigmatically:

> And thenne spak *spiritus sanctus* in Gabrieles mouthe
> To a mayde þat hihte Marie, a meke thyng withalle,
> That oen Jesus, a justices sone, most jouken in here chaumbre

Til *plenitudo temporis*-tyme ycome were
That Elde felde efte þe fruyt, or full to be rype   (123–7)
    jouken perch;   *felde* caused to fall;   *full* (it) chanced

In case the riddling nature of these lines should conceal the fact that he is setting out upon an account of the progress of Christ's life on earth, Langland continues with a straightforward paraphrase of Luke 1:38 ('Lo me his hondmayden . . .', 131–2), with a clear statement of how long Christ was in Mary's womb (133), with the fact of his birth (134) and (in the C-text only) with the characteristics of his *barnhoed* (*pueritia*), during which he was 'byg and abydyng (sturdy and steadfast), and bold' (135). These boyhood characteristics of Christ bring to mind the heroic child William of Palerne and other heroic 'infants' in late fourteenth-century alliterative romance,[3] and this association makes it seem altogether natural that Langland should go on to provide details of Christ's training in leechcraft. Leechcraft was one of the branches of knightly education, and we assume that after *pueritia* will come *adolescentia*; in this case, apparently, the *adolescentia* of a knight aspirant.[4] Once Langland has firmly established that he is moving through the series of the ages of Christ's life, he can rely on his readers to continue to supply the structure which underpins the narrative. A man is predictably under instruction during the stage of life which follows *barnhoed*, and because this is what we expect Langland is able to persuade us to accept the notion of Christ being 'taught' by Piers (in the B-text) or by *Liberum Arbitrium* (in the C-text), a notion which would otherwise tend to be resistant even to such a persuasive interpretation as David Aers places upon it, arguing 'that the Creator in his Incarnation is obliged to learn creaturely limitation, and to learn from a creaturely perspective' (p. 109).[5]

Aers' analysis of Langland's representation of Christ as learner is subtle enough for him to be forgiven for being a little impatient with more 'obvious' aspects of this part of the narrative of Christ's life. He takes it for granted that it 'concerns Christ in his Manhood' (p. 108) because he interprets manhood not as a stage of life but as the human condition, conjoined (in the case of this unique human being) with godhead. Admittedly, later in this same passus (B:16:220–4; C18:223–38), Langland draws out the parallel between manhood and godhead as part of Abraham-Faith's teaching about the nature of the Trinity, but the initial definition of manhood in the B-text, 'in þre persones is parfitliche pure manhede' (16:220), is by no means a commonplace or predictable one. Perfect manhood is here perceived as a figuring forth of the process of procreation in the trinity of man, woman and child. Manhood is not a condition but an action – Abel, in the C-text, 'of Adam and of his wyf Eve / Sprang forth' (229–30) – and this human act of manhood shows us what godhead is like:

So oute of þe syre and of þe sone þe seynt spirit of hem bothe
Is and ay were and worþ withouten ende.   (231–2)

Langland is not content, however, to leave manhood as a visible signifier
and godhead as an invisible signified. This passage about manhood and
godhead is an introduction to Faith's extraordinary autobiographical
revelation, and in the C-text Langland provides a bridge between the
exegetical and the narrative sections in the form of a startling metaphor:

In matrimonie aren thre and of o man cam alle thre
And to godhede goth thre and o god is alle thre.
Lo! *treys encountre treys* . . . in godhede and in manhede.   (236–8)

The trinity of manhood and the trinity of godhead are transformed into dice
on the gaming-table as the hazard-player's cry 'a three opposes a three'
irrupts into the carefully-balanced, step-by-step exegesis. This giddying
change of perspective, which is characteristic of the C-text, enables the
Dreamer to ask what would otherwise seem an irrational question, 'Hastow
ysey this . . . alle thre and o god?' (239) (*ysey* seen), providing a cue for
Faith's deceptively matter-of-fact 'in a somur y hym seyh' (240).

The relationship between manhood and godhead and the uniting of the
two in the person of Christ is unquestionably one of Langland's central
concerns in the Faith passus as a whole, but he does not choose to examine
either godhead or manhood within the framework of accepted definitions.
Having seen the three-in-one godhead 'one summer', long ago, Faith tells the
Dreamer that he is now searching for him, 'for I herde seyn late / Of a buyrn
þat baptised hym' (B16:249–50; cf. C18:267–8: 'for seynt Johann þe
Baptiste/Saide þat a seyh here þat sholde save us alle'). Throughout Faith's
narrative the singular pronouns 'he' and 'hym' apparently refer to the same
person, without any differentiation, so that by what is seemingly the
simplest of poetic devices, Langland transforms the triune God into the
Christ who is alive on earth and has only 'lately' been baptised, a
transformation which is dependent on the absence of semantic change. The
process of transformation does, however, end at one particular moment in
time, just as it begins with one specific revelation of God to man, the
visitation to Abraham which resulted in the conception of Isaac and the
genesis of God's people (Genesis 18:1–15). Faith's narrative ends as Christ is
baptised and begins his public ministry; in other words, as Christ reaches his
perfect age. Another kind of transformational process is at work here: not
only does God the Trinity become man, in the sense of taking upon himself
the human condition, but also man progresses from the moment of his
engendering, as a child of God and for God, to the perfect age of manhood.
Through Faith's narrative, Langland provides us with a redeemed and
redemptive series of the ages of man's life, and bonds together in an entirely

new way the topos of the ages of man's life and the topos of the ages of the world.

The fusion of divine and human history in Faith's narrative, the coming together of godhead and manhood as the perfect age is revealed in the fullness of time, makes this one of the most astonishing episodes in *Piers Plowman* in its own right, but the sense of delight and satisfaction we derive from it partly arises from the fact that Langland is obliquely but convincingly answering a question which has been implicit throughout the passus, a question about the nature and the timing of *plenitudo temporis*. At the point in the series of the ages of Christ's life where we expect the learning age, *adolescentia*, to be succeeded by *juventus*, manhood, Langland (in the C-text) says that '*plenitudo temporis* hy tyme aprochede' (18:138). This is the last of the three different English renderings of *plenitudo temporis* Langland offers during the series of Christ's ages. First Langland calls it '*plenitudo temporis*-tyme' (126, and cf. B16:93), a deliberately tautological name which indicates that *tempus* should be interpreted 'period of time' rather than 'time in general'; then he calls it 'fol tyme' (136, and cf. B16:102), a name which can scarcely be taken as an attempt at a literal translation ('fulnesse of tyme' would be the obvious phrase; see *MED, fulnes*, 1 and 3), but seems rather to be a calque on the age-name *ful age* (manhood, legal majority). The third name Langland gives *plenitudo temporis* in the B-text is 'plener tyme' (103), a simple variant of 'ful-tyme' in the previous line – though Langland is certainly also playing on the coincidence that this French adjective meaning 'full' happens to have an ending which looks like the inflexional ending of an English comparative adjective.

The third naming of *plenitudo temporis* in the C-text, '*plenitudo temporis* hy tyme aprochede', (138) is less riddling, but considerably more resonant. Because 'high time' has by now diminished into a cliché and 'approach' is a very common verb, the solemnity and the strangeness of this line are not immediately apparent, but in fact Langland's 'hy tyme' is a unique combination of two distinct Middle English phrases, 'heigh time' meaning 'solemn period of time' (*MED, heigh*, 4b) and 'heigh time' meaning 'fully time' (*MED, heigh*, 6b). Like 'fol tyme', 'hy tyme' has the grammatical structure of an age-name and does not literally mean 'the fullness of time' (malgré *MED*'s gloss on this line, *heigh*, 6b), but the equivalent age-name *heigh age* (-*elde*) in the sense of manhood or prime of life is extremely rare, and perhaps is not recorded at all (depending on how the Green Knight's *hyghe elde* be interpreted). In isolation, Langland's 'hy tyme' would suggest gravity and solemnity and also 'high time' in the still current sense, but it would not suggest a specific stage of man's life. Nevertheless, the cumulative effect of the three interpretive glosses on *plenitudo temporis* ensures that the phrase will have come to be firmly associated with manhood in the reader's mind by the time Christ completes his *adolescentia*, attains manhood and begins his fight against the devil (C18:139 ff.; B16:107 ff.).

Characteristically, Langland proceeds here by way of subtle insinuation rather than overt argument. If his English renderings of the Biblical phrase implant the idea of an association between manhood and the fullness of time, these interpretive glosses also occur in contexts which are designed to provoke the question '*when* is *plenitudo temporis*?' rather than to provide an unequivocal answer. At first it seems from Gabriel's reported words that Christ's birth will be the fullness of time (C18:125–6; B16:92–3); then a fight against the devil at some unspecified time in the future is specified as the fullness of time (C18:136; B16:102). Only after Langland has outlined the healing miracles of Christ do we realise that Christ's work as a 'surgien' and 'fisciscyen' is to be understood as the first part of his campaign against Satan:

> some Jewes saide with sorserie he wrouhte
> And thorw the myhte of Mahond and throw misbileve:
> *Demonium habes.*
> 'Thenne is Saton ȝoure saveour', quod Jesus, '& hath ysaved ȝow ofte.
> Ac y saved ȝow sondry tymes   (C18:149–52)

In the C-text, the narrative of Christ's life ends abruptly, in highly conventional dream-poem fashion, with the uproar as the Jews lead Christ away to stand trial. The last battle of Christ in his human manhood is reserved for later in the poem, and Langland leaves us uncertain whether 'hy tyme' has already come or is still to come.[6]

'Hy tyme' is the manhood of Christ; 'hy tyme' is Christ's entire life on earth: in the series of the ages of Christ's life Langland is intent on persuading us that both these definitions of *plenitudo temporis* are valid. The paradox itself is not Langland's invention, but the means by which it is presented and the poetic ends towards which it is directed are markedly idiosyncratic.[7] The whole thrust of the Faith passus is in the direction of the revelation of the perfect age in the manhood of Christ, but Langland is at the same time very far from wanting to suggest that the perfect age of Christ was preceded by imperfection, or that *plenitudo* was preceded by anything incomplete during Christ's progress through the ages. Quite remarkably, he is so determined to avoid any possibility of an association between imperfection and the early life of Christ that neither in this passage about Christ's movement through the ages nor anywhere else in *Piers Plowman* does he refer to the *youthe* of Christ as *yong*. When Langland wishes to refer to the pre-adult Christ during Conscience's discussion of the different names given to Jesus (B19:26-198; C21:26–198, unrevised), he anglicises *juventus*, puzzling some of the poem's copyists:[8]

> In his Juventee þis Jesus at Jewene feeste
> Water into wyn turnede   (B19:108–9)

While Christ is 'in his juventee' Langland describes him not as being *yong* but as being 'a fauntekyn' (B19:118), puzzling many of his copyists again.[9] The very words *yong* and *youthe*, it seems, are so tainted with pride and all kinds of imperfection in *Piers Plowman* that they can only be applied to a man who is moving through an imperfect and unredeemed series of the ages.

Christ's experience of living through the ages, in the Faith passus, is in every way represented as being unlike the Dreamer's experience of living through the ages in the land of Fortune, even to the names Langland chooses to give to the ages. If that opposition were all *Piers Plowman* offered, Langland would seem to be suggesting that man might as well despair of ever arriving at the perfect age, but Faith's innovative series of the ages begins with the conception of man and ends with the perfect age, '*Ecce agnus dei*' (C18:268a). If that beholding of the perfect age of manhood is still, for Faith, in the future – 'Forthy I seke hym' (267) – the poem as a whole persuaded us that seeking and seeing can scarcely be dissociated from one another.

Were we now to try to determine how the search for the perfect age of manhood in the central part of *Piers Plowman* relates to, sheds light on and is in turn illumined by the larger quest which provides the poem with its fictional framework, and which (it is tempting to think) represents the formal correlative of Langland's impulse towards revision after revision, an extended journey of interpretive exploration would be necessary. Such an enterprise would involve us in investigating areas of the poem in which the idea of the perfect age is scarcely relevant, or not relevant at all. Nevertheless, since we have just been considering the object of Faith's quest it would be quixotic to ignore the fact that, as the poem closes, Conscience sets off to search for Piers the Plowman. The 'hym' Faith is seeking, at first God-the-Trinity and at last Christ in his perfect age, is ultimately transformed into the figure who shares *humana natura* with the Dreamer, at one extreme, and with Christ, at the other; who functions, formally, as a *mene* 'mediator' between the two. There are implications for our understanding of the Piers-figure in what has been said already about the ages of the Dreamer and the ages of Christ; he remains, in spite of these implications, a profoundly mysterious presence.

These three persons, Piers, Christ and the Dreamer, are the only characters in this densely-populated poem who are ever represented as progressing from one age of man's life to another. We have seen how Langland carefully avoids contaminating Christ with *youthe*, an age-name indelibly imprinted, for him, with imperfection; he likewise refuses to associate personified *humana natura* with the imperfect age the Dreamer lives through in Fortune's domain. Like Christ, Piers is never *yong*; unlike Christ, on the other hand, he experiences old age:

The perfect age in Ricardian poetry

For now y am olde and hoer and have of myn owene,
To penaunce and to pilgrimages y wol passe with oþere
(C8:92–3, cf. B6:83–4)

By assigning Piers in the half-acre to the age which Christ never experienced in his earthly nature, Langland assures us that Piers partakes fully of doomed-to-die humankind, just as the Dreamer does. But there is a very marked contrast between the way in which Piers experiences the crossing of the threshold of the last of the ages and the way in which the Dreamer experiences the same threshold in the 'inner dream' of the Third Vision and at the beginning of the Ymaginatif passus in the B-text. Piers is neither menaced nor disoriented by *elde*; calmly and rationally he puts his affairs in order, 'y wol ar y wende do wryte my biqueste' (before I go I shall get my will drawn up; C.8:94), and then he proceeds with his *kyndely* activities as a pilgrim seeking *Treuthe*, ploughing on behalf of himself and everyone else. Because the age-territory which Piers-*humana natura* occupies in the latter part of the Visio in no way hinders him from carrying out the fruitful actions Langland asks us to associate with manhood, it seems perfectly appropriate that in the Vita he should be characterised as a person who acts rather than as a person assigned to a specific stage of life – just as it seems perfectly appropriate that the Dreamer, who fails to perform fruitful actions, should be characterised by his changing place in the series of the ages.

Idiosyncratic as Langland's 'hy tyme' – perfect age is, it recognisably possesses those characteristics which earlier chapters of this study have led us to associate with the idea of the perfect age. On the one hand, Langland insists that we conceive of the perfect age of manhood as an age which has its proper and accustomed place within the series of the ages, as a stage of life rather than as the state of being human. On the other hand, the perfect age in *Piers Plowman* separates itself from the series of the ages and assumes an independent existence. The Dreamer, remembering his dream about his own progress through the series of the ages, experiences the place where perfect age ought to be as the state of being without an age. Perfect age as Piers experiences it is not a stage of life but a state of life, and through his manhood-actions both in the Visio and in the Vita Langland insinuates the idea that the natural and fitting permanent condition of *humana natura* is the perfect age of manhood.

13

Myhty youthe in *Confessio Amantis*

ONCE a man has passed through youth, *Piers Plowman* gives us to understand, he may all of a sudden encounter old age, or he may experience a complete absence of age-identity, or even, perhaps, he may arrive at the perfect age. Langland's perception that man's progress through the ages is in itself fit matter for a story, an *aventure* in its own right rather than a predetermined and predictable structure on which a super-structure of narrative needs to be imposed, is a perception made possible by the ambiguity inherent in the idea of the perfect age. Langland's narrative of the search for the perfect age of manhood is unquestionably *sui generis*, but his sense of the chanciness of man's journey through the ages is shared, as I shall try to show, by Gower, by the poet of *Sir Gawain and the Green Knight* and by Chaucer. None of these Ricardian poets felt constrained to represent the life of the individual as an exemplary instance of a presupposed pattern of human ageing; all of them felt able to make the individual's experience of living through the stages of his life a significant aspect of narrative content.

What I have just said runs directly counter to the proposition which this study of perfect age took as its starting-point, Burrow's proposition that Chaucer, the *Gawain*-poet, Gower and Langland share the sense that there is an 'inevitable order in the unfolding of individual experience'.[1] The conflict between Burrow's argument and my own arises out of our very different understanding of the nature and role of perfect age in Ricardian poetry. We agree about its importance, but Burrow closely associates the prime of active life (his rendering of the age-name *hyghe eldee*) with the ethical ideal that we should 'take it weel that we may nat eschue' (*Canterbury Tales* 1:3041; Burrow quotes Theseus' words as an exemplification of the ideal of 'measure', p. 129). The things that men in the prime of active life in Ricardian narratives perceive as being inescapable, Burrow's argument runs, include the predetermined order in which the ages of man's life succeed one another.

By contrast, my examination of *Piers Plowman* has led to the conclusion that perfect age, by virtue of its ambiguous relation to the series of the ages, brings into question the very concept of a doctrine or a decorum of the ages. To be sure, Ricardian poets solemnly draw our attention to the

inevitability attendant upon the progression of the ages at those times when
and in those contexts where a weighty commonplace of this kind may serve a
particular and localised poetic purpose: the warning given to the Dreamer at
the beginning of *Piers Plowman* B 12 is a good case in point. Such reminders,
however, typically function ironically, providing a counterpoint to the way
in which man's movement through the ages is represented in the narrative as
a whole, for the idea of the perfect age enables Ricardian poets to question
whether indeed it is possible for man to know in advance what the stages of
his life will be. The ageing process itself is one of Ricardian poetry's most
characteristic *matières*. For Gower, in *Confessio Amantis*, it is the most
exciting *aventure* of all.

When Prince Apollonius flees from Tyre to escape the wrath of the
incestuous Antiochus, in the eighth book of Gower's *Confessio Amantis*, the
people he has abandoned give themselves up to lamenting:

> Helas, the lusti flour of youthe,
> Our Prince, oure heved, our governour,
> Thurgh whom we stoden in honour,
> Withoute the comun assent
> Thus sodeinliche is fro ous went! (490–4)[2]

Having lost their leader, 'thei of Tyr' (473) go into mourning 'for unlust of
that aventure' (481); they react as though they have been bereaved, but the
grief they express is in the first place grief for *juventus* personified, 'the lusti
flour of youthe', the embodiment of communal well-being and the envy of
those outside the 'commune'.

This is not an especially outstanding moment in Gower's version of the
romance of Apollonius of Tyre, which occupies the larger part of Book 8
(271–2008), but the oddities of emphasis in this passage may serve to alert us
to ways of thinking about the nature of *juventus* and about the series of the
ages which are peculiar to *Confessio Amantis*, although also characteristically
Ricardian in that they involve a questioning of accepted age-doctrine. There
are two, interrelated oddities of emphasis in this little incident: the stress on
the youth of Apollonius at the beginning of a lament for a sudden loss
perceived as death, and the stress on the physical being of Prince and youth
('oure heved . . . thurgh whom we stoden'). The body of the young man is
corporately recollected in this act of mourning. The more famous and more
crucial lament for youth in the same book of *Confessio Amantis*, the Lover's
lament after he has seen his decrepit face in Venus' mirror (2824–57), is cast
in the form of an individual complaint. In Book 8 as a whole, however, and
above all in the closing sequence of the poem, Gower explores the
correspondence between the experience of the *I*-figure and the communal
experience of mankind with an authoritative confidence and a grave
commitment found nowhere else in Ricardian poetry.

In *Ricardian Poetry*, Burrow argues that the closing sequence of the poem is a delicately humorous rendering of the topos of the '*senex amans* who sins against the decorum of the ages of man' (p. 118). The Lover renounces love because there is no other option available to him as an old man; the tone of the latter part of Book 8, as Burrow interprets it, is 'rueful' and 'quite unfanatical' (p. 119). In his recent discussion of 'The Portrayal of Amans in *Confessio Amantis*', Burrow provides a more subtle and more sympathetic reading of the 'beautiful closing pages' of the poem, but he continues to perceive the revelation of the Lover's age as the crucial moment within the framing narrative. [3] He is following C.S. Lewis in this, although Lewis fixes the roots of the Lover's cure firmly in Gower's own life rather than in any rhetorical age-topos:

[Gower] finds in his own experience – the experience of an old man – how Life itself manages the necessary palinode; and then manages his in the same way. It is Old Age which draws the sting of love, and his poem describes the process of this disappointing mercy.[4]

The word 'process' is the significant one here, for while the Lover's realisation of the need 'to make a beau retret' ('orderly withdrawal', as Burrow nicely translates it, p. 18) from love is a significant turning-point in the framing narrative – even if, as Donald Schueler argues, it has been anticipated from the start of the poem[5] – the number of different stages by which this realisation is at last achieved is hard to account for in terms of mere amplification. If the healing process were as inevitable and necessitated as Burrow claims, such a marked *dilatacio* could scarcely be warranted. Lewis, in his magisterial celebration of the palinode, explains its breadth of scale in terms of allegory culminating in myth:

We have here one of those rare passages in which medieval allegory rises to myth, in which the symbols, though fashioned to represent mere single concepts, take on new life and represent rather the principles – not otherwise accessible – which unite whole classes of concepts.[6]

In the context of this essentially Neoplatonistic interpretation, Lewis uses the telling word 'ritual' to describe the process the Lover undergoes. A Neoplatonistic ritual of death and new life, or *senex amans* learning to conform to age-decorum – both these interpretations seem to me to involve a radical misunderstanding and underestimation of this part of *Confessio Amantis*, because they predicate a known pattern and then proceed to discover it in the text. I therefore make no apology for looking at this much-discussed passage again, hoping to re-define it as a Ricardian *aventure* of the ages, Gower's unique representation of the way in which man experiences the ages of his life.

Gower carefully indicates where the process of realisation and healing which the Lover undergoes begins and ends, and both at the beginning and at the end he describes the condition of the Lover's mind and the condition of the Lover's body; both are sick, both are cured. At the beginning, *Amans* responds to Venus' 'derisoria exhortacio',[7] which concludes

> Forthi mi conseil is that thou
> Remembre wel hou thou art old   (2438–9)

by exercising his mind to find an escape: 'I bethoght was al aboute' (2441). Finding none, he falls into a swoon which has the appearance of death and is caused by grief of heart (2446–9).[8] At the end of the realisation-and-healing process, the Lover grieves for his own condition, for the condition of man ('status hominis', p. 463) and for the condition of the year, abruptly recovers from his swoon and very deliberately calls back his mental faculties:

> I was out of mi swoune affraied,
> Whereof I sih my wittes straied,
> And gan to clepe hem hom ayein.   (2858–60)
>
> *affraied* aroused;   *sih* saw

The last stage of the process, the visit of Resoun, follows at once:

> He cam to me the rihte weie
> And hath remued the sotie
> Of thilke unwise fantasie,
> Whereof that I was wont to pleigne,
> So that of thilke fyri peine
> I was mad sobre and hol ynowh.   (2864–9)
>
> *sotie* mad folly

According to the Latin summary of the healing process, the nature of the Lover's sickness is not a matter of doubt. He is suffering bodily from *concupiscencia*, which is cured by Cupid and Venus, and in the 'inner man' from mad folly, which is caused by love and cured by *Senectus*, with the aid of *Racio*.[9] This would seem to be confirmed by the blatant similarity between the healing acts of Resoun and Cupid. Cupid removes the burning spear from the Lover's heart –

> Me thoghte a fyri lancegay,
> Which whilom thurgh myn herte he caste,
> He pulleth oute–   (2798–80)[10]

as Resoun removes the burning pain of 'sotie' from the Lover's wits. The Latin summary describes the stages of the healing process accurately enough, then, on the purely literal level, which is the level to which Gower (or Gower's editor) confines his marginal annotations. The summaries are not in themselves, it hardly needs saying, of any profound significance – the nature of *Concessio Amantis* is not altered when they are omitted – but they helpfully highlight Gower's strategy in this episode (2377–2869). Here, paradoxically, the purely literal level is the unbroken allegorical surface of the framing narrative, the fictional *superficies* which accepts without question that the *I*-figure is the exact equivalent of *Amans*. These third-person summaries apparently authorise the reader to translate the *I*-discourse of the English poem into third-person narrative; to turn this episode into yet another exemplary tale. The very presence of the *I*-figure in the body of the text, however, ensures that the 'summaries' will seem to the reader to be interpretive glosses, glosses which provide a fictive account of the actual experiences of the first-person narrator, as the text reveals them.

At the end of the episode, Gower takes great pains to bring to his reader's attention the gap between the radically allegorical surface of the framing narrative, which is its literal meaning, and the interpretation which the text's *I* places upon the events which happen to him. Resoun makes haste to visit the Lover and cure him after he has heard from some unspecified third party ('it herde sein', 2862) that the Lover has already been cured of 'loves rage'. Because Gower is so careful not to disturb the episode's allegorical surface at this point, the *I*-figure's assured control over his own wits as soon as he starts out of his swoon impresses itself upon us even more than it would otherwise have done; the third-person fiction manifests itself as an unnecessary encumbrance upon a discourse which has the authority of first-person experience to validate it. The *Amans* of the Latin glosses has been named 'John Gower' already, just before this episode, when Venus prefaces her reply to the Lover's supplication by asking 'halvinge a game' (half jokingly, 2319) what his name is, and, as Burrow has well demonstrated (pp. 21–4), it is in the course of this episode that the *I* who equals the voice of the poet achieves full individuation. Once the poet has 'called his wits home again' and has been absolved by Genius, his cast of mind makes any further tarrying in Venus' court unthinkable; the Queen sends him away from her fictional territory, instructing him to go and live in the world of 'vertu moral' (2925) where his books have been long awaiting him (2926–7). John Gower's discovery of himself as the *I* of his own poem exiles him from the realm of impersonal narration but also persuades him that he and his writings should not be separated from one another. The text's *I* is John Gower, and John Gower is the *I* his poems represent; the poet's entire selfhood lends authority to the experiences detailed in the episode of realisation and healing.

The third-person *Amans*, to return for a moment to the fictional surface, is cured of the physical and mental manifestations of love by a series of allegorical healers, *Senectus* being only one of four. The process is lengthy, but the outcome is never in doubt. As far as the first-person narrator is concerned, on the other hand, not only is the outcome in doubt until the very end of the episode but the nature of the process is in doubt, as well. At the beginning he grieves because he knows he cannot be cured of old age:

> Tho wiste I wel withoute doute
> That ther was no recoverir;

> And as a man the blase of fyr
> With water quencheth, so ferd I   (2442–5)
>
> *recoverir* remedy

Already, in effect, he has been cured of the fiery pain of lust and infatuation by the deathly chill of sorrow.[11] The cure he needs is a cure for his grief, not a cure for love, and his vision of the 'parlement' (2454) of lovers, defined as a 'revelacion' (2806), only serves to make it more difficult for him to think in terms of a true cure. The vision makes it poignantly apparent that the condition of *elde* does not necessarily differ from the condition of *youthe*, except in superficial externals. Both young men and old men are subject to the chanciness of Venus' favour, and the fact of being old does not of itself bring release, or even the desire for release:

> I thoghte thanne how love is swete
> Which hath so wise men reclamed –   (2720–1)
>
> *reclamed* lured

even 'Ovide the poete' (2719). It seems that the petition of the community of old lovers 'and ek some of the yonge route' (2741) may have the effect of persuading Venus to allow John Gower to remain her subject, in good philosophic and poetic company, for ever.[12]

One possibility offered to John Gower in this episode, then, is to ignore Venus' exhortation – 'Remembre wel hou thou art old' – and to be incorporated into the body of lovers. Man is not bound to conform himself to the series of the ages, Gower suggests, unless he makes a conscious decision to do so. Like Langland in the Third Vision of Piers Plowman, Gower conceives of youth as one, essentially undivided age; like Langland, he envisages there being a clear dividing-line between youth and old age; unlike Langland, whose Dreamer, in the 'inner dream', crosses the threshold between *juventus* and *senectus* scarcely aware of what he is doing – 'I abandoned youth and ran into age' (C12:12) – Gower represents the threshold between the two ages as a place where consciousness of self begins. In *Confessio Amantis* it is by no means easy for the poet-narrator to pass from the one age to the other; even the bodily conditions of youth and age may not be instantly recognisable as a matter of course but may require skilled diagnosis. It takes the wisest of all the physicians of Ephesus, Maister Cerymon, to discover whether Apollonius' wife, who has been washed up on the shore in a 'cofre', is young or old, alive or dead:

> he, which knew what is to done,
> This noble clerk, with alle haste
> Began the veines forto taste,
> And sih hire age was of youthe,
> And with the craftes which he couthe
> He soghte and fond a signe of lif.   (1184–9)
>
> *taste* examine

The tale of Apollonius of Tyre is full of such strange and wonderful happenings, and the miraculous element in Cerymon's diagnosis follows naturally upon the miraculous arrival of the sea-chest at Ephesus, but John Gower's diagnosis of his own bodily condition is also recounted as a procedure requiring skill – and something more than ordinary skill. Blind Cupid has to remove the burning spear from the poet's heart by feel, at the end of the true vision; the vision ended, the poet (still in a swoon) needs to look into a 'wonder' (magic) mirror (2821) in order to see his own decrepit face with the eye of his heart.

When he has seen and realised his own condition, John Gower performs the first action he has performed in the framing narrative which is dictated by his own, individual will rather than willed upon him from outside himself:

> Mi will was tho to se nomore
> Outwith, for ther was no plesance;
> And thanne into my remembrance
> I drowh myn olde daies passed,
> And as reson it hath compassed,
> I made a liknesse of miselve
> Unto the sondri monthes twelve,
> Whereof the yeer in his astat
> Is mad (2832–40)

> *compassed* contrived

Earlier in this episode, as we have seen, he has been offered the possibility of ignoring his own decrepitude and of becoming a member of the company of Elde. Here, he turns away from contemplation of his own *elde* and, with the utmost deliberation, recollects the course of his life by way of a familiar age-topos.

As Gower solemnly announces the topos, we are led to expect a kalendar of the ages of man's life, twelve separate stages dutifully detailed. We are not expecting a lament for the man and the year whose state 'stant upon debat' (is rooted in contention, 2840). For man and for year, as the poet understands it, there are only two states: delight and despoliation, plenty and nakedness, *myhty youthe* (= *juventus*) and age. [13] He entangles man and year inextricably together. Man recollects *myhty youthe*, but it is the year's youth he recollects,

> In which the yeer hath his deduit
> Of gras, of lef, of flour, of fruit
> Of corn and of the wyny grape. (2847–9)

> *deduit* pleasure

Afterwards, the two halves of the year confront each other, with winter as the aggressor:

> The wynter wol no somer knowe.
> The grene lef is overthrowe (2853–4)

The perfect age in Ricardian poetry

Because the first half of the year has been represented as *myhty youthe*, the confrontation between youth and age is implicit in the confrontation between summer and winter, and the sense of loss and grief is thereby the greater in the last three, beautifully-judged lines of the lament, in which deliberate plainness and deliberate poeticism meet and comment on each other:

> The clothed erthe is thanne bare,
> Despuiled is the somerfare,
> That erst was hete is thanne chele.   (2855–7)
>
> *Despuiled is the* . . . summer is stripped of its apparel[14]

The last line of the lament turns the episode of realisation and healing full circle, so that John Gower's recovery from his swoon is not in the least unexpected, although the literal surface of the narrative suggests once again that the *I*-figure is acted upon rather than acting, 'I was . . . affraied' (2858).

Amans' supplication to Venus might have been granted. The *I* who is the centre of this episode might have been permitted by the text, by the poet, by the literary conventions of the period to remain 'the Lover', and to forgo the experience of living through the ages altogether. Instead, with immense effort and great grief the *I* discovers his own, individual will by choosing to incorporate himself not in Venus' ageless retinue but in the world of the ages, in which microcosm and macrocosm are not essentially different. The restless and chancy *aventure* of crossing the threshold between the ages is, for Gower, the opportunity which creates selfhood, and selfhood is inseparable from incorporation. In other words, Gower stands the concept of age-decorum on its head. At the same time, he re-defines the series of the ages. *Senectus* as grief and loss and nakedness is experienced only during the time of transition from one age to the next, in a swoon. The age which comes after *myhty youthe* is an age of rest and ease and peace, an age which anticipates a calm, unadventurous transition to the eighth age of the world, the age which is, as Ambrose says, 'una et perpetua' – not a stage but a lasting state.[15]

The eighth book of *Confessio Amantis* begins with an account of the laws governing human love in the successive ages of the world, and the poet's prayer at the end of the book again reminds us of the ages of the world, the ages of man's life and the ages of the soul:

> He which withinne daies sevene
> This large world forth with the hevene
> Of his eternal providence
> Hath mad, and thilke intelligence
> In mannes soule resonable
> Enspired to himself semblable
> Wherof the man of his feture
> Above alle erthly creature
> After the soule is immortal . . .   (2971–9; second recension)

132

Burrow is surely right when he suggests, in *Ricardian Poetry*, that this book may be 'meant to point beyond the "temporal state" represented in the other seven' (p. 60), but 'point beyond' is too tentative an expression for the boldness of Gower's design. The episode we have been discussing and its aftermath represent the poet living through the experience of incorporation into *juventus*, the age of restlessness, 'debat' and 'querele', the age to which worldly tales belong, and afterwards living through the experience of incorporation into an age free from chance and change, the perfect age which lives for ever blessed in the present tense. The two ages are not any longer, as in the fictional world, *juventus* and *senectus*; they are *myhty youthe* and perfect age. Passing from one to the other means not bodily death but grief for bodily loss; it means the will to be incorporated into the created world. The lament of the people of Tyre for the loss of 'the lusti flour of youthe' (490–1) fictively foreshadows the actual sorrow which enables fiction to be laid aside, and the *aventure* of Apollonius of Tyre is a type of the true story which is the framing narrative of *Confessio Amantis*.

14

Hyghe eldee in *Sir Gawain and the Green Knight*

AT THE END of *Confessio Amantis*, Gower – who is at this stage totally identified with the *I* of his poem – represents his own perfect age as an age which is mercifully free from *aventure*. Characteristically Ricardian in its rejection of age-doctrine and age-decorum, Gower's account of the experience of living through the ages is also gravely and unashamedly personal. *Sir Gawain and the Green Knight* can also be interpreted as a Ricardian *aventure* of the ages, but its poet is as intent on telling his story impersonally as Gower is on laying himself open to us. We have no way of knowing what the perfect age may have meant to the poet of *Sir Gawain* as an individual, but it is difficult to imagine him ever representing it to himself as an age bringing release from the world of 'wonderez'. Even life in and beyond the grave is full of strange happenings in the poems of the *Gawain*-poet: neither the just judge in *St Erkenwald* nor the maiden in *Pearl* experiences life after death as a predictable age of everlating rest.[1] Whereas Gower authenticates *Confessio Amantis* by testifying to its truth as a record of personal experience, the poet of *Sir Gawain* authenticates his poem by referring the reader to the testimony of 'þe best boke off romaunce' (2521) and 'þe Brutus bokez' (2523).[2] And yet, in spite of the fact that the poetic strategies of the two poets are so dissimilar, and in spite of the fact that their poems suggest that they had markedly different convictions about the integrity of the poetic text, both Gower and the *Gawain*-poet represent man's experience of the ages of his life as a peculiarly personal and unpredictable adventure, and they both make imaginative use of the paradox that the perfect age is a stage of life and, at the same time, an unchanging condition.

At this point, however, it is not enough just to reassert the ways of looking at the ages which the Ricardian poets have in common. An important distinction now needs to be made between Langland and Gower on the one hand and the *Gawain*-poet and Chaucer on the other – a distinction which, it is worth noting, cuts across the conventional distinction between alliterative and non-alliterative poets, native and non-native poetic traditions. In *Piers Plowman* and in *Confessio Amantis*, then, youth (that is to say *juventus*, which Langland calls *youthe* and Gower calls *youthe*, *lusti youthe* or *myhty youthe*) is perceived as being the age-territory man lives in until he arrives at the threshold of *elde*. For Langland, the whole of youth is associated with subjection to Fortune and with the vice of pride; for Gower, the whole of youth is associated with subjection to Venus and with the demands of worldly love. Neither Langland nor Gower allows us to associate any part of the youth of the first-person narrator with perfection or maturity, for in both *Piers Plowman* and *Confessio Amantis* the time of transition from the first age to the second age, from *youthe* to decrepitude, is the time which may, *par aventure*, open out into the perfect age. In both these poems, the representation of perfect age as a stage of life experienced by an individual – Christ's *manhod*, Gower's eighth age – leads to a questioning of the authoritative status of the text. Neither poet can imagine perfect age accommodated within a poem whole-heartedly acknowledged to be a 'makynge'.

The crossing of the threshold between *youthe* and *elde* is as significant an aspect of man's experience of the ages in *Sir Gawain and the Green Knight* and in Chaucer's poems as it is in *Piers Plowman* and *Confessio Amantis*, but Chaucer and the *Gawain*-poet do not see this as the only adventurous transition, or as the only possible means of entry into an age which is different in kind from the other ages. They are at least as interested in the potential for *aventure* associated with man's crossing of the threshold between the earlier and the later part of youth, and they are prepared (which is perhaps to put the same thing another way) to admit into their poems the possibility that the perfect age of completed maturity may be experienced even by a wholly imaginary character whose being is wholly contained within a fictional world.

The earlier and the later part of youth is a clumsy enough way of rendering *adolescencia* and *juventus*, but the age-name youth, as we have found again and again in the course of this study, always needs to be defined further if it is to be used with any kind of precision. In the Middle English period, the commonest way of perceiving man's life, as a movement through two, essentially opposed states – a habit of thought strongly influenced by Augustine – continually thrust the emphasis forwards on to the consummation of growth and on to the extremity of decay. As a result, the age-name *youthe* increasingly tended to suggest full maturity, and the age-name *elde* increasingly tended to suggest impotent senility. Middle English age-terminology is an extraordinarily slippery area, and the *MED* is not a reliable guide, but my investigation into age-terminology in the second half of the fourteenth century leads me to believe that during this period new age-names were being created in response to the lexical drift of *youthe* towards *juventus* and *elde* towards *senium*, age-names which could express precisely-conceived distinctions within the two stages of man's life.

In particular, there is evidence in late Middle English of an impulse to find an age-name to denote the first part of youth, that part of man's life between the end of childhood and the beginning of completed maturity. The Latin age-name *adolescentia* was not accepted into English as *adolescence* or *adolesceni* until the fifteenth century, and even then it was commonly paired with an age-name containing *yong* or *youthe*, as if still perceived as a foreign word: the literal translation *wexing age* is extremely rare.[3] Translating Bartholomeus Anglicus' division of the ages, in the 1390s, Trevisa first gives 'þe age of a yonge stripelinge' as the equivalent of *adholoscencia* and then, a few lines later, turns this phrase into a proper age-name, 'striplynges age'.[4] This age-name became very common in the sixteenth and seventeenth centuries, often including 'springal' as a synonym for stripling, but I do not know of any other medieval examples.[5] Trevisa chooses a different translation for *adolescentia*, 'þe firste 30wthe', in his translation of Ranulph Higden's *Polychronicon*.[6] This age-name may well have its origins in Bartholomeus Anglicus' chapter 'De etate', where man is said to have two childhoods (*infancia* and *puericia*) and two old ages (*senecta* and *senectus* or *senium*).[7] Bartholomeus does not explicitly say that man has two youths as well, for he is concerned to establish that *juventus* is the middle age of man's life rather than the second youth, but the way in which he talks about adolescence makes it clear that he thinks of it as the first phase of youth, 'able to fonge my3t and strengþe' (Trevisa's translation, p. 292).

(The) *first youthe* is not a common age-name, but a somewhat more common age-name, *first age* (− *elde*) came to be associated with it; partly, perhaps, because of its authoritative origins in *De Proprietatibus Rerum*. (The) *first age* existed as an age-name, *seo æreste ildu*, in the Old English period, and in all periods of English it may mean nothing more than the first of a numbered series of ages, or of an implied series of ages (in which case it typically spans infancy, childhood and adolescence), but in the late fourteenth century it comes to have a more precise meaning, as well. Like *first youthe*, it signifies the early part of youth, after childhood and before full maturity.[8] This, to return to *Sir Gawain*, is the stage of life the *Gawain*-poet is putting his audience in mind of when he says at the beginning of his poem, with reference to the entire Arthurian court, 'al watz þis fayre folk in her first age' (54). Neither Norman Davis' gloss, 'in the flower of their youth', nor the *MED*'s definition for this context, 'early adulthood', is sufficiently precise, for the former is blurred by a suggestion of 'the best age' and the latter inclines too much towards the second part of youth, and away from early adolescence.[9] *First age* is not, as our 'prime' is, a fuzzily nostalgic age-name for the best part of man's life: to the *Gawain*-poet's original audience it must have seemed unexpectedly specific. They would not have been surprised if the whole of Arthur's court had been assigned to *youthe* rather than *elde*, for they were no doubt well acquainted with the conventions of romance, but to discover 'lordez and ladies' one and all confined within much narrower age-boundaries would have been – and still is – distinctly startling.

The effect of this crucial line, then, is to set us thinking about the boundaries of *first age*. The poet immediately gives us further encouragement to do so by drawing attention to the King's resolute determination ('hyȝest mon of wylle', 57) and the company's valour ('so hardy a here', 59) – calling to mind the strength of the second part of youth – and then by drawing attention to the newness of the New Year, 'so ȝep þat' by a blatant tautology 'hit watz nwe cummen' (60) – calling to mind the sharp exuberance of the second part of childhood. The much-discussed phrase 'sumquat childgered' (86) ought not, therefore, to 'jolt us out of the eulogistic tone of the first five stanzas', as Patricia Moody claims it does.[10] Arthur's court is an ideal court, but it is experiencing an actual stage of life. The surprise in the phrase 'sumquat childgered' derives not from the adjective itself, which I take to mean 'boyishly changeable', but from the modifier, highly characteristic of this poet as a device for gaining attention, and from the fact that the poet is compelling us to realise that Arthur the King is in his *first age*, too; not separated, except by rank, from those around him.[11] At the end of the same stanza, a stanza which is all concerned with restless action, *aventure* and hazard, the poet again reminds us of the boundaries of *first age*, at one end verging on boyhood and, at the other end, verging on *juventus*:

> þerfore of face so fere
> He stiȝtlez stif in stalle,
> Full ȝep in þat Nw ȝere
> Much mirthe he mas withalle. (103–6)[12]
>
> *fere* bold;   *stiȝtlez* stands firm;   *mas* makes

The whole of the first section of *Sir Gawain*, before the Green Knight 'hales in', represents the *first age* of the court, and of Arthur and Gawain (who has not yet been identified as the hero), as an age in which other ages meet and mingle, in which the apparent hero can be like a sturdy man in one line and like a fresh boy in the next, in which there is no conflict or opposition betweeen one end of *first age* and the other. The first suggestion in the poem that there is a barrier between *first age* and the second part of youth comes with the Green Knight's refusal of Arthur's martial challenge:

> Hit arn aboute on þis bench bot berdlez chylder.
> If I were hasped in armes on a heȝe stede,
> Here is no mon me to mach, for myȝtez so wayke. (280–2)
>
> *wayke* feeble

This almost-more-than-naturally large knight, picturing himself on the back of a huge war-horse, banishes the court to the earliest end of youth, offering them a 'gomen' instead of a manly combat.

This game, which is the whole of the rest of *Sir Gawain*, is a game about life and death, certainly, but it is also a game about the ages of man's life. The passage at the beginning of the second fitt representing the course of the year makes this amply obvious, the New Year now being not 'ȝep' *like* a young man but actually 'ȝonge' itself (492). As Burrow points out, however, passages comparing the seasons with the ages habitually begin at the beginning of the zodiacal year, the season of the creation of the world, and end with decrepitude in the depths of winter. Here, the mid-winter season is both 'ȝonge' and like extreme old age (527–30).[13] So strong is the implication that the ages of man's life are being figured forth as the seasons of the year that it seems strangely, even disturbingly incongruous that Gawain does not undergo any change in age as the year passes. He is still in his *first age* in Bertilak's castle on Christmas Eve, but now his age is represented as a season of the year rather than the other way round. Nearly everyone who looks upon him (again, the characteristic modifier) imagines that it is not mid-winter but spring:

> þe ver by his visage verayly hit semed
> Welneȝ to uche haþel, alle on hwes
> Lowande, and lufly alle his lymmez under   (866–8)
>
> *lowlande* glowing

Gawain's spring-age is like a blazing fire, lovely to look at and to be near in the heart of winter, but this is at 'þe fyniment' of a stanza, and it is necessary to look back to 'þe forme' of the same stanza where, surely in deliberate apposition, the poet associates the Green Knight with an age-name for the first and only time. The 'bolde burne' who has the castle in his charge is – or, rather, so he seems to Gawain, looking at him – 'of hyghe eldee' (844). *Hyghe eldee* is not recorded elsewhere, and the customary glosses, 'the prime of life' and 'mature age', are unhelpful in that they substitute what are to us familiar but vague age-names for an age-name which the *Gawain*-poet's audience must have found unfamiliar, and not so much vague as ambiguous.[14] The adjective 'hyghe' apparently means 'full, completed, perfected', as it does in the quasi-age-name *hy tyme* in the C-text of *Piers Plowman* (18:138), and it may therefore be interpreted as a synonym for *ful age*, 'legal majority, adulthood' or, with no specifically legal reference, simply 'manhood'.[15] This would have been one, natural way for the *Gawain*-poet's audience to understand *hyghe eldee*, and it seems to be confirmed by the adjectives 'sturne' and 'stif' (846). On the other hand, as Eiichi Suzuki points out, the only Middle English age-description at all analogous in wording to *hyghe eldee* is the phrase 'hyȝe out of age' in *Cleanness* (656). This phrase seems to be a translation of the Vulgate's *provectaeque aetatis* (Genesis 18:11), and it certainly means 'advanced in age'.[16] At the very end of the second fitt, an emphatic position, the Green Knight is described as 'þe olde lorde of þat leude' (1124). 'Olde' may be interpreted in various ways, most relevantly as 'mature, adult' (*MED*, *old*, 1C, a, thus defines it for some contexts, though not this one), but I agree with Suzuki (pp. 28–9) that it is more reasonable to give 'olde' here its obvious meaning – as the primary meaning, at least.

In assigning the Green Knight to *hyghe eldee*, the poet of *Sir Gawain* is only apparently, not really, enabling us to place him in the series of the ages. He is exploiting the ambiguity which is potentially present in all age-names including the idea of fullness or completion, an ambiguity which is only avoidable when such an age-name becomes so well-established that one or other of the meanings of 'full, complete', either 'adult' or 'aged', is cancelled out. *Ful age*, then, is not ambiguous in late Middle English; it no longer suggests 'full of age, old'. The Latin age-name *aevi plenus*, 'full of age', is not ambiguous, either, but when Chaucer translates this age-name, which Boethius applies to Philosophia, he has to incorporate an explanatory gloss. Boethius' 'aevi plena foret ut nullo modo nostrae crederetur aetatis' becomes 'sche was ful of *so greet* age that men ne wolden not trowen in no manere that sche were of our elde'.[17] The Green Knight's *hyghe eldee*, then, carries with it the twin ideas of full manhood and old age – but if old age, not withered decrepitude; rather, an old age of 'undiminished vigour', like Philosophia's.

By associating the Green Knight with an age-name, the *Gawain*-poet encourages us to think about the stage of life Gawain's host has reached, but we cannot even be sure whether he is in his *juventus* or his *senectus*, only that there seems to be every reason to associate him with the season of Christmas and New Year, and no reason to associate him with any other season, with change, or with decay. Then a few lines later, as we have seen, Gawain is identified as a figure of spring, a gorgeously and resplendently inapposite intruder, both re-establishing age-decorum and making age-decorum itself seem a 'wonder'. When Gawain encounters the two ladies of the castle three stanzas further on, one 'ȝep' and one 'ȝolȝe' (withered, 951), one 'displayed' (955) and one 'enfoubled' (muffled up, 959), decorum dictates that age will call to age and that Gawain and the young girl will find each other's company consoling (1011). Yet the kind of age-decorum which binds 'ȝep' and 'ȝep' together and thrusts *juventus* and *senectus*, in this case the first youth and the second old age, apart, does not seem altogether decorous, or altogether natural, in Bertilak's castle. The 'magic' girdle which encircles the young girl's body and then Gawain's seems calculated to incorporate the Knight into the 'chance' of the series of the ages, ending in decreptitude and death, rather than to preserve life at the end of the year.

The Green Knight preserves *Gawain* from death, but the theme of the *aventure* of the ages in *Sir Gawain* is not, I think, the Renaissance theme suggested by Philippa Tristram, 'the triumph of Youth and Life'.[18] When

the game of the girdle is over, when Gawain has received his superficial
wound and the Green Knight has delivered his judgment, Gawain is no
longer – or seems no longer to be – in his first, spring-embodying age. The
experiences he has lived through in the course of a cycle of the seasons have
led him, or so the poet insinuates, from the early part of youth to *elde*. This is
not the place to enter into the debate about the nature, extent and
significance of Gawain's 'fault', but when we look at the poem as a Ricardian
aventure of the ages (and obviously this is only one of many possible ways of
looking at it) it becomes clear that incorporation into the cycle of the seasons
means incorporation into the characteristics of each successive age. The
vices of which Gawain accuses himself most bitterly, cowardice and (as a
result) covetousness (2374 and 2379–80), are characteristics especially
associated with an excess of the melancholy humour, and therefore with old
age.[19] The 'clene cortays carp closed fro fylþe' (1013) with which friends
comfort each other in the spring of life leads inexorably to repudiation and
vituperation in the winter of life:

> Bot hit is no ferly þaʒ a fole madde,
> And þurʒ wyles of wymmen be wonen to sorʒe   (2414–15)
> *ferly* marvel

The heroes deceived by the tricks of women belong, in *Confessio Amantis*
8:2689–2719, in the company of Elde.

   The ageing of the hero in *Sir Gawain*, then, is guilefully conveyed through
a series of ideas associated with old age, as it is in the fifth book of *Troilus and
Criseyde*. After Criseyde has left Troy, Troilus exhibits symptoms of
melancholy illness, jealousy (1212–14), desire for solitude (1217) and anger
(1223). Reduced to decrepitude, he expects to die:

> He so defet was, that no manere man
> Unneth hym myghte knowen ther he wente;
> So was he lene, and therto pale and wan,
> And feble, that he walketh by potente   (1219–22)
> *defet* disfigured;   *potente* crutch

Although Troilus' death is in fact a premature death, the death of a warrior in
battle cut down in his full strength, we feel it to be an expected death, closing
a life which has completed its humoral course. *Sir Gawain*, however, is a
comedy, and Gawain returns to the place from which he set out, having
undergone his individual *aventure* of the ages. When the courtiers honour
him by choosing to wear a girdle like his, they too incorporate themselves
into the series of the ages. For them, as for Gawain, *juventus* and *senectus* will
never co-exist in the unchanging, perfect age of *hyghe eldee*. But the court at
the end of the poem is still in its *first age*; the journey to *elde* is yet to be
undertaken; a new 'wonder' is surely about to begin.

15

The *ryght yong* man and Lady Perfect Age in the *Book of the Duchess*

G AWAIN'S RETURN to Arthur's court ensures that the hazardous cycle of the ages will begin all over again, and that there will be a new *aventure* which will be as strange as his own 'chaunce' at the Green Chapel. Burrow's sense of the ending of *Sir Gawain*, however, is very different; he sees in it a characteristically Ricardian narrative closure:

> [Ricardian poems] turn back towards their starting place and reach there a muted and often doubtful conclusion . . . Octavian, in the *Book of the Duchess*, returns to his castle; Gawain returns to Camelot; Gower's Amans returns home; and the Canterbury pilgrims would have returned to Southwark. Whatever achievement there may be seems a matter . . . of coming to terms with everyday realities and better understanding one's own nature and that of the world around one.[1]

Burrow proceeds to argue that 'this unheroic sense of the cyclic and repetitive character of human experience is associated with the cycle of the seasons of the year' (p. 101) and with the ages of man's life (pp. 117–20).

We have now looked at three cyclically-structured Ricardian narratives, *Piers Plowman*, *Confessio Amantis* and *Sir Gawain*, and our argument has in each case tended towards the conclusion that the circularity of structure serves to counterpoint the essentially *un*repetitive and unpredictable nature of the individual man's experience of the ages and of the seasons. The journey through the ages is itself, in these Ricardian narratives, a heroic *aventure*, and the correspondence between the course of life and the course of the year can by no means be taken for granted. If Amans returns home 'a softe pas' at the end of *Confessio Amantis*, Gower experiences a wholly new kind of age; if Gawain returns to Camelot, the court responds with a wholly unexpected action, which signifies that what seems to be the end is in fact a new beginning. As for the return of the Canterbury pilgrims, if Chaucer sketches the outline of the feast which will close the pilgrimage at Southwark, at the end of the General Prologue, this true-to-life ending is never as literally believable as the allegorical ending of the pilgrimage anticipated in the Parson's Prologue (10:48–51), and again in the closing paragraph of his Tale:

Thanne shal men understonde what is the fruyt of penaunce; and, after the word of Jhesu
Crist, it is the endeless blisse of hevene, ther joye hath no contrarioustee of wo ne
grevaunce   (10: 1075–6)

By disposing of the putative return from pilgrimage before the journey has
even begun, Chaucer frees himself to introduce the unexpected, the
indecorous and the uniquely individual wherever he wishes in the *Canterbury
Tales* – but to substantiate that claim another book would need to be written.

The last Ricardian *aventure* of the ages we shall look at here takes us back to
the first phase of Chaucer's poetic career. The *Book of the Duchess* is almost
certainly the earliest of the four Ricardian narratives chosen for this study,
but I leave it until the end because it is in many ways the most difficult to
penetrate; only recently has criticism begun to come to terms with the
sophistication of its manner and its subject.[2] As Burrow says, the end of the
dream-vision in the Book of the Duchess is represented as being a return:

> me thoghte that this kyng
> Gan homwardes for to ryde
> Unto a place, was ther besyde,
> Which was from us but a lyte.
> A long castel with walles white,
> Be seynt Johan! on a ryche hil
> As me mette   (1314–20)

'This kyng' is returning from the hunt, but the 'man in blak', whose
relationship with 'this kyng' (and with 'th' emperour Octovyen', 368) is
quite unclear, has not until this point seemed to be the kind of creature who
needs an ordinary, human home. His proper place has seemed to be the heart
of the wood, where the poet finds him using the trunk of a huge oak-tree as a
chair-back. Yet when the nearby castle, with its apocalyptic and its
specifically personal, Lancaster and Richmond associations, suddenly comes
into our field of vision, we realise at once that this white home is where the
man dressed in black belongs, and that the wood could not, after all, have
been his natural dwelling-place. The homeward ride at the end of the dream
seems simultaneously a return and a journey to a new and more appropriate
habitation. It is hard to see how this particular return, which follows the
summary, almost impatient dismissal of White's death and of the hart hunt
(1309–13), could be taken to suggest the 'repetitious character of human
experience' or the inevitability of the progression of the seasons and the
ages. While 'heroic' would scarcely be the right word for the image of man
this dream presents, Burrow's 'unheroic' and 'everyday' are far from
appropriate; the poet's own adjective for his dream, 'queynt' (strange,
curious, 1330) indicates a more profitable direction for our discussion.

When the poet reaches the heart of his dream and comes across the man in
black, he is confronted by a figure who presents himself as the embodiment

of two opposed ages and two opposed seasons; he is a living contradiction of the concept of decorum. Clothed all in black, the colour of *cholera nigra*, he is 'ful pitous pale' (470) and his formal 'compleynte' has a 'dedly sorwful soun' (462). Suffering from an excess of melancholy, he is like a man in his old age; cold and on the verge of death, he is under the malign influence of Saturn; his stage of life corresponds to the depths of winter. As such, he is an incongruous figure in a May-time wood where the poet, recalling his dreams, thinks he might have expected to meet the deities of the season:

> For both Flora and Zephirus,
> They two that make floures growe,
> Had mad her dwellynge ther, I trowe   (402–4)

The cold and suffering of winter are not only past but 'forgeten' (413) as though they had never been – the last thing we anticipate is that they will almost at once be made visible again, or that the man who makes his dwelling in the forest will be a May-aged man in whom winter-age is nevertheless still 'sene'. That he is in actual fact at the same stage of life as the year, the poet firmly establishes through a succession of precise details; unexpectedly precise because they follow immediately after some phrases suggesting enthusiastic but very general approval:

> Than found I sitte even upryght
> A wonder wel-farynge knyght –
> By the maner me thoghte so –
> Of good mochel, and ryght yong therto,
> Of the age of foure and twenty yer,
> Upon hys berd but lytel her   (451–6)

Then – in case our first sense of incongruity should have become blunted – a reminder: 'And he was clothed al in blak' (457).

Commentary on this passage was sent off in an unhelpful direction by Walter Skeat, who took it for granted that the man in black is a portrait of John of Gaunt and that either Chaucer himself made a mistake about John of Gaunt's age at the time of Blanche's death or a scribe copied the number xxviiij incorrectly. Helen Phillips, the most recent editor of the *Book of the Duchess*, repeats Skeat's note with a few refinements of detail.[3] The three, surprisingly exact details about the man in black's age ought, however, to be taken together as providing an unmistakable indication that he is in the first part of youth and not in the age of completed maturity, with the actual number of years being perhaps the least telling and the 'ryght yong' the most telling detail. Twenty-four is not an age with any particular associations, but it is in the middle of the fourth hebdomad, and therefore of the later part of *adolescentia*, according to Isidore.[4] In his early youth, then, the man in black chooses to incorporate himself into wintry old age, a season which in the wood, his chosen setting, is already over and forgotten.

The perfect age in Ricardian poetry

If it is surprising that the poet should offer us such a carefully-defined description of the man in black's age, it is even more remarkable how often and how precisely the man in black talks about his own youth. He says nothing at all about the age he has reached in the present tense of the poem, relating himself only to his excruciating sorrow and longed-for death—

> For whoso seeth me first on morwe
> May seyn he hath met with sorwe,
> For y am sorwe, and sorwe ys y—   (595–7)

as though by an act of rhetorical will he could turn himself from the representation of melancholy into the 'kyndely' reality, with all its correspondences. In his own, past-tense narrative, on the other hand, when the poet is sitting beside him and adopting his narrative perspective (for as far as he is concerned there is no action and therefore there can be no narrative in the present tense), he fixes everything he says about himself by relating it to his stage of life.

The beginning of his narrative is so extraordinary that it is worth quoting it in full:[5]

> 'Syr,' quod he, 'sith first I kouthe
> Have any maner wyt fro youthe,
> Or kyndely understondyng
> To comprehende, in any thyng,
> What love was, in myn owne wyt,
> Dredeles, I have ever yit
> Be tributarye and yiven rente
> To Love, hooly with good entente,
> And throgh plesaunce become his thral
> With good wille, body, hert, and al.
> Al this I putte in his servage,
> As to my lord, and dide homage;
> And ful devoutly I prayed hym to,
> He shulde besette myn herte so
> That hyt plesance to him were,
> And worship to my lady dere.
> And this was longe, and many a yer,
> Or that myn herte was set owher,
> That I dide thus, and nyste why;
> I trowe hit cam me kyndely.'   (759–78)

comprehende apprehend with the intellect;   tributarye feudal vassal

The impression we receive as we read from the begining of this narrative as far as 'my lady dere' is that the man in black is talking about successive stages of his life, starting with his earliest youth and at last arriving at *adolescentia*, the age conventionally associated with love-service. His 'sith *first* I kouthe . . . *fro* youthe' leads us to expect the syntactical progression 'and then . . . and then', and this expectation is reinforced by the fact that the kinds of experience he is describing are kinds of experience closely linked with the notion of development and progression. We are accustomed to being told about the growing awareness of the power of love, which culminates 'kyndely' in the choice of the desired object of love; we are accustomed to being told, in a different, Aristotelean context, about the gradual evolution of the mental faculties, which culminates in the *vis intellectiva* during the third and fourth hebdomads of a man's life.[6] The scholastic language in this passage is so intertwined with the language of love that it seems altogether natural that the goal of intellectual apprehension should also be the goal of erotic endeavour, though this is in fact a most unusual proposition. As soon as we read on from 'And this was longe . . .', however, we find that we have been mistaken. There has been no succession of stages of life, for 'this' (775), everything so far recounted, happened all at one time, long ago in the past; there has been no choice of the desired object of love, for at that time his heart was still not 'set'; there has been no understanding through intellection, for then he had an instinctive, unlearned faculty for comprehending love:

> therto most able,
> As a whit wal or a table,
> For hit ys redy to cacche and take
> Al that men wil theryn make   (779–82)[7]

Our sense of the movement of time through the narrative from distant past to nearer past is bewilderingly disrupted; we can no longer be at all confident that we have understood the nature of the goal of the process of development, since there seems to have been no process of development, after all. The man in black's narrative continues to give the impression of being the story of his movement through successive stages of life and learning towards love, from the distant past towards the present tense of the rest of the poem, but the many indications of his stage of life he offers all assign him to one age, *firste youthe* (799). Throughout his narrative he belongs to that immature part of youth which is governed by others rather than being self-governing.[8] Within that one age, however, he undergoes a change of the greatest possible significance; he sees White. Before he sees her he is governed by the ruler of his age-territory, and is boyishly changeable:

> For that tyme Yowthe, my maistresse,
> Governed me in ydelnesse;
> For hyt was in my firste youthe,
> And thoo ful lytel good y couthe,
> For al my werkes were flyttynge
> That tyme, and al my thoght varyinge.   (797–802)

After he sees her, he is no longer governed by his age, with its intrinsic instability and lack of purpose, but by White.[9] 'I loved her', he says, 'in no gere' (in no changeable fashion):[10]

> In al my yowthe, in al chaunce,
> She took me in hir governaunce.
> Therwyth she was alway so trewe,
> Our joye was ever ylyche newe (1285–8)

The man in black does not, then, pass from one stage of life to another during the course of his narrative. For all the references to the passing of many years, he is 'ryght yong' (1090) when he first sees his lady and 'ryght yong' (454) when he tells his story to the poet; his age is the present-tense age of the wood, not the aged, inherently melancholy age he attempts to establish in his past-tense area of the *Book of the Duchess*. But, unexpected and disorienting as this is, it is not as surprising as the fact that his lady, 'goode faire White' (948), is never at any point associated with an age-name or an age-description of any kind. If she were a goddess – and she is indeed associated very deliberately with Nature (871) and with Reason (922; 1010–1),[11] as well as with the Virgin Mary (946; 982; 1003–5) – we should not think of her in terms of a human age. White is assuredly a human woman, however, in spite of all these more-than-human associations, and her human lover is again and again associated with a specific age. Most readers of the poem have taken her to be an idealised portrait of Blanche of Lancaster, and have therefore been happy to accept as applicable to her the historical facts about Blanche's age: the more so since Blanche was some six years younger than her husband, an age-difference between husband and wife which suits twentieth-century conventions about what is 'normal'. If for 'White' we read 'Blanche', Froissart's miniature portrait of her in *Le Joli Buisson de Jonece* could be regarded as an adequate précis of the *Book of the Duchess* portrait:

> Elle morut jone et jolie,
> Environ de .xxii. ans;
> Gaie, lié, frisce, esbatans,
> Douce, simple, d'umble samblance

(she died young and lovely, aged about twenty-two years; gay, joyful, fresh, delightful, sweet, straightforward and modest.)[12]

The charming girl of Froissart's lines is like a hundred others; there is only one White. She is no more a portrait of Blanche than the man in black is a portrait of John of Gaunt, and we have already seen that the historical facts about John of Gaunt's age are not reproduced in Chaucer's poem.

Chaucer invites us to think about White's age because of the emphasis the man in black places on his own age, but he does not give us any indication of the stage of life she has reached. If he had assigned her to a named age, the strange tension of the man in black's narrative would have been dissipated: it is only in relation to his unique experience that the passing of years and the processes of learning and loving fail to bring about the transition from immaturity to the second part of youth. On the other hand, it is precisely because of this tension throughout his narrative that we become increasingly anxious for the state of completed maturity to be unambiguously represented in the poem. Chaucer encourages us to want to perceive White not only as the man in black's personal *aventure* but also as the 'kyndely' culmination of every natural process of development, intellectual and erotic. He encourages us to want to believe that her completed perfection includes her stage of life. When the poet gently suggests that White's perfection existed only in her lover's subjective view—

> 'I leve yow wel, that trewely
> Yow thoghte that she was the beste,
> And to beholde the alderfayreste,
> Whoso had loked hir with your eyen'   (1048-51)
>
> *alderfayreste* loveliest of all

we, like the man in black, are concerned that this error should be refuted:

> 'With myn? nay, alle that hir seyen
> Seyde and sworen hyt was soo.'   (1052-3)

White does not change her stage of life any more than the man in black changes his stage of life, and yet there is nothing in the least unnatural, incongruous or surprising about her unchanging, perfect age. Although White is part of the man in black's past-tense narrative, it is the representation of her completed maturity in the poem which makes it possible for present-tense narrative to be restored at the end of the dream-vision, and which makes it possible for all the oppositions in the poem to be harmoniously resolved. When the man in black says 'she ys ded' (1309), past tense and present tense work in harmony as vehicles of narrative for the first time. The rhetoric of grief and melancholy can now be put away and forgotten, as the May wood forgot its winter sorrow. Early youth and old, old age no longer need to oppose each other in the same, incongruous figure, for in the new narrative present of the end of the dream the man found all in black under the oak-tree can return home to his white-walled castle, where he now undoubtedly belongs.

White's perfect and unchanging age, newly created in the man in black's narrative, restores the natural series of the ages which had been brought to a standstill by her death. The new series of the ages begins with *first youthe* and decrepitude, ends with the perfect age and establishes a continuing present tense. Chaucer takes the wheel of the 'chaunce' of man's life out of the hands of Lady Fortune, in the *Book of the Duchess*, and puts it into the hands of Lady Perfect Age, 'goode faire White', instead. If this boldest and most unexpected of gestures is not heroic, it is nevertheless so extraordinary that this poem deserves to be recognised as one of the most unconventional and unpredictable of all the Ricardian poems which challenge the commonplaces associated with the ages of man's life, and turn the ages into a curious *aventure*.

Notes

PART 1

1. In the middle of the way

1 *Ricardian Poetry: Chaucer, Gower, Langland and the 'Gawain' poet* (London: Routledge, 1971), p. 119.

2 This quotation is, in context, a characterisation of Clergy's role in *Piers Plowman* B13:198–214, but Burrow makes it clear that he regards Clergy's 'dry humour' as being typically Ricardian.

3 For *gravitas* used as an age-name, see Augustine, *De Diversis Quaestionibus*, 58 and 64; *PL*, 40, cols. 43 and 55; also *Epist.* 213, 1; *PL*, 33, col. 966. Eyben, 'Die Einteilung des menschlichen Lebens', p. 185, notes that *gravitas* is very rarely found as an age-name in classical Latin, though as a moral quality it is commonly associated with the *aetas senioris*. See also De Ghellinck (ref. in n. following). In English, gravity (from c.16 onwards) is frequently associated with sobriety and staidness, and all three are associated with the earlier part of old age and contrasted with the qualities of youth.

4 *Studia Mediaevalia in honorem . . . Raymundi Josephi Martin* (Bruges, 1948), p. 40.

5 B12:7; discussed in chap. 11.

6 This age-name is discussed in chap. 14. Since this is the only occurrence of this age-name, I prefer to retain its MS spelling.

7 See chaps. 9 and 10.

8 Philippa Tristram discusses the Pride of Life in *Figures of Life and Death in Medieval English Literature* (London: Elek, 1976), pp. 34–48 (with drama as the focus) and pls. 2 and 5.

9 *Figures of Life and Death*, p. 92. (Tristram does not discuss Gower's treatment of the ages.) A further distinction is made between Chaucer's 'humane and secular vision', which 'endures into the Renaissance', and the peculiarly medieval vision of Langland and the *Gawain*-poet.

10 He is 'in al his wele and in his mooste pride' at 1:895. At 1:1812–13 he distances himself from youth (immediately after dividing the ages into youth and old age).

11 On the associations of the colour green, see J.A. Burrow, *A Reading of Sir Gawain and the Green Knight* (London: Routledge, 1965), pp. 14–17.

12 At Wood Eaton, Oxon. (for instance), the painting of St Christopher is accompanied by the legend (depending from the Christ-child) 'Ki cest image verra le jur de male mort ne murra'; see E.W. Tristram, *English Wall Painting of the Fourteeth Century* (London: Routledge, 1955), p. 268.

2. Numbering ages and naming the middle age

1 *The Treasurie of Auncient and Moderne Times . . . Translated out of . . . Pedro Mexio*, etc. London: W. Jaggard, 1613; *STC*, no. 17936, p. 336.

2 *Archaeologia*, 35, p. 167.

3 Discussed in chap. 4.

4 *De Opificio Mundi*, trans. F.H. Colson and G.H. Whitaker (London: Heinemann, 1929), section 103. Solon's poem is quoted in section 104 and Hippocrates' division of the ages in section 105. On the association of the number seven with the ages, see also Franz Boll, 'Die Lebensalter', *Neue jahrbücher für das klassische Altertum*, 31 (1913), pp. 112–18, and Eyben, 'Roman Notes on the Course of Life', pp. 228–9.

5 'Die Lebensalter', p. 112.

6 Ed. A.L. Mayhew, EETS, e.s. 102 (1908), col. 3. The six ages here derive from a conflation of Isidore's *Etymologiae*, ed. W.M. Lindsay, Scriptorum Classicorum Bibliotheca Oxoniensis (Oxford, 1911), Book 11, chap. 2, with his *Differentiarum*; *PL*, 83, cols. 81–2.

7 MS Ff. 2.38, fol. 20v; Brown and Robbins, *Index*, no. 1259, *inc.* 'How mankinde dooþ bigynne'; ed. E.C. York, 'The Mirror of the Periods of Man's Life', Diss. Pennsylvania, 1957. See also Brian S. Lee, 'A Poem "Clepid the Sevene Ages"', in *An English Miscellany Presented to W.S. Mackie* (Cape Town: Oxford, 1977), pp. 72–92.

8 For Baret's will, see S. Tymms, *Wills and Inventories from . . . Bury*, Camden Society, 49 (1850), p. 33. Other references to tapestries depicting the seven ages may be found in Joan Evans, *English Art: 1307–1461*, Oxford History of English Art, vol. 5 (1949), p. 93, and in R. Van Marle, *Iconographie de L'Art Profane au Moyen-Age et à la Renaissance*, 1932, vol. 2, p. 159.

9 Written in 1600 according to the title-page. See also Chew, *The Pilgrimage of Life* (New Haven: Yale and London, 1962), p. 166.

10 *The Touchstone of Complexions* (London: Thos. Marsh; *STC*, no. 15456), fols. 29r–v. See also Chew, *The Pilgrimage of Life*, p. 170.

11 Cambridge: John Legate; *STC*, no. 5900, sig. C2r.

12 London: Tho.Newcomb; Wing, no. B3334, sig. B6v.

13 London: Henry Bonwicke.

14 Henry Cuffe, *The Differences of the Ages of Mans Life* (London: Arnold Hatfield for Martin Clearke, 1607; *STC*, no. 6103), p. 120.

15 London: Nath.Crouch; Wing, no. C7355; see also Chew, *The Pilgrimage of Life*, p. 168. In the following century it was rewritten in heroic couplets and printed as a chapbook, entitled *The Vanity and Vain Glory of Mortals* (B.L. 11601. d. 29, 3).

16 London: J. Blare; see also Chew, *The Pilgrimage of Life*, p. 168. The running title changes at p. 11.

17 T.W. Baldwin's discussion of 'All the world's a stage', in his *William Shakespere's Small Latine and Less Greeke*, vol. 1 (Urbana, 1944), pp. 652–73, suffers from this emphasis on the correctness of Shakespeare's division of the ages, although the source-material he assembles is interesting and valuable. See also Chew, *The Pilgrimage of Life*, pp. 145 and 358–9.

18 [sub-title] *A Surveigh of Rare and Excellent Matters* (London: Richard Badger; *STC*, no. 19781), Book 5, tr. 1, p. 2. See also Chew, *The Pilgrimage of Life*, p. 166.

19 Examples of perfect age meaning 'legal majority' are given in *MED*, *parfit*, adj. 3(c) and *OED*, *perfect*, adj. B,1,c.

20 *The French Academie, wherin is discoursed the institution of maners*, 3rd edn (London: Geor.Bishop, 1594; *STC*, no. 15235), p. 537.

21 Although they are implied in G.K. Hunter's gloss, 'being fully mature and adult' (Harmondsworth, 1972), p. 200.

22 In his revision of the edition by J.R.R. Tolkien and E.V. Gordon (Oxford, 1967), p. 161. *GGK*, 54 and Davis' gloss are discussed in chap. 14.

23 *The Spared Houres of a Souldier in his Travels* (Dort: Nicholas Vincentz for George Waters, 1623; *STC*, no. 25939), p. 362.

24 Important studies include (arranged chronologically): A. Hofmeister, 'Puer, iuvenis, senex', in *Papsttum und Kaisertum* (for) *P. Kehr*, ed. A. Brackmann (Munich, 1926), pp. 287–316; Joseph de Ghellinck, *Studia Mediaevalia* (see chap. 1, n. 4), pp. 39–59; B. Axelson, 'Die synonyme *adulescens* und *iuvenis*', in *Mélanges de philologie . . . offerts à J. Marouzeau* (Paris, 1948), pp. 7–17; E. Eyben, 'Die Einteilung des menschlichen Lebens in römischen Altertum', *Rheinisches Museum für Philologie*, 116 (1973), pp. 185–90.

25 In Timothe Kendall's *Flowers of Epigrammes* (London: J. Kingston for J. Shepperd, 1577; *STC*, no. 14927), fol. 92v.

26 *Complete Prose Works*, ed. E. Sirluck (New Haven, 1959), vol. 2, p. 558 (and see n. on 'muing', *ibid.*); Gower uses *myhty youthe* as an age-name in *Confessio Amantis* 8:2846, see chap. 13.

27 Book 7, chap. 1; St Omer, 1620; *STC*, no. 910, p. 281. See also chap. 6.

28 (New Haven, 1977), p. 143. In this sonnet Shakespeare surely has in mind Martianus Capella's well-known version of the correspondence between man's journey through the ages and the sun's journey through the heavens: 'Facie autem mox ut [sol] ingressus est, pueri renitentis, incessu medio juvenis anheli, in fine senis apparebat occidui', *De Nuptiis Philologiae et Mercurii*, I, 76; ed. U.F. Kopp (Frankfurt, 1836), pp. 119–20.

29 For further discussion, see chap. 12.

30 *On the Properties of Things*, ed. M.C. Seymour, et al. (Oxford, 1975), vol. 1, book 6, chap. 1, p. 292. See also J.A. Burrow, 'Langland *Nel Mezzo Del Cammin*', in *Medieval Studies for J.A.W. Bennett: aetatis suae LXX*, ed. P.L. Heyworth (Oxford, 1981), p. 27.

31 *Works*, Book 5; ed. E. Vinaver, vol. 1 (Oxford, 1967), p. 189. The phrase is borrowed from the alliterative *Morte Arthure*, ed. Valerie Krishna (New York, 1976), line 301. Krishna notes other interpretations, p. 169.

32 Bodl. MS Lat.theol.d.1, fol. 171r (*SC*, 29746): see Siegfried Wenzel, 'Unrecorded M.E. Verses', *Anglia*, 92 (1974), 63. Other examples of *middel age = juventus* are cited in *MED*, *middel*, adj., 2(a) and sb., 4.

33 The King James Bible has 'all those that were in their best age' at 2 Maccabees 5:24. *MED* also cites an example from Trevisa's trans. of Bartholomeus Anglicus (see n. 30 above).

34 For *se fulfremeda wæstm*, see Ælfric's homily on the parable of the vineyard, ed. Dorothy Whitelock, *Sweet's Anglo-Saxon Reader* (Oxford, 1967), p. 64, line 96.

35 For a concise survey of *perfecta aetas* in patristic writings, see Eyben, 'Die Einteilung des menschlichen Lebens', pp. 153–63.

36 Brown and Robbins, *Index*, no. 931; ed. O. Glauning, *Lydgate's Minor Poems*, EETS, e.s. 80 (1900), pp. 1–15. The quotations are from the prose introduction, p. 1. (The poem is almost certainly not by Lydgate.)

37 See chap. 7.

3. The ages of woman's life

1 (London: Adam Islip for Richard Watkins; *STC*, no. 13890), p. 274.

2 On the creation of Adam at the pefect age, see chap. 7, esp. n. 14.

3 Trans. Haven C. Krueger (Springfield, Illinois, 1963), p. 17.
4 Ed. E.T. Gilby (London: Eyre and Spottiswoode, 1975), vol. 57, part 3a, chap. 72, section 8; pp. 210–15.
5 This section of the *Summa* is discussed further in chap. 6. The quotation about women's spiritual strength derives from Chrysostom.
6 (London: [H. Middleton for] Raufe Newberie; *STC*, no. 19151), p. 22.
7 For well stayde age, see *The Foreste, or Collection of Histories* (London: John Kyngston for Willyam Jones, 1571; *STC*, no. 17849), fol. 39v. The *aetas consistentiae* is discussed in Part I, chap. 5.
8 See M. Manzalaoui, 'The pseudo-Aristotelian *Kitāb Sirr al-asrār*. Facts and problems', *Oriens* (Leiden), 23–4 (1974), pp. 147–257. Phillipus Tripolitanus' Latin trans. of the 'Long Form' of *KSa* (mid c.13) is ed. R. Möller, in parallel with Hiltgart von Hürnheim's MHG trans. (Berlin, 1963). For further discussion of *SS*, see chap. 7.
9 Ed. R. Steele, *Three Prose Versions of the SS*, EETS, e.s. 74 (1898), pp. 243–4.
10 Ed. J.H. Stevenson, *Gilbert of the Haye's Prose MS*, Scottish Text Society (1914), vol. 2, p. 132. The treatise is here entitled *The Buke of the Governaunce of Princis*.
11 On the sanguine complexion as the 'best tempred' see Newton's trans. of Lemnius (chap. 2, n. 10, above), fols. 29v, 86v and 87v; also Raymond Klibansky, Erwin Panofsky and Fritz Saxl, *Saturn and Melancholy* (London: Nelson, 1964), esp. pp. 69 and 103. See also chap. 4, nn. 29–30, below.
12 *The Interpreter* (see chap. 2, n. 11, above), sig. C2r.
13 B.L.12350. cc.6, p. 43. This is vol. 3 of the treatise; vol. 1 is B.L.012357.i.44 (I have not located vol. 2).

4. 'Maturity, full of ripenesse'

1 'Seven Ages', in *Selected Poems* (London: Hutchinson, 1979), p. 152.
2 Edward Wilson, *A descriptive index of the English lyrics in John of Grimestone's preaching book*, Medium Ævum Monographs, n.s. 2 (Oxford: Blackwell, 1973), p. 11. 'Eþe for to fillen' renders 'parvo saciati'.
3 *De Medicina*, Book 2, chap. 1; trans. W.G. Spencer (London: Heinemann, 1935), p. 94.
4 On the classical age-name *media aetas*, see Eyben, 'Die Einteilung des menschlichen Lebens', pp. 156, 163 and 167. Thomas Sheafe, in *Vindiciae Senectutis, or, a plea for Old-Age* (London: George Miller, 1639; rev. *STC*, no. 22391.8), first refers to 'mature, or middle-age' at the end of the work (p. 204), having previously used the age-names 'mature age', 'man's age' and 'ripe age'.
5 See Boll, 'Die Lebensalter', pp. 93–4.
6 Ed. J.M. Osborn (Oxford, 1961), p. 117. I have normalised Whythorne's spelling less thoroughly than Osborn does.
7 H.V. Dicks, in a *New Society* Social Studies Reader entitled *The Seven Ages of Man*. Middle age is the sixth age (42–60 years).
8 *Rhetoric*, Book 2, chaps. 12–14; trans. J.H. Freese (London: Heinemann, 1926), pp. 246–57. See also Boll, 'Die Lebensalter', pp. 99–101.
9 According to Philo, *De Opificio Mundi* (see chap. 2, n. 4, above), section 104. The quotation here is from the trans. by W.A. Merrill, Univ. of California Publications in Classical Philology 6 (Berkeley, 1919), p. 147 – see also Merrill, pp. 208–9, on the relationship between Solon's poems and Aristotle's *Politics*.

10 Book 1, chap. 6, section 75; trans. W.H. Stahl (New York: Columbia, 1952), p. 115; see also Stahl's nn. on Macrobius' sources.

11 According to Solon *via* Philo, 'in the fourth period of seven years, every man is at the prime of his physical strength'; according to Hippocrates *via* Philo, section 105, the *akmē* begins at 29 and extends to 49.

12 Book 7, chap. 9, sections 5–6; trans. B. Jowett (Oxford, 1905), p. 275.

13 Book 4, chap. 10; trans. J.M. Ashmand (London: Davis, 1822), p. 203.

14 *De Arte Poetica (Epistola ad Pisones)*, lines 153–78.

15 *Vita Sancti Anselmi*, ed. and trans. R.W. Southern (London: Nelson, 1962), p. 20.

16 See E. Eyben, 'Die Einteilung des menschlichen Lebens in römischen Altertum', *Rheinisches Museum für Philologie*, 116 (1973), pp. 181–3.

17 *The Spared Houres of a Souldier* (see chap. 2, n. 23, above), p. 373. *OED, virility*, misprints Wodroephe's 'fift' as 'first'.

18 *Vindiciae Senectutis* (see n. 4, above), p. 103, but see also the discussion of this work in chap. 5.

19 (London: William Hope; *STC*, no. 10693); sig. G6r.

20 *Saturn and Melancholy* (see chap. 3, n.11, above).

21 See Boll, 'Die Lebensalter', pp. 102–6.

22 *Pseudogaleni in Hippocratis de Septimanis Commentarium ab Hunaino Q.F. Arabice versum*, chap. 29; ed. w. German trans. G. Bergstraesser, Corpus medicorum graecorum, XI, 2, 1 (Leipzig and Berlin, 1914), p. 57. My quotations derive from the German trans.

23 *Witts New Dyall: Or, a Schollers Prize* (London: W.W[hite] for John Browne; *STC*, no. 22426), sig, M4v.

24 *Quinti Horatii Flacci Emblemata . . . studio Othonis Vaenii* (Antwerp, 1607), pp. 206–7; see also Chew, *The Pilgrimage of Life*, p. 154.

25 *The xv. Bookes of P. Ovidius Naso, entytuled Metamorphosis*, rev.ed. (London: Willyam Seres, 1575; *STC*, no. 18597), fol. 190r; see also Chew, *The Pilgrimage of Life*, pp. 154–5.

26 See *Saturn and Melancholy* (chap. 3, n. 11, above), pp. 293–4 and pl. 97; also Boll, 'Die Lebensalter', pp. 103–4 and pl. 1. The series of the seasons as the ages of woman's life in the *Secretum Secretorum* is discussed in chap. 3, above.

27 Book 7, chap. 1; *PL*, 111, cols. 179–85. The miniature discussed here is on p. 150 of Bibl. Casinensis MS 132; the miniatures of this MS are reproduced in *Miniature Sacre e Profane . . . illustranti l'enciclopedia di Rabano Mauro* (Montecassino, 1896). The ages are not named in the miniature, but are taken from the body of the chapter.

28 *Lectures* (London: Warburg Institute, 1957), vol. 1, pp. 234–41; quotation, p. 239.

29 'Sunt enim quattuor humores in homine, qui imitantur diversa elementa; crescunt in diversis temporibus, regnant in diversis aetatibus. Sanguis imitatur aerem, crescit in vere, regnat in pueritia. Cholera imitatur ignem, crescit in aestate, regnat in adolescentia. Melancholia imitatur terram, crescit in autumno, regnat in maturitate. Phlegma imitatur aquam, crescit in hieme, regnat in senectute.' *PL*, 90, col. 881. According to the authors of *Saturn and Melancholy* (see chap. 3, n. 11, above), *De Mundi Constitutione* was the work of one of the immediate predecessors of William of Conches (p. 183).

30 The macrocosm/microcosm figures reproduced and discussed by E. Wickersheimer, 'Figures médico-astrologiques des IXe, Xe et XIe siècles', *Janus*, 18 (1914), pp. 157–62, all follow this sequence; see also Klibansky, *Saturn and Melancholy*, pp. 10–11 and p. 293. For other sequences, see Boll, 'Die Lebensalter', pp. 104–6, and Philippa Tristram, *Figures of Life and Death* (chap.1, n. 8, above), p. 82.

31 Their table illustrating characteristics attributed to the humours from Galen to Bede, pp. 62–3, is particularly useful in this context.

32 See Klibansky, *Saturn and Melancholy*, pp. 127–95.

33 *Libri de Vita Triplici*, 2, 15; quoted in Klibansky, *Saturn and Melancholy*, p. 272.

34 'Similis est autumno . . . ut imitetur . . . frugum maturitatem . . Crescit in autumno, id est, in sensu maturo. In quantum enim plus attendis maturitatem sensus et aetatis, in tantum magis debet crescere immensitas doloris de peccati perpetratione', *PL*, 176, col. 1191; see also Klibansky, *Saturn and Melancholy*, pp. 106–9.

35 'ad deprimendam superbiam, que caput est omnium vitiorum'; ed. M. Maccarrone (Lugano, 1955), p. 3.

36 'The Nightingale' is discussed in chap. 2, above. On the thirty-five year middle of life, see Dante, *Convivio*, treatise 4, chap. 23.

37 On the *puer senex* topos, see J.A. Burrow, 'Young Saint, Old Devil: Reflections on a Medieval Proverb', *Review of English Studies*, n.s. 30, no. 120 (1979), pp. 385–96; Eyben, 'Roman Notes of the Course of Life', *Ancient Society* (Louvain), 4 (1973), pp. 237–8, and Christian Gnilka, *Aetas Spiritalis: Die Überwindung der natürlichen Altersstufen als Ideal frühchristlichen Lebens* (Bonn, 1972).

38 Robert Robinson's book of epigrams, Bodl. MS Rawlinson poet. 218, p. 115; dated 1660 on title-page.

5. 'Secrete diminution'

1 R.M. Belbin, in a *New Society* Social Studies Reader entitled *The Seven Ages of Man*.

2 *Kalendarium Humanae Vitae* (see chap. 4, n. 19, above), sig. E6r.

3 *Solomons Sermon: Of Mans Chief Felicitie* (Oxford, 1586; *STC*, no. 2762), p. iii r.

4 Both *adolescentia* and *iuventus* are here, in the King James Bible, trans. 'youth': on the ambiguity of these age-names, see chap. 2, above. At 11:10, the Vulgate reads 'adolescentia enim et voluptas vana sunt'.

5 *Vindiciae Senectutis* (see chap. 4, n. 4 above), sig. A5r. The 'great climacteric' is explained by Thomas Bowes in his trans. of Pierre de la Primaudaye, *The French Academie* (see chap. 2, n. 20, above): 'in the whole course of our life we live under only one climate, which is either from seven, or from nine yeeres, except in the yeere of 63, wherein two terminations or climates ende . . . and therefore this yeere is called climatericall, wherein we may note out of histories the death of many great men, and the change of estates and kingdomes' (p. 531).

6 *Kalendarium Humanae Vitae*, sig. H6r.

7 (London: Nathaniel Crouch; Wing, no. C7355), pp. 10–11.

8 Bartholomeus, *On the Properties of Things* (chap. 2, n. 30, above), p. 292. Stephen Bateman's clumsy trans. (*Batman uppon Bartholome*, London: T. East, 1582; *STC*, no. 1538, fol. 70v) highlights the precision of Trevisa's.

9 *Differentiarum*, Book 2, chap. 20; *PL*, 83, col. 81. See also Augustine, *De Genesi contra Manichaeos*, chap. 23; *PL*, 34, col. 191. The context in which Augustine discusses *declinatio* (the fifth age) is considered in chap. 8.

10 See chap. 11 and chap. 11, nn. 11 and 14, below.

11 The translations here derive from Stephen of Antioch's Latin version of *Al-Kitābu'l-Malakī, Liber regalis dispositio nominatus in arte medicine* (Venice, 1492), Book 1, part 1, chap. 21.

12 See Emiel Eyben, 'Antiquity's View of Puberty', *Latomus*, 31 (1972), pp. 678–82.

13 Avicenna's division of the ages and complexions is found in the *Canon*, Book 1, part 1, thesis 3, sections 51–62; trans. O.C. Gruner (London: Luzac, 1930), pp. 68–75. For details of Fortescue's trans. of Mexia, see chap. 3, n. 7, above; quotations, fol. 48r.

14 Aristotle, *De Anima*, Book 3, chap. 12; slightly elaborated by Fortescue in line with what Aristotle says elsewhere.

15 (London: Tho.Flesher; Wing, no. B372). Browne translated from John Williams' ed. (Oxford, 1590).

16 'hoc videtur Aristoteli impossibile quod medicine, que corruptioni et alterationi subiacent, conservent corpora humana in sanitate et naturalem humiditatem, ne cito dissolvatur ante tempus et defendant homines ab accidentibus senectutis et senii . . . Et cum [hec medicina] est preparata preparatione meliori tunc facit operationes nobiles', *De Retardatione*, ed. A.G. Little and E. Withington, British Society of Fransiscan Studies (Oxford, 1928), vol. 14, p. 45.

17 (London: Robert Wyer; *STC*, no. 777.) The reader is encouraged to avoid 'suche accidentall causes as do induce age, as sorowe, study, hevynes, desperation, over much venery, labour, traveyl, or rest', sig. A2v.

18 'bibit senex agricultor in regno Cicilie . . . et mutatus est . . . in equalem complexionem et in etatem 30 annorum in apparentia, et factus est maioris discretionis et memorie et intelligentie', *De Retardatione* (see n. 16, above), pp. 45–6.

PART II

6. The perfect age and the ages of the soul

1 Book 1, chap. 26; *CSEL*, 36, p. 121.

2 *Ennead* 2:9:17; trans. S. MacKenna, rev. B.S. Page, 4th edn (London: Faber, 1969), p. 151.

3 *Avencebrolis Fons Vitae ex arabico in latinum translatus ab Johanne Hispano et Dominico Gundissalino*, ed. Clemens Baeumker, Beiträge zur Geschichte der Philosophie des Mittelalters, 1 (Münster, 1892–5), tract 5, chap. 32; p. 317.

4 In the *Rasā-il*, for instance; see below.

5 *Fons Vitae* (see n. 3, above), tract 5, chap. 34; pp. 319–20.

6 Ed. from the Latin trans. made in Toledo in the mid c.12, 2 vols. (Leiden, Books 4–5, 1968; Books 1–3, 1972); quotation from 1972 vol., p. 14*.

7 Book 1, chap. 5; pp. 81–2. I do not discuss here, since it is not directly relevant, the c.13 scholastic controversy over whether the soul was created complete in its three faculties of nutrition, sensation and intellection (argued by Aquinas), or whether the different faculties follow each other in order until *intellectus* is reached in the *perfectus homo* (argued by Roger Bacon and Robert Kilwardby). On this controversy, see T. Crowley, *Roger Bacon: The Problem of the Soul in his Philosophical Commentaries* (Louvain and Dublin, 1950), pp. 153–9. The 'serial' belief seems to have been influenced by the topos of the ages of the soul.

8 I do not wish to imply that belief in the survival of the physical body was confined to Christian philosophers: on (e.g.) pagan beliefs about astral bodies, see A.H. Armstrong and R.A. Markus, *Christian Belief and Greek Philosophy* (London: Darton, 1960), pp. 47–9.

9 See chap. 3, n. 4, above.

10 See Christian Gnilka, *Aetas Spiritalis: Die Uberwindung der natürlichen Altersstufen als Ideal frühchristlichen Lebens* (Bonn, 1972).

11 Chap. 8, section 8; *PL*, 38, col. 1081; see also Eyben, 'Roman Notes on the Course of Life', p. 225.

12 See also *Enarrationes in Psalmos* 127: 15; *PL*, 37, col. 1681, and Eyben, 'Roman Notes on the Course of Life', pp. 226–7.

13 Chap. 26, sections 48–9; *CCL*, 32, pp. 217–19; see also Eyben, 'Roman Notes on the Course of Life', p. 225.

14 Book 7, chap. 1; St Omer, 1620; *STC*, no. 910, pp. 281–2.

15 Chap. 33; *PL*, 32, cols. 1073–7.

16 'Augustine. Man: body and soul', in *The Cambridge History of Later Greek and Early Medieval Philosophy*, ed. A.H. Armstrong (Cambridge, 1967), p. 360.

17 Book 9, 580–2; trans. F.M. Cornford (Oxford, 1941), pp. 299–302. Plato implies an age-division when he says 'all the advantage lies with the philosopher, who cannot help experiencing both the other kinds of pleasure from childhood up' (p. 581). See also *Averroes' Commentary on Plato's Republic*, ed. and trans. E.I.J. Rosenthal (Cambridge, 1956), p. 140.

18 Chap. 2, section 7; trans. Y. Marquet, *La Philosophie des Iḥwān al-ṣafa*, Etudes Musulmanes, ed. E. Gilson and L. Gardet, no. 19 (Algiers, 1975). pp. 266–7 and pp. 272–4.

19 *The Greatness of the Soul* (Westminster, Maryland, 1950), pp. 101–2.

7. The perfect age and the perfect man

1 *Secretum Secretorum cum glossis et notulis*, ed. R. Steele, Opera hactenus inedita Rogeri Baconi, Fasc. 5 (Oxford, 1920), p. 131. On Bacon's title, see p. xxiii.

2 Part 3, chap. 7; pp. 130–2. On the derivation of this chapter, see M. Manzalaoui, 'The pseudo-Aristotelian *Kitāb Sirr al-asrār*. Facts and problems', *Oriens* (Leiden), 23–4 (1974), pp. 147–257, esp. pp. 180–1. The Latin trans. of the 'Long Form' dates from the second quarter of c.13.

3 For further comment, see S.C. Easton, *Roger Bacon and his Search for a Universal Science* (Oxford: Blackwell, 1952), pp. 78–86, and Manzalaoui, 'The pseudo-Aristotelian *Kitāb Sirr al-asrār*', p. 487.

4 In *Compendium Studii Philosophiae*, however, 30 is the end of a *juventus* characterised by *luxuria* and the beginning of a *provecta aetas* characterised by 'peccata spiritualia, quae nequioria sunt . . . ambitio honorum, et cupiditas, et avaritia', chap. 2; ed. J.S. Brewer, *Fr. Rogeri Bacon Opera*, Rolls Series, 15 (London, 1859), vol. 1, p. 412.

5 *CCL*, 78 (1958), pp. 499–500.

6 This is repeated by Isidore in his *Etymologiae*, Book 11, chap. 2, 16; ed. W.M. Lindsay, Scriptorum Classicorum Bibliotheca Oxoniensis (Oxford, 1911), n.pag.

7 See Gregory the Great, *Homiliarum in Ezechielem*, Book 1, sections 2–3; *PL*, 76, col. 796; Abelard's preface to his *Expositio in Hexaemeron*, *PL*, 178, col. 731; Gregory of Elvira's preface to his *In Canticum Canticorum*, *CCL*, 69 (1967), p. 169.

8 Part 3, chap. 25; *PL*, 77, col. 98.

9 *Epist.* 82, section 8; *CSEL*, 55 (1912), pp. 114–15. On 30 as the minimum age for ordination, see also Eyben, 'Die Einteilung des menschlichen Lebens', n. 68.

10 *Anglo-Saxon England*, 3rd edn (Oxford, 1971), p. 368.

11 *PL*, 178, col. 731.

12 From Venantius Fortunatus' hymn 'Pange, lingua, gloriosi proelium certaminis', ed. G.M. Dreves, *Analecta Hymnica Medii Aevi* (Leipzig, 1907), vol. 50, p. 71. The pun does not survive in J.M. Neale's trans. 'his appointed time fulfilled'.

13 *Commentarium in Epist. ad Ephesios*, Book 2, chap. 4; *PL*, 26, col. 502.

14 *Contra Joannem Hierosolymitanum*, section 32; *PL*, 23, col. 384. Cf. also Thomas Browne, *Religio Medici*, part 1, chap. 39: 'Some divines count Adam thirty years old at his creation, because they suppose him created in the perfect age and stature of man', *Works*, ed. Geoffrey Keynes (London: Faber, 1928), vol. 1, p. 50.

15 On the meaning of this text, and on Patristic ideas of resurrection at the perfect age, see Gnilka, *Aetas Spiritalis*, pp. 148–62.

16 Chap. 56, para. 7; ed. J.H. Waszink (Amsterdam, 1947), pp. 75–6; see also Waszink's commentary, p. 572.

17 Book 22, chap. 15; trans. W.M. Greene (London: Heinemann, 1972), vol. 7, pp. 276–7.

18 Eyben, 'Die Einteilung des menschlichen Lebens', p. 176, suggests that Augustine may have in mind Varro's division of the ages.

19 I depart from Greene's trans. here.

20 See his *Comment. in Esaiam* 65: 20; *CCL*, 73A, p. 762, and Gnilka, *Aetas Spiritalis*, pp. 155–8. On the triad of perfection, see Eyben, 'Die Einteilung des menschlichen Lebens', p. 176, and chap. 11, esp. n. 13, and chapter 12, n. 2.

21 Treatise 4, chap. 24, para. 6; ed. G. Busnelli and G. Vandelli (Florence, 1937), p. 311.

8. The perfect age and the ages of the world

1 *PL*, 34, cols. 190–3; the quotation comes from section 38.

2 On the godless triad of 1 John 2:16, see Donald R. Howard, *The Three Temptations* (Princeton, 1966), pp. 43–75, and also chapter 11.

3 *Chronica*, prologue to Book 5; ed. W. Lammers and A. Schmidt (Berlin, 1960), p. 374; see further M.D. Chenu, 'Theology and the New Awareness of History', in *Nature, Man, and Society in the Twelfth Century*, ed. and trans. J. Taylor and L.K. Little (Chicago, 1968), pp. 162–201. (Chenu dismisses the Ages of Man as a 'cliché'.)

On the origins of the comparison between the evolution of the state and the ages of man's life in Roman historians, see Eyben, 'Roman Notes on the Course of Life', pp. 222–3, and on Christian versions of the topos, see R. Schmidt, '*Aetates mundi*. Die Weltalter als Gliedrungsprinzip der Geschichte', *Zeitschrift für Kirchengeschichte*, 67 (1956), 288–317; also Eyben, pp. 223–5.

4 For medieval commentators, the comparison between the ages of the world and the ages of man's life seems to have been valued above all for the evidence it provided of a correspondence between macrocosm and microcosm: see, e.g., the discussion of the macrocosm/microcosm diagrams in some MSS of Lambert of St Omer's *Liber Floridus*, in F. Saxl, *Lectures* (London: Warburg Institute, 1957), vol. 1, pp. 243–4. The 'original' MS, Ghent Univ. Lib. 197, has a macrocosm diagram showing 6 *mundi etates*; then, under the heading 'microcosm hoc est minor mundus', a 'descriptio etatis hominis' with 7 ages: see *Liber Floridus*, ed. A. Derolez (Ghent, 1968), pl. 42.

5 Gnilka discusses the concept of rejuvenation in *Aetas Spiritalis*, pp. 244–54. Chenu discusses political and eschatological interpretations of Isaiah 40:30–1 in the later Middle Ages in 'Nature, Man, and Society', pp. 182–4.

6 *Hymnarius Paraclitensis*, ed. Joseph Szövérffy (Albany, N.Y. and Brookline, Mass., 1975), vol. 2, pp. 58–78 (nos. 18–29). For Abelard's abbreviated version of Augustine's comparison, see *Expositio in Hexaemeron*, PL, 178, cols. 771–3.

7 Trans. J.M. Neale.

8 Abelard refers to the fourth age as 'juventus, id est virilis aetas' in *Expositio in Hexaemeron*, col. 772.

9 See Szövérffy, *Hymnarius Paraclitensis*, p. 67, for further comment on these lines.

10 *De Vita Sancti Geraldi Auriliacensis Comitis*, Book 2, 1; *PL*,133, col. 669. See also Alexander Murray, *Reason and Society in the Middle Ages* (Oxford, 1978), p. 360.

11 The Douai Bible follows the Vulgate ('in the middle of my days'); the Great Bible, Geneva Bible, Bishops' Bible and King James Bible share the variant reading 'in the cutting off of my dayes' (KJ).

A typically Renaissance ambivalence about the notion of *best age* is found in Valentine Leigh's *The plesaunt playne and pythye Pathewaye* (London: Nicolas Hyll for John Case, 1550?; *STC*, no. 15421): *best age* is at one point 21 years (sig. B3r) and at another, 'grave and sage man's state' (sig. C4v).

9. The perfect age and the image of the wheel

1 *Inc.* 'Opon a somer soneday se I þe sonne'; Brown and Robbins *Index*, no. 3838. The most accessible text is in R.H. Robbins (ed.), *Historical Poems of the XIV and XV Centuries* (New York: Columbia, 1959), pp. 98–102, nn. on pp. 301–3; see also T.M. Smallwood, 'The Interpretation of Somer Soneday', *Medium Ævum*, 42 (1973), pp. 238–43, for comments on Robbins' and other earlier editions (particularly p. 238 and p. 242, n. 1). On the date of the poem, see Smallwood, p. 242 (mid c.14) and T. Turville-Petre, *The Alliterative Revival* (Woodbridge, Suffolk, 1977), p. 35 (late c.14). I incline towards the earlier date, on linguistic grounds.

2 'The Interpretation of *SS*', pp. 240–1.

3 *Inc.* 'Alle wandreths, welthis and lykingis'; Brown and Robbins, *Index* no. 230. Ed. C. Horstmann, *Yorkshire Writers: Richard Rolle of Hampole and his followers* (London: Macmillan, 1896), vol. 2, pp. 70–1. See also Smallwood, p. 239. Space has been allowed for the image of the wheel in the MS, but it has been left blank.

4 *The Goddess Fortuna in Medieval Literature* (Cambridge, Mass., 1927), pp. 164–6.

5 B.L. MS Add. 47682, fol. 1v; see W.O. Hassall, *The Holkham Bible Picture Book* (London: Dropmore, 1954), pp. 55–6, and F.P. Pickering, *The Anglo-Norman Text of HBPB*, Anglo-Norman Text Society, 23 (1971), pp. 70–1.

6 *Literature and Art in the Middle Ages* (London: Macmillan, 1970), p. 191, n. 1. See also pp. 211–22 for a useful Wheel of Fortune bibliography.

7 *Reason and Society in the Middle Ages* (Oxford, 1978), p. 100.

8 Ed. K.S. Block, EETS, e.s. 120 (1922), p. 173, lines 135–9.

9 *Literature and Art*, pp. 191, 215–16 (I boast, raised up on high; I go down, enfeebled; pressed down by the axle, I am at the lowest point; once more I am carried to the heights); Walther, *Initia*, no. 7251. In this elaborated version of the 'formula of four' it is surely deliberate that the reigning king speaks first – a recognition of the fact that our eyes are first drawn to him.

10 For examples, see Smallwood, 'The Interpretation of *SS*', pp. 238–9.

11 Dionysius of Fourna's manual has been edited from Leningrad, Saltykov-Shchedrin State Public Lib. MS gr. 708 by A. Papadopoulo-Kérameus, *Hermeneia tes zographikes technes* (St Petersburg, 1909). P. Hetherington uses the same MS for his trans. and commentary, *The 'Painter's Manual' of Dionysius of Fourna* (London: Sagittarius, 1974).

On the title and date of the manual see Hetherington, pp. II and V.

For the picture of 'the vain life of this world' see Papadopoulo-Kérameus, pp. 213–15 and Hetherington, p. 83. Translations from the manual are my own, though I am much indebted to Hetherington's trans.

12 Papadopoula-Kérameus, *Hermeneia*, p. 3; Hetherington, *The Painter's Manual*, pp. III, 2 and 91.

13 See his article 'Symbolique Chrétienne: La Vie Humaine', *Annales archéologiques*, 1 (1844), pp. 240–8.

14 *Manuel d'Iconographie Chrétienne greque et latine*, trans. P. Durand (Paris, 1845); commentary, pp. 411–17.

15 Smallwood, 'The Interpretion of *SS*', pp. 239–40, provides other examples. See also the De Brailes Wheel of Fortune, plate 10.

16 Rosalie Green *et al.*, eds., Studies of the Warburg Institute, 36 (London and Leiden, 1979), vol. 2, p. 349, item 737, fol. 213v; see Walther, *Initia*, no. 16256.

17 *Proceedings of the Society of Antiquaries*, 26 (1914), 60.

18 On the 'Rota Vite Alias Fortune' see F. Saxl, 'A Spiritual Encyclopedia of the Later M.As', *JWCI*, 5 (1942), pp. 97–8, and on the 'Rota Vite Que Fortuna Vocatur' see John Winter Jones, 'Observations on the Origin of the Division of Man's Life into Stages', *Archaeologia*, 35 (1853), pp. 186–8 and plate 6. There is no general agreement about how the Wheel of Fortune and Wheel of Life should be distinguished from one another, but the attempt to classify all wheels with age-differentiation as wheels of life is made by (e.g.) Karl Weinhold, 'Glücksrad und Lebensrad', *Abhandlungen der königlichen Akademie der Wissenschaften zu Berlin*: Philosophisch-historische Classe (1892), pp. 1–27. Weinhold recognises, however, that the two 'kinds' of wheel are closely related (p. 21).

19 'Infans dicor' (Walther, *Initia*, no. 9300), p. 421; 'Sum modo natus' (Walther, *Initia*, no. 18714), p. 422; 'Iam mentis ingenio' (Walther, *Initia*, no. 9709), p. 423 and 'Hanc, homo, cerne rotam' (not recorded by Walther), p. 425. The poems have not been printed.

10. The perfect age and the De Lisle Psalter

1 The text is recorded by G. McN. Rushforth (see chap. 9, n. 17, above), pp. 48–52, and by Lucy Freeman Sandler, *The Psalter of Robert de Lisle in the British Library* (London: Harvey Miller and Oxford, 1983), p. 125. I have supplied the age-names from internal evidence and by analogy with other age-poems (see also n. 8, below). The four figures at the corners of the picture are named *infantia, juventus, senectus* and *decrepitus: juventus* is crowned.

2 For Sandler's discussion of the Madonna Master, see *The Psalter of Robert de Lisle in the British Library* (London: Harvey Miller and Oxford, 1983), pp. 14–17, and for her discussion of the Majesty Master, pp. 17–19.

3 F. Saxl discusses the diagrams associated with the *Speculum Theologie* in 'A spiritual encyclopedia', pp. 107–15; see also Sandler, *Psalter of Robert de Lisle*, pp. 23–7, and her appendix of related MSS, pp. 134–9. According to Sandler's reconstruction of the original order of the leaves, p. 29, the *Speculum* diagrams would all follow the present fols. 126r–127r.

4 Reproduced here from Bodl. MS Laud misc. 156, fol. 66r; see also Camb. U.L. MS Gg. 4.32, fol. 15r and B.L. MS Arundel 83 (I), fol. 4r.

5 See G. McN. Rushforth, *Proceedings of the Society of Antiquaries*, 26 (1914), pp. 52–5 and

fig. 3. E.W. Tristram, in *English Medieval Wall Painting: The Thirteenth Century* (Oxford, 1950), vol. 1, p. 262, dates the Leominster wheel late c.13 (believing it to be contemporary with the De Lisle wheel); Rushforth also suggests late c.13 (p. 48). The verses were not written around the medallions of the Leominster wheel, but instead on (and on scrolls projecting outside) the rim (Rushforth, *Proceedings*, p. 52).

6 For details of the Kempley Wheel of Life, see Rushforth, *Proceedings*, p. 47 and fig. 1; for details of the c.12 frescoes, see E.W. Tristram, *English Medieval Wall Painting: The Twelfth Century* (Oxford, 1944), pp. 134–6 and plates 56–66 and 89.

7 Brown and Robbins, *Index*, no. 4277 (*inc.* 'Young and tender childe I am'). The text has not been printed and no other MS is recorded. Linc. Cath. Lib. MS 66 is a paper vol. of c.15 date and probable northern provenance. The language of '3ing and tender child' is northern.

8 *Inc.* 'In pannis iaceo; vivo de lacte papille', fols. 84r-v pp. 167–8; not recorded by Walther. The age-names are the same as I have supplied for '3ing and tender child' except for the last three, 'languidus', 'mortuus' and 'sepulturus'. The ages are paralleled with 'aurora', 'prima', 'tercia', 'sexta', 'nona', 'decima', 'undecima', 'vespera', 'completorum' and 'nox'.

9 E.W. Tristram provides a good introduction to the complexities of the image of the three living and the three dead in *English Wall Painting of the Fourteenth Century* (London: Routledge, 1955), pp. 112–14. For details of the Wickhampton painting see pp. 263–4, and for a list of churches where the image is (or was) visible, see p. 303. The De Lisle picture is discussed by R. Freyhan in 'English Influences on Parisian Painting of about 1300', *Burlington Magazine*, 54 (1929), pp. 320–30. (Freyhan dates the De Lisle Psalter *c.*1285.)

10 See E.W. Tristram, *Wall Painting of the Fourteenth Century*, p. 114, and Philippa Tristram, *Figures of Life and Death in Medieval English Literature* (London: Elek, 1976), p. 163. The language of the quatrain here shows S.E. colouring.

11 The De Lisle text is printed by S. Glixelli in *Les Cinq Poèmes des Trois Morts et des Trois Vifs* (Paris, 1914), pp. 118–20; the long form of the poem is ed. pp. 83–91. See also P. Tristram, *Figures of Life and Death in Medieval English Literature* (London: Elek, 1976) pp. 162–7, on the image's literary ramifications.

12 On the relationship between poem and picture see Freyhan, 'English Influences' (see n. 9 above), esp. p. 326.

13 There are five known copies of the poem 'Parvule, cur ploras':
  i Cambridge Univ. Lib. MS Gg. 4.32, fol. 15v = *C* (see plate 9)
  Turris sapiencie is written on the contents-page of this c.14 miscellany, but the title (in a c.15 hand) may be intended to refer only to the first part of the MS, which contains *Speculum Theologie* diagrams (fols. 10v–12v and 15r), though not now the *turris sapiencie* itself. Our poem, here *inc.* 'Parvule, quid ploras', entitled *Speculum etatis hominis*, is apparently intended to be associated with these diagrams, for it is written in tabular form on the reverse of a *rota altercacionis oppositorum* (fol. 15r). The poem has been printed from this MS, not wholly accurately, by C. Sayle, *The Ages of Man* (London: Murray, 1916), p.xiii. See also Sandler, *The Psalter of Robert de Lisle*, p. 134.
  ii British Library MS Arundel 83 (II), fol. 126r = *L*
  The poem is here entitled *Duodecim proprietates condicionis humane*.
  iii Lincoln Cathedral Library MS 210, fol. 194r = *Lc*
  This c.15 paper MS consists chiefly of Latin devotional works. 'Parvule, cur ploras'

is written in tablular form (*Quaestio* replacing the *Racio* of the other copies), and entitled *Versus de etatibus hominis*. Immediately following the poem is an ages poem *inc.* 'Duxit Natura de semine me genitali' (Walther, *Initia*, no. 5046), in which nine ages speak in turn (fols. 194r–v), and by another poem, now indecipherable, beginning with the words of *Infans* (fol. 194v).

iv Bodleian MS Laud misc. 156, fol. 66v = O

This early c.15 MS, which comes from the Hospital of St John the Baptist, Exeter (fol. 5r), contains Old Testament schemes (fols. 5r–15r), a Biblical *tabula* (fols. 16r–60r) attributed here to Nicholas de Lyra, and *Speculum Theologie* diagrams (fols. 61r–66r). Our poem, entitled as in *L*, is written, as copy *C* is, in tabular form on the reverse of a *rota altercacionis oppositorum* (fol. 66r). Although Rushforth suggested (p. 58) that the *Speculum Theologie* diagrams in this MS were copied from B.L. MS Arundel 83, the text of our poem is not a copy of *L*, nor is the visual presentation the same. Ref.: O. Pächt and J.J.G. Alexander, *Illuminated MSS in the Bodleian Library* (Oxford, 1973), vol. 3, p. 72. See also Sandler, *The Psalter of Robert de Lisle*, pp. 136–7.

v Bibliothèque de Tours MS 331, fols. 54r–v = T

This c.14 MS preserves a corrupt text of our poem, here entitled as in *L* and *O* and written in tabular form. Ref.: A. Dorange, *Catalogue Descriptif . . . des MSS de la Bibl. de Tours* (Tours, 1875), p. 186.

'Parvule, cur ploras' is recorded in Walther, *Initia*, nos. 13757 and 13759. (Copies *L* and *O* are not noted.) (See also Sandler, *The Psalter of Robert de Lisle*, p. 105, n. 83, for a related poem.) The De Lisle text (*L*) contains some corrupt readings, and it has been corrected from *C* where necessary. All instances in which *L* readings have been rejected in favour of other MS readings are recorded in the textual footnotes, and some of the more significant variants are also noted.

14 Described by S.C. Cockerell, *The Work of W. De Brailes* (Cambridge: Roxburghe Club, 1930), pp. 16–18. This detached leaf is now Fitzwilliam Museum, Cambridge, MS 330(4).

15 The frescoes are described by M. Salmi, 'Gli affreschi del Palazzo Trinci a Foligno', *Bollettino d'Arte del Ministero della Pubblica Istruzione*, Rome, series 1, year 13 (Dec. 1919), pp. 153–5 and figs. 11–13; also Van Marle, *L'Art Profane*, vol. 2, p. 156, figs. 186–7. Some of Salmi's readings of the inscriptions do not make sense as they stand, but can readily be reconstructed (see nn. following).

16 Salmi: '. . . ont va a fin forque bien f . . .' (p. 154, n. 6).

17 Salmi: 'voici(?)' (p. 154, n. 4). Perhaps *jovenes* by analogy with the 21-year-old *jovencaus*.

18 Salmi: 'reus dous coment as tu vesqut' (p. 154, n. 6).

19 The question put to the fifth age (60-year-old) and his reply are both indecipherable.

20 'The Wall-Paintings at Longthorpe Tower, near Peterborough', *Archaeologia*, 96 (1955), 1–57; quotation from p. 1. See also E.W. Tristram, *Wall Painting of the Fourteenth Century*, pp. 219–21.

21 On the date, see Rouse and Baker, pp. 6–7 and 31–2, and on the stylistic affinities, pp. 15–22.

22 See Rouse and Baker, p. 10 and pls. 7, 8b, 15a and 16b. The '. . . or' which I complete as *senior* is my own reading, and *juvenis* is my own supposition: Rouse suggests *vir* and *mediaevus* (!)

PART III

11. *Myddel age* in *Piers Plowman*

1 Brown and Robbins, *Index*, no. 349. The quotation is taken from F.J. Furnivall's edition of the Lambeth copy, *Hymns to the Virgin and Christ*, EETS, o.s. 24 (1867), pp. 83–5. For further comment, see Philippa Tristram, *Figures of Life and Death*, p. 80, and Brian S. Lee, *An English Miscellany Presented to W.S. Mackie* (Cape Town: Oxford, 1977), pp. 81–2.

2 *PP: an edition of the C-text* (London: Arnold, 1978), p. 16.

3 'The Role of the Dreamer in *PP*', in *PP: Critical Approaches*, ed. S.S. Hussey (London: Methuen, 1969), p. 185.

4 Quotations from the B-text are taken from the edition by George Kane and E. Talbot Donaldson (London: Athlone, 1975); quotations from the C-text are taken from the forthcoming edition by George Russell.

5 John F. Adams, for instance, in his article '*PP* and the Three Ages of Man', *Journal of English and Germanic Philology*, 61 (1962), pp. 23–41, attempts to show that the Vita is organised around the successive youth, middle age and old age of the Dreamer.

6 *Medieval Studies for J.A.W. Bennett*, p. 35.

7 'Langland *Nel Mezzo Del Cammin*', pp. 22–4. To n. 5 on Gregory's use of *adolescentia* as a synonym for *juventus* may be added a ref. to Eyben, 'Die Einteilung des menschlichen Lebens', pp. 185–90, and see chap. 2, n. 24.

8 Ed. B. Assmann, *Angelsächsische Homilien und Heiligenleben*, Bibliothek der angelsächsische Prosa, 3 (repr. Darmstadt, 1964), p. 52. See also Burrow, 'Langland *Nel Mezzo Del Cammin*', p. 23.

9 *XL Homiliarum in Evangelia*, Book 1, homily 13; *PL* 76, col. 1125. See also Burrow, 'Langland *Nel Mezzo Del Cammin*', pp. 22–3.

10 Ed. J.S. Westlake, EETS, o.s. 143 (1913), p. 86. Cicero's 'ferocitas iuvenum' (*De Senectute*, x, 33) evidently lies behind *PLA*'s 'wildenes'.

11 For medieval refs. to 45 as the end of *juventus*, see Burrow, 'Langland *Nel Mezzo Del Cammin*', pp. 25–8. The ballad, in the British Library collection, was printed in Glasgow by I. and M. Robertson.

12 Quotations from *PTA* are taken from the edition of the Thornton text by M.Y. Offord, EETS, 246 (1959).

13 'The Three Ages of *PTA*', *Chaucer Review*, 9 (1975), pp. 342–52. On the triad of perfection see also Eyben, 'Die Einteilung des menschlichen Lebens', p. 176.

14 On 60 as the onset of old age, see (*inter multa alia*) Eyben, 'Die Einteilung des menschlichen Lebens', p. 169 and W. Wackernagel, *Die Lebensalter* (Basle, 1862), p. 66. On 60 as the end of the period of male fertility see Rowland, 'The Three Ages of *PTA*', p. 347 and n. 31.

15 See, e.g., *Troilus and Criseyde* 4: 1368–9 and *Middle English Sermons*, ed. W.O. Ross, EETS, o.s. 209 (1940), p. 210.

16 'The Ages of Man in *PTA*', *Medium Ævum*, 46 (1977), p. 73.

17 It is just possible that we are dealing with direct influence here: certainly the description of the assault of Elde, *PTA*, 283–9, has sufficient points of similarity with *PP* B 20:183–92 to tempt one to think that *PP* influenced *PTA* here. Offord suggests a date 'before 1370' for *PTA* (p. xxxvi), but more recent studies are disinclined to be

more precise than late c.14 (see, e.g., Thorlac Turville-Petre, *The Alliterative Revival*, Woodbridge, Suffolk, 1977, p. 5).

To do justice to the poet's overall design, a full discussion of the numerological aspects of *PTA* would be necessary (including the way in which pagan and Christian perfect numbers interact with each other, the pagan 81 being raised to the Christian 100). Here, I have confined myself to those aspects of the poem that bear directly on *PP*.

18 The 'inner dream' extends from B11:5–404 and C11:165 – 13:214. See also Pearsall's notes on C11:168 and C13: 213.

19 Burrow, 'Langland *Nel Mezzo Del Cammin*', pp. 29–30.

20 An extremely common alliterative phrase: see, e.g., *PTA* 134 (etc.), and, for an interesting variation, *Wynnere and Wastoure*, ed. I. Gollancz (Oxford, 1921): 'What, he was ʒongeste of ʒeris and ʒapest of witt' (119).

21 On medieval interpretations of the godless triad of 1 John 2:16, see Donald R. Howard, *The Three Temptations* (Princeton, 1966), pp. 43–75, and Pearsall's note on C1:37–8.

22 For a summary of the reasons suggested for Langland's expansion of the role of Rechelesnesse in the C-text, see Pearsall's note on C11:196.

23 The relationship between Rechelesnesse and Sir Wanhope is stated in C11:196 and explained in C11:198 ff.

24 Although covetousness was proverbially associated with old age in the later Middle Ages (see n. 15, above: also p. 22, above), it also came to be regarded as the characteristic vice of the latter part of *juventus*, insofar as that age was protracted until it met decrepit old age. Perhaps it would be both simpler and more accurate to say that avarice was perceived as the characteristic vice of that period of life when lust is no longer a temptation (see *2 Henry IV*, I, ii, 228–30: 'A man can no more separate age and covetousness than a can part young limbs and lechery').

25 Rather than 'childishness' (Pearsall's gloss).

26 *Boece*, Book 2, *prosa*, 1, lines 114–15.

27 The C-text reading is a notable improvement on B11:15.

28 Latin commentators variously render the Vulgate *superbia vitae* as *ambitio seculi*, *jactantia vitae* and *superbia hujus vitae*. The literal meaning of the Greek would seem to be 'ostentatious pride in the possession of worldly resources'. See further Howard, *The Three Temptations*, pp. 43–75.

29 See *MED, foryeten* 4(c); but possibly = *forʒede* (passed right through), see Kane and Donaldson's reading at B11:60, and Pearsall's note on C12:12.

30 See Kane and Donaldson's variants at B13:2.

31 See his note on C15:5–24. 'This meteles' (C15:4) seems to include only part of the Third Vision, and Langland makes no attempt to distinguish between the 'inner dream' (see n. 18, above) and the 'outer dream'. See Pearsall, p. 17.

32 On the emblematic interpretation of *vix* as the wounds of Christ, see Pearsall's note on C15:22–3.

33 *PP as a Fourteenth Century Apocalypse* (New Jersey: Rutgers, 1961), and '*PP* and the Three Grades of Chastity', *Anglia*, 76 (1958), pp. 227–53.

12. Hy tyme in *Piers Plowman*

1 The best discussion of this section of the poem is that by David Aers, *PP and Christian Allegory* (London: Arnold, 1975), pp. 79–107. See also Peter Dronke, 'Arbor

Caritatis', in *Medieval Studies for J.A.W. Bennett* (see chap. 2, n. 30, above), pp. 209–20.

2 See '*PP and the Three Grades of Chastity*' and chap. 11, n. 13, above.

3 *The Romance of William of Palerne*, ed. W.W. Skeat, *EETS*, e.s. 1 (1867), line 18 (etc.). There is undoubtedly an underlying reference to Luke 2:40 in C18:135, but R.E. Kaske is surely mistaken when he says ('Patristic Exegesis: The Defense', in *Critical Approaches to Medieval Literature*, ed. Dorothy Bethurum, New York, 1960, p. 44) that this line of *PP* allegorises the Biblical verse systematically.

4 See M.A. Martindale, 'The Treatment of the Life of Christ in *PP*', unpublished B. Litt. Diss., Oxford, 1978, pp. 48–54.

5 Aers also discusses B18:220–3, B16:192–3 and 214–15 and B19: 92–7 in the context of his elucidation of this passage, pp. 107–9.

6 The uncertainty is not present in the B-text (16:160–6). The C-text is decidedly superior at this point.

7 For a discussion of medieval interpretations of *plenitudo temporis*, see Martindale, 'Life of Christ in *PP*', pp. 29–36.

8 See Kane and Donaldson's variants, and *MED*, *juvent* and *juventē*.

9 See Kane and Donaldson's variants.

13. *Myhty youthe* in Confessio Amantis

1 *Ricardian Poetry*, p. 119.

2 Quotations from *CA* are from the edition by G.C. Macaulay, EETS, e.s. 81–2 (1900–1).

3 In *Gower's 'Confessio Amantis': Responses and Reassessments*, ed. A.J. Minnis, (Woodbridge, Suffolk, 1983), pp. 5–24, quotation, p. 16.

4 *The Allegory of Love* (Oxford, 1936), p. 218.

5 'The Age of the Lover in Gower's *CA*', *Medium Ævum*, 36 (1967), pp. 152–8. Schueler perhaps overstates his case, but it provides a useful counterbalance.

For a detailed critique of Schueler, see Burrow, 'The Portrayal of Amans', (see n. 3, above), pp. 12–14, and Jacquelyn Hardwick, 'Amans, Genius, " John Gower" and the Poet: A Consideration of the Relationship between these Four Figures in *CA*', unpublished M.A. Diss., La Trobe (Melbourne), 1979, esp. pp. 18–45. Hardwick argues that the relationship between Lover and poet is 'far more delicate and complicated than Schueler makes out' (p. 35).

6 *The Allegory of Love*, pp. 220–1.

7 From the marginal summary beside 2440, p. 452. My argument assumes that (but does not depend upon the fact that) the Latin summaries are Gower's; see Macaulay's account of the MSS in *The Complete Works of John Gower*, vol. 1 (Oxford, 1899), pp. cxxxviii-clxxi.

8 'contristatus Amans quasi mortuus in terram corruit', p. 452.

9 'provisa Senectus, racionem invocans, hominem interiorem per prius amore infatuatum mentis sanitati plenius restauravit', p. 461.

10 The definition of *launcegai* in *MED*, for this context only, as 'Cupid's dart', does Gower less than justice. It is a real weapon here, not an allegorical stage-property (by contrast, at 1:144 it *is* a dart).

11 Although Lewis is aware of this (*The Allegory of Love*, p. 221), his definition of the theme of *CA* as 'Love cured by Age' (p. 219) makes it clear that he does not distinguish between first-person and third-person narrative in this episode as a whole.

12 On Gower's attitude to the company of Elde, see Hardwick, 'Amans, Genius, "John Gower" and the Poet' (see n. 5 above), pp. 162–4.

13 This age-name is not recorded in *MED*. See also chap. 2, n. 26.

14 See *MED*, *fare*, 9.

15 *Epist.* 44, section 14; *PL*, 16, col. 1189. Ambrose proceeds to give a rendering of Ephesians 4:13. See also Burrow, *Ricardian Poetry*, chap. 2, n. 43.

14. *Hyghe eldee* in *Sir Gawain and the Green Knight*

1 I think it highly likely that the *Gawain*-poet also wrote *Pearl* and *St Erkenwald*, although the evidence cannot be regarded as conclusive. My argument about the representation of the ages and of perfect age in *GGK* does not depend upon any theory of common authorship of the poems of B.L. MS Cotton Nero A.X., or of these poems and *St E*.

2 Quotations from *GGK* are taken from the edition by J.R.R. Tolkien and E.V. Gordon, rev. Norman Davis (Oxford, 1967).

3 The reference to Trevisa should be omitted from *MED*, *adolescenci*, since Trevisa gives the age-name in its Latin form and proceeds to translate it (see n. following). For examples of the pairing of adolescence with an age-name containing *yong* or *youthe*, see *MED*: for *wexing age*, see *MED adolescence* and *manhed*, 3(b).

4 *On the Properties of Things*, ed. M.C. Seymour, *et al.*, vol. 1 (Oxford, 1975), p. 291, line 30; p. 292, line 9.

5 Thomas Milles, for instance, defines *adolescentia* as 'the springall or stripling estate of a youth', p. 337.

6 Ed. E.C. Babington, *Rolls Series*, 41 (London, 1869), vol. 2, p. 371. The whole phrase rather confusingly reads 'þe first ȝowþe of manhede is cruel as a lyoun', but the context makes it clear that *manhede* here means the state of being human, not a stage of life.

7 *On the Properties of Things* (see n. 4 above), Book 6, chap. 1; pp. 291–3.

8 See *MED*, *first*, ord.num., 2a(c), *first elde*, but 'the prime of life' is not an exact definition. This sense survived into the c.16, as Thomas Bowes' trans. of Pierre de la Primaudaye's *French Academie* attests: 'in their first age they usually provide teachers for them sending them to colledges', 3rd edn (London: G. Bishop, 1594; *STC*, no. 15235), p. 529.

9 For Davis' gloss, see *GGK*, p. 161, *age*; the note on line 54 (p. 74) suggests 'the "springtime" of their lives'. For the *MED* definition see *age* 1b(b).

Under *first*, ord.num., 2a(c), *first age*, *MED*'s only definition is 'the Golden Age', which is clearly correct for the context cited. Unfortunately it led Martin Stevens to read *GGK* 54 as though it referred to the golden age ('Laughter and Game in *GGK*', *Speculum*, 47, 1972, p. 67). Apart from contextual arguments against this, the possessive adj. *her* makes it certain that *first age* is to be taken as an age-name.

10 'The *Childgered* Arthur of *GGK*', *Studies in Medieval Culture* (W. Michigan), 8–9 (1976), p. 174.

11 *Childgered* is discussed by Davis in *GGK*, p. 75, and by Moody, pp. 174–5. Although the precise implications of *-gered* are in doubt, *MED*'s 'boyish, light-hearted', *child*, 13(d), seems inadequate. Nevertheless, to say that boyhood is 'changeable, restless' or even 'wild' does not 'undoubtedly imply a criticism', as Burrow asserts (*A Reading of GGK*, London: Routledge, 1965, p. 7), unless (as Burrow does) we take Arthur to be a mature adult, behaving in a way which is inappropriate to his age.

12 *Fere* < OF *f(i)ers* is commonly associated with the early part of youth: Henry de Beauchamp, who died aged twenty, is lamented as 'a myghty prince, lusty, yonge and fiers' in 'The Nightingale' (*inc.* 'Go lityll quayere'; Brown and Robbins, *Index*, no. 931; ed. O. Glauning, *Lydgate's Minor Poems*, vol. 1, EETS, e.s 80, 1900, line 330). Cf. also *Piers Plowman* B5:66, and *MED, first*, ord.num., 2a(c).

    Stif is associated with manhood in Walter Hilton's *Qui Habitat*, ed. B. Wallner (Lund, 1954): 'þou schalt fulliche & mekelich hopen in þe help of god and stiflich & monliche holde forþ þi purpos' (p. 16). Cf. also Thomas Sheafe, *Vindiciae Senectutis* (London: G. Miller, 1639; rev. *STC*, no. 22391.8): 'man's age' is 'more staid . . . but yet more stiffe in everything'(p. 103).

13 *A Reading of GGK*, pp. 33–5.

14 *Hyghe eldee* is glossed 'the prime of life' by Davis, by Burrow (*A Reading of GGK*, p. 69) and by many others. It is defined as 'mature age' in *MED, heigh*, adj., 6(b).

15 On *ful age*, see the examples given in *MED, ful*, adj. 5(a) and *man*, 3(b).

16 'A Note on the Age of the Green Knight', *Neuphilologische Mitteilungen*, 78 (1977), 29. *MED, out(e) of*, 10(a), defines *out of age* for this context as 'past childbearing age'; this seems unjustifiably specific.

17 *Philosophiae Consolatio*, Book 1, *prosa* 1; ed. L. Bieler, *CCL*, 94 (1957), p. 2; *Boece*, p. 321.

18 *Figures of Life and Death in Medieval English Literature* (London: Elek, 1976), p. 92.

19 On old age and *coveitise*, see p. 22 and chap. 11, nn, 15 and 24, above. Cowardice is rooted in sluggishness and sloth (see *MED, couardise*, 2). All these symptoms are characteristic of those suffering from an excess of the melancholy humour and of those in the cold and dry age: see Raymond Klibansky, Erwin Panofsky and Fritz Saxl, *Saturn and Melancholy* (London: Nelson, 1964), chaps. 1 and 2, esp. pp. 62–3 and 100. See also Part 1, chap. 4.

15. The *ryght yonge* man and Lady Perfect Age in the *Book of the Duchess*

1 *Ricardian Poetry*, pp. 100–1.

2 Helen Phillips' edition, Durham and St Andrews Medieval Texts, no. 3 (1982), while not offering a new interpretation of *BD*, acknowledges the extreme complexity of the poem and provides a much fuller commentary than has hitherto been available. I take it that *BD* very probably pre-dates the completed B-text of *Piers Plowman* (*c.*1377), but I do not accept Phillips' argument that *BD* 'must have been written between the autumn of 1368 and 1371' (p. 5).

3 For Skeat's note on *BD* 455, see *The Complete Works of Geoffrey Chaucer*, 2nd edn (Oxford, 1899), vol. 1, p. 476. Although Phillips repeats the tradition that *BD* 'was almost certainly written as an elegy for Blanche, Duchess of Lancaster' (p. 3), she also says that its three main characters 'are not the Duchess, the Duke and Chaucer' but 'figures with a wider reference . . . not directly representing any particular real–life situation' (p. 6).

4 *Differentiarum*, Book 2, chap. 19; *PL*, 83, col. 81; see also *On the Properties of Things*, p. 292.

5 Robinson expresses the more usual view in his note on lines 759 ff., when he states that 'the following account of the service of the God of Love is thoroughly conventional' (p. 776).

6 According, for instance, to Roger Bacon, *Secretum Secretorum*, ed. R. Steele, Opera hactenus inedita Rogeri Baconi, fasc. 5 (Oxford, 1920), p. 131. See chap. 7.

7 The 'whit wal or a table' suggests both the Aristotelean *tabula rasa* and actual whitewashed walls and tables: see Phillips, p. 158

8 This immaturity is confirmed by 'yonge childly wyt' (1095), meaning 'boyish' rather than 'childlike', the gloss offered for *childly* in Norman Davis *et al.*, *A Chaucer Glossary* (Oxford, 1979).

9 Note especially, as evidence of this, 'for to kepe me fro ydelnesse' (1155).

10 See *A Chaucer Glossary*, *ge(e)re*; also, chap. 14, n. 11, above.

11 'And resoun gladly she understood' (1011) does not mean 'she gladly acceded to the arguments of reason' (Phillips, p. 162), but rather 'she apprehended and adhered to reason as a matter of course'.

12 Ed. A. Fourrier (Geneva, 1975), lines 246–9.

Select Bibliography

This list contains only works which are particularly rich sources of reference or which have particular bearing on the argument of this book.

Aers, David. *Piers Plowman and Christian Allegory*. London: Arnold, 1975.

Bartholomeus Anglicus (Bartholomew of Glanville). *De Proprietatibus Rerum*, trans. John Trevisa, *On the Properties of Things*, ed. M.C. Seymour *et al.*, 2 vols. Oxford, 1975 (esp. Book 6, chapter 1).

Bloomfield, Morton. *Piers Plowman as a Fourteenth Century Apocalypse*. New Jersey: Rutgers, 1961.

Boll, Franz. 'Die Lebensalter', *Neue Jahrbücher für das klassische Altertum*, 31 (1913), pp. 89–145.

Burrow, J.A. 'Langland *Nel Mezzo Del Cammin*', in *Medieval Studies for J.A.W. Bennett: aetatis suae LXX*, ed. P.L. Heyworth. Oxford, 1981, pp. 21–41.

Ricardian Poetry: Chaucer, Gower, Langland and the 'Gawain' Poet. London: Routledge and Kegan Paul, 1971.

'Young Saint, Old Devil: Reflections on a Medieval Proverb', *Review of English Studies*, n.s. 30, no. 120 (1979), pp. 385–96.

Chew, Samuel C. *The Pilgrimage of Life*. New Haven: Yale and London, 1962 (esp. pp. 144–74).

Cuffe, Henry. *The Differences of the Ages of Mans Life*. London: Arnold Hatfield for Martin Clearke, 1607. *STC*, no. 6103.

Didron, Adolphe N. 'Symbolique Chrétienne: La Vie Humaine', *Annales archéologiques*, 1 (1844), pp. 240–51.

Eyben, Emiel. 'Antiquity's View of Puberty', *Latomus*, 31 (1972), pp. 677–97.

'Die Einteilung des menschlichen Lebens in römischen Altertum', *Rheinisches Museum für Philologie*, 116 (1973), pp. 150–90.

'Roman Notes on the Course of Life', *Ancient Society* (Louvain), 4 (1973), pp. 213–38.

Gnilka, Christian. *Aetas Spiritalis: Die Uberwindung der natürlichen Altersstufen als Ideal früchristlichen Lebens*. Bonn, 1972.

Jones, John Winter. 'Observations on the Origin of the Division of Man's Life into Stages', *Archaeologia*, 35 (1853), pp. 167–89.

Klibansky, Raymond, Erwin Panofsky and Fritz Saxl. *Saturn and Melancholy: Studies in the History of Natural Philosophy, Religion and Art*. London: Nelson, 1964.

Milles, Thomas. *The Treasurie of Aunciend and Moderne Times* . . . Translated out of . . . Pedro Mexio, etc. London: W. Jaggard, 1613. *STC*, no. 17936.

Pickering, F.P. *Literature and Art in the Middle Ages*. London: Macmillan, 1970 (esp. pp. 168–222).

Rowland, Beryl. 'The Three Ages of the *Parlement of the Thre Ages*', *Chaucer Review*, 9 (1975), pp. 342–52.

Bibliography

Rushforth, G.McN. *Proceedings of the Society of Antiquaries*, 26 (1914), pp. 47–60 (The De Lisle Wheel of Life).

Sandler, Lucy Freeman. *The Psalter of Robert de Lisle in the British Library*. London: Harvey Miller and Oxford, 1983.

Schmidt, R. 'Aetates Mundi. Die Weltalter als Gliedrungsprinzip der Geschichte', *Zeitschrift für Kirkengeschichte*, 67 (1956), pp. 288–317.

Smallwood, T.M. 'The Interpretation of *Somer Soneday*', *Medium Ævum*, 42 (1973), pp. 238–43.

Suzuki, Eiichi. 'A Note on the Age of the Green Knight', *Neuphilologische Mitteilungen*, 78 (1977), pp. 27–30.

Tristram, Philippa. *Figures of Life and Death in Medieval English Literature*. London: Elek, 1976.

Turville–Petre, Thorlac. 'The Ages of Man in the *Parlement of the Thre Ages*', *Medium Ævum*, 46 (1977), pp. 66–76.

Van Marle, Raimond. *Iconogaphie de l'Art Profane au Moyen–Age et à la Renaissance*, in *Allégories et Symboles*. La Haye: Nijhoff, 1932, vol. 2 (esp. pp. 153–66 and 189–200).

Wackernagel, W. *Die Lebensalter*. Basle, 1862.

Weinhold, Karl. 'Glücksrad und Lebensrad', *Abhandlungen der königlichen Akademie der Wissenschaften zu Berlin*: Philosophisch-historische Classe (1892), pp. 1–27.

Wickersheimer, E. 'Figures médico-astrologiques des IXe, Xe et XIe Siècles', *Janus*, 18 (1914), pp. 157–77.

Index of authors and works

Abelard, Peter, *Expositio in Hexaemeron*, 57; *Hymnarius Paraclitensis* ('Aetates temporum nostrique corporis'), 63–5
Adam, created at the perfect age, 57
Ælfric, 17, 108
Al-ʿIbādī, *see* Hunain ibn-Isḥāḳ
Aquinas, Thomas, *see* Thomas Aquinas
Aristotle, 28–9, 40, 41–2
'As I gan wandre in my walkinge', 103
Augustine, 135; *Confessiones*, 16, 50; *Retractiones*, 45; sermon CCXVI, 48–9; *De Vera Religione*, 49–50; *De Quantitate Animae*, 50–2; *De Civitate Dei*, 58–9; *De Genesi contra Manichaeos*, 60–3; on *gravitas*, 45, 62–3; on sinfulness of *juventus*, 49–50; on resurrection at the perfect age, 58; on old age, 58–9; on *juventus* as king of the ages, 60–3; on adolescence, 60; on *declinatio*, 60–1; on rejuvenation, 62
Avicebiron, 46–7
Avicenna, *Poem on Medicine*, 21; *Canon*, 41–2; *Liber de Anima*, 46–7

Bacon, Roger, *De Retardatione Accidentium Senectutis*, 42; *Liber Decem Scienciarum*, 53–4; *Compendium Studii Philosophiae*, 54; on preservation of *juventus*, 42; on the 30-year-old, 53–4
Bartholomeus Anglicus, 16–17, 39–40, 136
Bartholomew of Glanville, *see* Bartholomeus Anglicus
Beer, Patricia, 26
Bible, 53–4; Genesis, 60–3, 138; Ecclesiastes, 37–8, 56; Song of Songs, 55–6; Isaiah, 62, 65–6; Ezekiel, 55; 2 Maccabees, 17; Matthew, 61, 110;

Mark, 54–5; Ephesians, 57–8; 1 Peter, 116; 1 John, 61, 113, 114
Bowes, Thomas, 14
De Brailes Wheel of Fortune, 94–5, plate 10
Browne, Richard, 42
Burton, Richard, *see* Crouch, Nathaniel

Carew, Richard, 21
Celsus, 26–7
Chaucer, Geoffrey, 4, 7, 125, 134–5; *Book of the Duchess*, 7, 104, 141–7; age of man in black, 143–6; age of White, 146–7; General Prologue, 8–9, 141; Knight's Tale, 4, 7, 65, 125; Miller's Tale, 71; Parson' Prologue and Tale, 141–2; *Troilus and Criseyde*, 4, 7, 140
'Compaynouns, veez ceo ke jeo voy' (accompanying three living and three dead), 87–8
de Coro, Antonio, 37
Coverdale, Miles, 66
Crouch, Nathaniel, 12, 39
Cuffe, Henry, 11, 12, 23, 34–5

Dante, 59
David, King of Israel, 60, 61, 63; as figure of *caritas perfecta*, 63–4
Didron, Adolphe, 74–5
Dionysius of Fourna, 73–5

Edgar, King of the English, 56
'Enfes, que demande tu?', 96–8, plate 11
Eve, created 'perfect in her sex', 21

Farley, Robert, 30, 37
Fortescue, Thomas, 41–2

169

Froissart, Jean, 146

Gawain-poet, 4, 134; see also *Pearl*, *St Erkenwald*, *Sir Gawain and the Green Knight*
Gerald, count of Aurillac, 65–6
Gilbert of the Haye, 22–3
Googe, Barnabe, 22
Gower, John, *Confessio Amantis*, 4, 7, 16, 104, 125–35, 140, 141; interpretations of the lover's cure, 127; third-person framing narrative, 127–8; first-person framing narrative, 128–31; lament for man and year, 131–2; perfect age in, 132–3
Gregory the Great, 56, 108
'ȝing and tender child I am', 85–6

Haddon, Walter, 15–16
Hali Abbas, 40–1
Herod, 71
Herrad of Hohenbourg, 75, 85
Hezekiah, King of Israel, 65–6
Hippocrates, 10, 28, 30
Holkham Bible Picture Book, 68, 71, 75, plate 3
Horace, *De Arte Poetica*, 29; *Carmina*, 31–2
Hortus Deliciarum, 75, 85
Huarte, Juan, 21
Hugo de Folieto, 35
Ḥunain ibn-Isḥāḳ, 30

Ibn Gabirol, *see* Avicebiron
'Ich am afert' (accompanying three living and three dead), 87
Iḥwan al-ṣafa, see *Rasā-il*
Innocent III, 35–6
Isidore of Seville, 11, 32, 39–40, 143

Jerome, 58, 59; *Tractatus in Marci Evangelium*, 54–5; *Epist.* 82, 56; *Contra Joannem Hierosolymitanum*, 57; on number thirty, 54–7; on age of ordination, 56; on resurrection at the perfect age, 57; on resurrection at one hundred years, 59
John of Grimestone, 26
John of Metz, 81; *see also* De Lisle Psalter, *Speculum Theologie*

'labilis ut ventus sic transit leta juventus', 75
Langland, William, *Piers Plowman*, 4, 6, 7, 16, 103–26, 130, 134–5, 138, 141; *manhod* in, 105–6, 111, 116–24; Ymaginatyf, 105–6, 107–9, 111–12; *myddel age* in, 109, 111–12; dream of Fortune and Elde, 112–15; recapitulation of Third Vision, 115–17; Tree of Charity, 118–19; ages of Christ's life, 119–20, 122–4; *hy tyme* in, 121–2; Piers, 123–4
De Lisle Psalter, 80–100; Madonna Master, 80; Majesty Master, 80; provenance, 80; Wheel of Life, 80–90, plate 5; *Speculum Theologie* diagrams, 81–4, 92, 94, plate 7; three living and three dead, 82, 86–8, plate 6; 'Mitis sum et humilis', text and translation, 80, discussion, 89; 'Parvule, cur ploras', edition and translation, 90–2, discussion, 92–6, 98, plates 8 and 9
De Lisle, Robert, 80; *see also* De Lisle Psalter
Longthorpe Wheel of Life, 98–100, plate 12
Lotario dei Segni, 35–6
Ludus Coventriae, 71
Lusty Juventus, 16

Macrobius, 28
manuscripts, Cambridge: Corpus Christi Coll. 481, 76, 78–9; Univ. Lib. Gg.4.32, 92, 159 n.13, plate 9; London: BL Arundel 83 (I) (Howard Psalter and Hours), 81; BL Arundel 83 (II) (*see* De Lisle Psalter); Lincoln; Cath. Lib. 66, 85–6; Cath. Lib. 210, 159–60 n.13; Oxford: Bodl. Laud misc. 156, 92, 160 n.13; plate 7; Tours: Bibl. de la Ville 331, 92, 160 n.13
Meditations on the Several Ages of Man's Life, 12, 18
Mexia, Pedro, 29; *see also* Milles, Thomas
Milles, Thomas, 10, 20–1, 29
'The Myrrour of Mankind', 11
'Mitis sum et humilis', *see* De Lisle Psalter

Index of authors and works

'The Nightingale', 18, 36

Odo of Cluny, 65–6
Ovid, 10, 32, 130

Parlement of the Three Ages, 109–11, 113
'Parvule, cur ploras', *see* De Lisle Psalter
Pearl, 134
Pie, Thomas, 37–8
Plato, 59
Plotinus, 45–6
de la Primaudaye, Pierre, 14
Promptorium Parvulorum, 11
Ptolemy, 29
Pythagoras, 30, 34

'Quod fortuna fidem non servat', 75

Rabanus Maurus, 32–3, plate 2
Rasā'il, 51–4

St Erkenwald, 134
Secretum Secretorum, 22–3; *see also*

Bacon, Roger, *Liber Decem Scienciarum*
Shakespeare, 10; *King Lear*, 13–14; 18–19; sonnets, 16, 24–5; *Twelfth Night*, 23–4; *As You Like It*, 36
Sheafe, Thomas, 38–9
Sherley, Anthony, 30
Sir Gawain and the Green Knight, 4, 5, 7, 14, 104, 125, 134–41; *first age* in, 14, 136–8; age of the Green Knight, 138–9; 'ageing' of Gawain, 139–40
Solon, 10
Somer Soneday, 67–73, 75, 78
Speculum Theologie, *see* De Lisle Psalter

Tertullian, 6, 57–8
Thomas Aquinas, 21–2, 47–8
Trevisa, John, 16–17, 39–40, 136
'þo Whele of Fortune', 68, 70, 72–3, 75

Van Veen, Otto, 31–2, plate 1

Whythorne, Thomas, 27
Wodroephe, John, 15, 29

Yonge, James, 22

Index of age-names and subjects

adolescence, adolescenci(e), 136, see
also *adolescens*

adolescens, ad(h)olescentia, 32–3, 40,
65, 78; relationship with *juventus*, 15;
relationship with youth, 15, 18; in
Bartholomeus Anglicus, 16;
wantonness of, 18; trans. youth-
hood, 20; choler dominant in, 34; in
'Mitis sum et humilis', 80, 85; in
'ʒing and tender child I am', 85; in
Piers Plowman, 119, 121; as English
age-name, 135–6; in Trevisa, 136; in
Book of the Duchess, 143; see also *juvenis*

adolescentulus/-a, 56, 75

adulta aetas, 17

aerestu ildu, 136

aevi plenus, 139; see also *ful age*

age farre spent, 30

age, definitions of, 11–12

'the age(s) of man', 11

akmē, 28–9

alacritas, 45, 62

barnhoed, 119; *see also* childhood,
infancy and *puer*

best age, 17 n.33, 66

bidmi yamai, 66

boyhood, see *puer*

childhood, 18, 20 26, 29;
correspondence with spring, 30;
vanity of, 38; see also *barnhoed*,
infancy and *puer*

choler, humour and temperament, 34

Christ, perfect age of, 6, 17–18, 54–9

cildhad, 108

cold weak age, 27

consistentiae aetas, 22, 41–2, 47

creation at the perfect age, 21, 57

declinatio/-nis aetas, Avicenna's third
age, 41–2; Augustine's fifth age, 61

decrepitatus, decrepitus, decrepitude,
80, 90, 96, 99; see also *senilis aetas*

decrepit crooked age, 35

diminutio, 28; see also *declinatio*

eighth age, 132, 135

elde, 18, 36, 59; meaning in Middle
English, 40, 135, *see also* old age and
senectus

Elde, in *Piers Plowman*, 104, 106, 107,
111–13, 115, 116; in *Parlement of the
Thre Ages*, 110; in *Confessio Amantis*,
131, 140

'excellence and flour', 65

fauntekyn, 123

fauntelete, 113

first age/-elde, in *Sir Gawain and the
Green Knight*, 14, 136–8; meaning first
part of old age, 40; meaning in
Middle English, 136

first youth(e), 136, 145

fol tyme, 121, see also *ful age*

Fortune, 67, 75, 114; in *Piers Plowman*,
104, 106, 107, 112–16; *see also* Wheel
of Fortune

forweredu ildu, 108

four humours, correspondence with the
ages, 34; changing balance of
associated with ageing, 26, 40–1; *see
also* choler, melancholy, phlegm,
sanguine humour

four seasons, correspondence with ages,
22–3, 29–32, 34–5, 39; in *Confessio
Amantis*, 131–2; in *Sir Gawain and the*

Green Knight, 138, 140; in *Book of the Duchess*, 142–3
ful age, 16, 121, 138–9
fulfremed waestm, 17
full ripe age, 30

grandiorum aetas, 40
gravitas, 5, 32–3; contrasted with *alacritas*, 45, 62
great climacteric/climactericall yeare, 38, 153 n.5

hyghe eldee, 'high eld', 4, 5, 121, 125, 138–9
'*hyȝe out of age*', 138; see also *provecta aetas hy tyme*, 121–2

infancy, *infans/infantia*, 20, 32, 80, 90, 99; see also *barnhoed*, childhood and *puer*

juvenis, *juventus*, yo(u)ng (man), youth, 58; ambiguity of age-name 'youth', 15; youth as pre-adolescence, 15, 18; relationship with *adolscentia*, 31; Renaissance English equivalents of *juventus*, 15–16; youth meaning *juventus*, 16; folly of, 18; instability of, 18, 37, 145; vice of, 18, 37–9, 108; *neotes* in Aristotle, 28–9; correspondence with summer, 30; association with pride, 36, 37, 39, 114–15, 123; correspondence with air, 36; vanity of, 38; correspondence with spring, 39; medieval protraction of, 40; degree of heat in, 41; in Augustine, 49–50, 52, 60–3; thirty years as upward limit, 58; in Abelard, 63–5; as King of Wheel of Life, 75–6; in poems associated with Wheel of Life, 78; in *Piers Plowman*, 108–9, 112–15, 122–3; forty-five years as upward limit, 109; association with Three Temptations, 113–15; 'young' in conjunction with 'yep', 113, 137, 138, 139, 162, n.20; in *Confessio Amantis*, 126, 131–3; meaning in late Middle English, 135; in *Sir Gawain and the Green Knight*, 136–8; 'young' in conjunction with 'fere', 137; in *Book*

of the Duchess, 143–6: see also *manhoed*, *maturitas*, *middel age*, *perfecta aetas*, *vir*
juventee, 16, 122–3
juventus, see *juvenis*

'lustie flour of youthe', 126
lusti youth(e), 15, 18
manho(o)d, *monheed*, *manhood*, 15, 20, 29, 30, 75; in *Piers Plowman*, 105–6, 116–17, 119–23; see also *juvenis*, *maturitas*, *middel age*, *perfecta aetas*, vir
man('s) age/ – (e)state, 13, 14, 29, 35
mans malignant age, 38
maturitas, **maturity**, *maturus*, 26–38, 65; correspondence with autumn, 30–2, 34–5; under influence of Saturn, 30, 34; correspondence with earth, 34–6; melancholy dominant in, 34–6; protraction of, 39–40; see also *juvenis*, *manho(o)d*, *perfecta aetas*, *vir*
media aetas, 6, 26–7, 38, 40; see also *middel age*
Medill Elde, in *Parlement of the Thre Ages*, 109–11, 113
melancholy, humour and temperament, 34–8; association with phlegmatic temperament, 34–5; dominance in *maturitas*, 34–6; dominance in old age, 38, 140, 143
memento mori, implicit in the Ages of Man, 33, 42, 45, 49; in *Piers Plowman*, 107–9; in *Parlement of the Thre Ages*, 110; in *Confessio Amantis*, 131
Mercury, influence on children, 20
middel age/-elde, meaning in Middle English, 16–17, 39–40, 109; in *Piers Plowman*, 5, 107, 109, 112; in *Parlement of the Thre Ages*, 109–11; see also *media aetas*
Moon, influence on infants, 20
*myhty youthe/*mighty youth, 16, 131–3
more confirmed youth, 16, 50

novus homo, 49

old age, 26, 27, 28, 35; covetousness of, 22, 110, 140, 162 n.24;

old age (*cont.*)
correspondence with winter, 34;
correspondence with phlegm, 34;
correspondence with earth, 36;
praise of, 38; under influence of
Saturn, 34–6, 38; dryness of, 41;
wisdom of, 48, 53, 92; of Piers in
Piers Plowman, 123–4; in *Confessio
Amantis*, 127–31; cowardice of, 140;
see also *elde* and *senectus*
'**olde**', in *Sir Gawaine and the Green
Knight*, 138–9

parfit age/*-elde*, (the) perfect age,
definition of, 13–14, 17–19; see also
perfecta aetas
perfecta aetas, perfecti viri aetas,
perfection, *vir perfectus*, 13–14, 17,
21, 40, 80, 85, 86; in Shakespeare,
13–14, 19, 23–5; in Thomas
Aquinas, 21–2, 47–8, in Augustine,
50, 52; Christ's perfect age, 54–9;
resurrection at perfect age, 57–9;
Plato as *vir perfectus*, 59
perfecta maturaque aetas, 57
phlegm, humour and temperament,
34; woman's characteristic
disposition, 21, 23; association with
short life, 23; moisture extrinsic in
old age, 41
plener tyme, 121
plenitudo temporis-tyme, 121–2
Pride of Life, 6, 25, 39, 70–1, 114–15
prime, 3, 15, 37, 39
provecta/*provectior aetas*, 30, 138
puer, puerilis aetas, **puerilitie**,
pueritia, followed by *adolescentia*, 15,
40; followed by youth, 15;
covetousness of, 22; sacrament of
confirmation in, 21, 47;
correspondence with air and spring,
34; dominance of sanguine humour
in, 34; degree of heat in, 41; in
'Mitis sum et humilis', 80, 85;
pravitates of, 108; of Christ in *Piers
Plowman*, 119; see also childhood and
infancy
puer senex, 36

Racio, in 'Parvule, cur ploras', 90–8, 100

rejuvenation, 42, 62–3, 156 n.5
ressurection at the perfect age, 57–9
'**ryght yong**', in *Book of the Duchess*, 143,
146
ripe age, 29

sanguine humour and temperament,
correspondence with spring and
youth; 8, 30, 36; association with
long life, 23; correspondence with
air, 34; dominance in *pueritia*, 34
Saturn, influence on *maturitas* 30, 34;
influence on old age, 34–6, 38
secrete diminution, see *declinatio*
senecta, 16–17, 40, 136
senectus, senex, 32, 33, 40, 80, 90, 99,
136; see also *elde* and old age
Senectus, in *Confessio Amantis*, 128, 129,
132
senex amans, 127
senilis aetas, senium, 40, 48, 58–9, 135,
136; see also *decrepitatus* and old age
senior, 99
senium, see *senilis aetas*
seven ages, 10–13
series aetatum, 22–3, 30–4, 48–9
'**six severall ages**' of woman's life, 23
soul, ages of, 45–54; in Plotinus, 45–6;
in Avicebiron, 46–7; in Avicenna,
46–7; Christian attitudes towards,
47; in Aquinas, 47–8; in Augustine,
48–52; in *Rasā'il*, 51–2, 53–4; in
Roger Bacon, 53–4
springal, 136
striplynges age, 16, 136
strong youth, 16
'**sumquat childgered**', in *Sir Gawain
and the Green Knight*, 137

three living and three dead, 82, 86–8,
plate 6
three temptations, 61, 113, 114
three watches and three ages, 107–9
triad of perfection, 59, 110–11, 118

vanitas vanitatum ages of man, 38, 39
vergens aetas, 40
vetus homo, 49
vir/*-ilis aetas*, **virilitie**, 29, 64, 78, 90,
94, 95; see also man(s) age, *manho(o)d*
and *perfecta aetas vir perfectus*, see

perfecta aetas and *vir*

weaxend cnihthad, 108
well stayde age, see *consistentiae aetas*
wexing age, 136
Wheel of Fortune, in *Somer Soneday*,
67–73, 74, 75, 78; origins of, 68;
'formula of four', 68–9, 72, 73, 94;
idea of, 70; 'glorior elatus' formula,
73, 94; in Dionysius of Fourna,
73–5; relationship with Wheel of
Life, 75–6; De Brailes Wheel, 9–5,
plates 3 and 10
Wheel of Life, in Dionysius of Fourna,
73–5; relationship with Wheel of
Fortune, 75–6; verbal formulae
associated with, 76, 78–9; poems
associated with, 76, 78–9, 80, 85–6,
89, 90–6, 100, 103–4; in De Lisle
Psalter, 80–90; Leominster Wheel,
84–5; Kempley Wheel, 84; problems
associated with image, 86, 88–90;
De Brailes Wheel, 94–5, plates 5, 10
and 12
'within two ayges', in Malory, 17
world, ages of, 60–6; in Augustine,
60–3; in Abelard, 63–5; in *Piers
Plowman*, 120–1

young manhood, 20, see also *adolescens*
and *juvenis*
youth, *see juvenis*
Youthe, in *Parlement of the Thre Ages*,
110–11, 113
youth-hood, 20, 29; see also *adolescens*
and *juvenis*